WHO DO PEOPLE SAY I AM?

WHO DO PEOPLE SAY I AM?

Rewriting Gospel in Emerging Christianity

Vernon K. Robbins

WILLIAM B. EERDMANS PUBLISHING COMPANY
GRAND RAPIDS, MICHIGAN / CAMBRIDGE, U.K.

Published 2013 by
Wm. B. Eerdmans Publishing Co.
2140 Oak Industrial Drive N.E., Grand Rapids, Michigan 49505 /
P.O. Box 163, Cambridge CB3 9PU U.K.
www.eerdmans.com

Printed in the United States of America

18 17 16 15 14 13   7 6 5 4 3 2 1

Library of Congress Cataloging-in-Publication Data

Robbins, Vernon K. (Vernon Kay), 1939-
Who do people say I am?: rewriting gospel in emerging Christianity /
Vernon K. Robbins.
pages   cm
ISBN 978-0-8028-6839-8 (pbk.: alk. paper)
1. Jesus Christ — Person and offices.   I. Title.

BT203.R625   2013
232 — dc23
2013008086

To my sister Martha
and the leaders and congregation of
Central Presbyterian Church
Atlanta, Georgia

Contents

Preface

I have had a special fascination with the Gospels for years, and many people and groups have contributed to my interpretation of them. Professors Irvin W. Batdorf and Harold H. Platz deepened my interest with inspiring courses on the Synoptic Gospels when I was a student at United Theological Seminary in Dayton, Ohio. I still have the copy of Ernest DeWitt Burton and Edgar J. Goodspeed's *Harmony of the Synoptic Gospels* in which I underlined all the words in common with different colors. Alongside my signature I wrote the date of purchase as 3-24-1961. Since we read Conzelmann's *Die Mitte der Zeit* (1954) in English translation (1960) during a course with Dr. Platz, I was well prepared to study redaction criticism under Norman Perrin when I started my M.A.-Ph.D. work at the University of Chicago Divinity School during Fall of 1964 (Perrin 1969).

As a result of my special interest in apocryphal Gospels, when Dennis C. Duling and I divided up our research assistant activities for Norman Perrin's *Rediscovering the Teaching of Jesus* (1967), I agreed to compile the bibliography on the Gospel of Thomas at the end of the volume. Also during this time, I took Robert M. Grant's course on Early Christian Writings and read his book *The Secret Sayings of Jesus* (1960). This little book contained William R. Schoedel's English translation of the Gospel of Thomas. Later, Prof. Schoedel moved from Brown University to the University of Illinois at Urbana-Champaign and became my colleague in Classics and Religious Studies there from 1970 to 1984. I am grateful for these mentors during the earliest stages of my scholarly life. They remain with me both in my memory and in their published writings.

Teaching adult Sunday School classes at First Urbana Presbyterian

Church and attending McKinley Presbyterian Church in Champaign, Illinois, helped me with my journey into the world in which we live beyond the horizons of the Bible itself. Also, teaching at United Methodist churches, Ministers' Conferences, and Bible Camps in Illinois and Iowa; at Presbyterian Camp in Indiana; and at St. Mary's College, St. Mary of the Woods, Indiana, provided special opportunities for me to become acquainted with many leaders and speakers in various denominations and Christian traditions. So many people contributed to my life in those contexts, and I am truly thankful for them.

I became more and more fascinated with Gospels outside the New Testament during my time at the University of Illinois. Underneath my signature in my copy of M. R. James' *The Apocryphal New Testament* I wrote the year of purchase as 1975. In the same year I published my essay on "The We-Passages in Acts and Ancient Sea Voyages" (Robbins 2010: 47-81). My context in the Classics Department at UIUC was encouraging me to venture into Mediterranean literature outside the New Testament, and the apocryphal New Testament was a natural part of that broader world.

Soon after I started teaching at Emory University in 1984, I began teaching a course on Jesus and the Gospels. Many of the insights in this book emerged either in my preparation for these courses or in discussions with my students in the classroom. I will always be grateful for the students who have populated these classes over the years.

In the midst of teaching Emory College students and the many amazing students in the Ph.D. program in the Graduate Division of Religion, I have continued to teach series of studies on Gospels inside and outside the New Testament in local churches. Among these are St. Anne's Episcopal Church and Trinity Presbyterian Church. Since 1984, I have not only been welcomed as a fellow traveler but as a welcome teacher at Central Presbyterian Church. The people in this community, including its wonderful leaders, continue to amaze me by their dedication to people who are marginalized in all kinds of ways in our world today. I am so indebted to them for the way they bless my life on a continual basis.

I am deeply grateful to April D. DeConick for inviting me to lead a workshop and give a lecture sponsored with Andrew Mellon funds at Rice University during January, 2012. This gave me a special opportunity to work out some of the nuances of differences between the Gospel of John and the Gospel of Thomas and to consult with one of the world's great authorities on the apocryphal Gospels of Thomas and Judas. April has been a wonderful friend for many years, and I treasure her friendship and scholarly dedication to understanding emerging Christianity in all its diversity and fullness.

I acknowledge with special gratitude the members of the Rhetoric of Religious Antiquity research group who have helped nurture me since our first meetings in 1999. While their influence on this book may not be explicitly evident, they have contributed to it in many ways. Among this group I must especially express my appreciation to my friend Roy R. Jeal for our regular Skype sessions during the final months of completing this book.

I want to give special thanks to Eric Moore for reading through each chapter and writing most of the Learning Activities. His help made it possible for me to complete this book in an expeditious manner. Brandon Wason also made recommendations on a few of the chapters. I am grateful to him also.

My wife Deanna read through all the chapters, including the conclusion and preface. She has not only helped me learn how to write for a broader audience but also given sage guidance about certain things that should and should not be included. I am grateful to her beyond words during this very special year of her life.

Vernon K. Robbins
Emory University
July 10, 2012

BIBLIOGRAPHY

Burton, Ernest DeWitt. 1945. *A Harmony of the Synoptic Gospels for Historical and Critical Study.* New York: Charles Scribner's Sons.

Conzelmann, Hans. 1960. *The Theology of St. Luke.* New York: Harper & Brothers.

Grant, Robert M. 1960. *The Secret Sayings of Jesus.* In collaboration with David Noel Freedman. With an English translation by William R. Schoedel. Garden City, NY: Doubleday.

James, M. R. 1924. *The Apocryphal New Testament.* Oxford: Clarendon Press.

Perrin, Norman. 1967. *Rediscovering the Teaching of Jesus.* New York: Harper and Row.

Perrin, Norman. 1969. *What Is Redaction Criticism?* Philadelphia: Fortress Press.

Robbins, Vernon K. 2009. *The Invention of Christian Discourse.* Volume 1. Blandford Forum, UK: Deo Publishing.

Robbins, Vernon K. 2010. *Sea Voyages and Beyond: Emerging Strategies in Socio-Rhetorical Interpretation.* Blandford Forum, UK: Deo Publishing.

Introduction

Who is Jesus? People throughout twenty centuries have claimed to know who he is. But they claim so many different things. Some have a ready answer today, usually from being taught by someone at church or at home, or by a friend, or by all of these. "Jesus is so important because Jesus is God," many of my present-day college students say. But others say, "Jesus is important, because he was truly a friend of tax collectors, sinners, prostitutes, lepers, people possessed with demons, blind people, and lame people." Still others say, "Jesus became important when he healed people. As soon as he healed people, it was obvious he was the Messiah." And by "the Messiah" they might mean that Jesus was God!

I have to admit that many of the things people say about Jesus make me uneasy. To be specific, "Messiah" does not mean "God" to me; it means a physical human being whom God chose to perform specific tasks on earth and whom God "anointed" with gifts and responsibilities to perform those tasks. Also, for me "Son of God" does not automatically mean "God"; it refers first and foremost to someone like King David, whose kingship made him God's son and made God his father (2 Sam 7:11-14). For another, "Son of Man" does not first and foremost mean for me "a human being," but a heavenly being who will come on clouds from heaven to earth accompanied by angels. This means that many things are upside down for me, or else they are upside down for other people.

In the midst of what I experience as the chaos of beliefs and politics in our present-day world, the array of Gospels inside and outside the New Testament helps me keep my sanity. Why is this so? Well, if early Christianity came into being with the wide array of beliefs and politics in the

Gospels inside and outside the New Testament, then maybe our present-day world is not that much worse than the world two thousand years ago. It seems to me that humans now are about as equally prone to be good and helpful, and to be violent and destructive, as they were twenty centuries ago. I wish people were better now than they were then, but it is very difficult for me to find evidence that they are. Many people are remarkably loving and committed to helping others; many other people are remarkably violent and committed to destroying others. And the problem is that I am talking about people in my own nation!

So what does this have to do with Jesus? Well, perhaps it is fair to say that I was born with Jesus on my mind, so almost everything has to do with Jesus. This is not something I chose. It was chosen for me by my mother and father. They took me and my two brothers, and later also my little sister, to church every Sunday morning and evening. And then during Revival Week we went to church every night of the week. I could hardly wait until I was twelve years old so I could stay a week at Church Camp at Milford, Nebraska, twenty-five miles west of Lincoln. And it was wonderful. All the girls for one thing! But also it was a wonderful time away from milking the six cows by hand and feeding the calves, pigs, sheep, chickens, and horses. I remember sitting on the empty cream can when I came back from camp as my Dad drove the Model A Ford in the ruts in the half-mile mud lane back to our house in the middle of the section of land on the sand hill. I had been in a beautiful never-never land for a week at church camp! And now I was returning to the routine of milking the cows and all that other daily work. Jesus provided a wonderful world for me away from all the work I had to do at home on a daily basis. Perhaps this is one of the reasons I thought Jesus was so wonderful.

James Carroll quotes William Faulkner as saying, "The past is never dead, it is not even past" (2001: 62). With a little adjustment it can be said that for Christians Jesus is never dead, he is not even Jesus. In other words, people make Jesus into who they want him to be. Often their Jesus seems to have little or no "real" relation to who the historical Jesus actually was. In 1986, Robert W. Funk invited me to become a founding member of the Jesus Seminar to study and work on the historical Jesus. Dennis C. Duling and I had been research assistants for Norman Perrin at the University of Chicago Divinity School when he wrote his *Rediscovering the Teaching of Jesus* (1967), so early in my scholarly life I had participated in the excitement and pitfalls of studying the historical Jesus. By the 1980s I was enjoying my investigations of the emergence of Christianity in the broader

Mediterranean world, and I was reluctant to turn away from them. After significant hesitation about Funk's invitation, I finally agreed to join the Jesus Seminar. It was one of the most exciting and exasperating times in my life. The research and discussions were wonderful. The headlines were frustrating: in my view they never "really" told the story of how we made our decisions. Sonoma, California, is a wonderful place to go at least once a year, and the Jesus Seminar provided this opportunity for me. I was at Emory University at the time, and I did not realize that Funk had taught at Emory University's Candler School of Theology for a few years during the early part of his teaching career, and he badly wanted someone from Emory on the inside of the Jesus Seminar.

To participate in something as big as the Jesus Seminar is to be involved in something with such strong forces at work that a person is simply one grain of sand in a very large sandbox. I had no idea how the situation would "use" me even as I participated in it to grow in my understanding of the significance of studying the historical Jesus in our modern world. I did not quite realize how situations and traditions "use" people, even as people use situations and traditions. This is a major insight I want to bring to the forefront in this little book. This is why I have given it the subtitle: *Rewriting Gospel in Emerging Christianity.* My thesis is that as early Christians used Gospels, those Gospels used them. In other words, influences are very subtle. Once something comes into the domain of our experience, it influences us and we influence it. Take the Gospel of John for example. Once we have read it, we are not quite the same afterwards. It influences the way we think about Jesus no matter what we do. But that said, the Gospel of John is also "what we decide it to be." I have friends and students who love the Gospel of John. I also have friends and students who virtually "cannot stand" the Gospel of John. For some of my friends, Jesus gets too self-oriented in the Gospel of John: egotistical, if you will. In contrast, some of my friends think the Gospel of Mark is really great, especially because of the way it confronts our own involvement in ourselves. Jesus says in Mark that "those who want to save their life will lose it" (8:35). Still some other friends think the Gospel of Luke is really the great Gospel, because of the way Jesus focuses on those who are poor and those who are not accepted by others.

I have come to understand that it is important to remember how people use other people and occasions as we ask the question, "Who do people say Jesus is?" I started all this by thinking about how Jesus used occasions during his earthly life to be who he wanted to be and about how Gospel

writers used Jesus to be who they wanted him to be, and to be who they
themselves wanted to be. This book explores ways people presented stories
about Jesus not only during the time the New Testament was being written
but during three centuries afterwards.

But why do I care about Gospels outside the New Testament? I have
come to realize the answer lies deeply within me. When I grew up as a boy
in the Ebenezer Evangelical Church in Ithaca, Nebraska, during the 1940s,[1]
we sang "What a friend we have in Jesus" and "I come to the garden alone,
while the dew is still on the roses." I never had a "high Christology." In
other words, I never talked seriously with my brother Lanny about Jesus as
"the Word who was with God and was God." At least if I did I don't remember it. Jesus made God available to us, but it was never a big deal to argue
that Jesus actually "was" God. I have learned later that I had a "low Christology" rather than a "high Christology" when I talked about Jesus.

By 1946 the Evangelical Church had merged with the United Brethren
in Christ Church, so after that we were "EUBs," members of the Evangelical United Brethren Church. When I asked my father what we believed as
Evangelicals, he said the important thing to remember is that we are not
Pentecostals, who get loud and emotional, and we are not Fundamental-
ists, who become rigid and unwilling to listen to other people's ideas. Our
beliefs are based on the Bible, he said. This means that no list of beliefs
made by a group of "leaders" is more important than what it says in the Bible itself. Also it means we are to use our minds to try to understand the
Bible and not be led too far into "public demonstrations" that the Holy
Spirit is present in us, or into "unmovable beliefs" that we are "completely
certain" about.

During the 1970s the word "evangelical" lost its true meaning, so far as
I am concerned. For most people now, "evangelical" means Fundamental-
ist. What a corruption of the word, which really is based on the word "gospel"! But as the world goes, so go words. Sometimes I get depressed about
things like this, and sometimes I feel a bit overwhelmed with new forms of
excitement and politics that completely corrupt earlier meanings of words
and earlier forms of belief.

The goal of this book is to use scenes in Gospels both inside and out-

---

1. After a merger with the Church of the United Brethren in Christ in 1946, my church
became the Ebenezer Evangelical United Brethren Church. Then in 1968, when we merged
with the Methodist Church, it became the First United Methodist Church of Ithaca, Nebraska.

side the New Testament to explore ways early followers of Jesus tried to explain their understanding of the special nature of Jesus. A key to their procedure was to compare Jesus to other well-known types of people with whom they were familiar from biblical, Jewish, Greek, Roman, and broader Mediterranean literature and traditions. In most instances their approach was to talk about Jesus as "greater than" people of a certain kind known to humans from the traditions of their heritage. In other words, Jesus was greater than Moses, Elijah, Solomon, or Jonah, and he was greater than Socrates, King Codrus of Athens, who died for his people disguised as a regular soldier, or Apollonius of Tyana, who traveled around the Mediterranean world gathering disciples and teaching and healing people until he was arrested in Rome. As the portrayals of Jesus in the Gospels grew, early Christians blended concepts together in ways that created new, emergent structures for thinking and talking about Jesus. In some instances, truly remarkable ways of talking about Jesus emerged. Who could have anticipated, for example, that people would talk about Jesus as "the light that is over all things," or as the one who "came from the immortal Aeon of Barbelo"?

When I first started to teach Gospels outside the New Testament in my college classes, very few other teachers were doing this. So the texts themselves, as well as good textbooks on them, were hard to find. The present situation is truly a dream come true! By 1984, when I wanted to include Gospels outside the New Testament in my Emory College class, it was easier to do so because Ron Cameron had published a little book called *The Other Gospels* (1982). Before that time, M. R. James' *The New Testament Apocrypha* (1924) made the most complete set of texts available, but it was difficult to expect students to buy it when we were only going to read some of the apocryphal Gospels. The same went for the Hennecke-Schneemelcher two-volume set (1964). James M. Robinson's successful publication in 1978 of Gnostic Gospels from Nag Hammadi in English translation had helped to create a great amount of interest, but this book did not contain other well-known apocryphal Gospels. By 1993 J. K. Elliott produced *The Apocryphal New Testament*, but the price was far too expensive for my college students. But already in 1992, Robert J. Miller's *The Complete Gospels* had made most of the texts available, and it has been updated regularly since. Today the Gospels outside the New Testament I interpret in this book are readily available to people even online (see the bibliography below), and there are complete commentaries on a number of them!

Also, during the 1980s there was much less scholarly clarity about many of the Gospels outside the New Testament than there is today. When I first included Gospels outside the New Testament in my "Jesus and the Gospels" course at Emory University, a number of students indicated that their parents were unsure they should be reading these Gospels. But so many students have learned so much in the course over the years that I have been motivated to teach it more often. I have regularly joked in private that the course I teach really is "Jesus and the Twelve Gospels." I know such an approach still is a challenge for many people today, but I know that for others reading beyond the four Gospels in the New Testament brings insights about early Christianity that they value highly. Once Dan Brown's *The Da Vinci Code* (2003) came out, and especially after it became a movie (2006), things turned decisively around for my teaching of Gospels outside the New Testament. Since that time a number of students have told me their parents are very excited that their child can take a class in college that includes Gospels outside the New Testament. And often they ask me if it is alright if they share information from my lectures with one or both of their parents, because their parents are truly interested to try to understand the Gospels outside the New Testament.

When I had completed writing about two-thirds of this book and was in the midst of the varying ways different Gospels portray Jesus, I began to think more and more about the differences between two early Christian hymns in the New Testament. In Paul's letter to the Philippians, a Christian hymn describes Jesus on earth as "empty" of divine form. Philippians 2:7-8 says that Jesus "[took] the form of a slave, being born in human likeness. And being found in human form, he humbled himself and became obedient to the point of death — even death on a cross." As a result of this obedience while in human form, the hymn goes on to say, God "highly exalted" Jesus, giving him the name of Lord, "so that at the name of Jesus every knee should bend, in heaven and on earth and under the earth, and every tongue should confess that Jesus Christ is Lord, to the glory of God the Father" (vv. 10-11). The emphasis on Jesus as a human who was obedient to God sounds to me a lot like the Synoptic Gospels: Mark, Matthew, and Luke.

In contrast to the Philippians hymn, there is a hymn in Colossians 1:15-20 that asserts that in Jesus "all the fullness of God was pleased to dwell." This hymn sounds to me like the Gospel of John, which presents Jesus during his time on earth in flesh, but "full" of divine grace and truth all the time. As a result of the "fullness [of God]" in Jesus, John asserts, "we have seen his glory, the glory as of a father's only son" (1:14). Then it says, "No one has ever seen God. It is the only Son, who is close to the Father's heart, who has made him known" (v. 18, NRSV mg.). The difference between these two hymns seems to me to exhibit two significantly alternative ways that Christ groups presented Jesus in emerging Christianity. For some Christ groups, Jesus was significantly "empty" of divinity while he was on earth. For some other Christ groups, Jesus was "full" of divinity during his time on earth.

By the 4th century c.e., Christian leaders decided that "proper" belief should be an assertion that Jesus is both "truly God" and "truly man" *(Definition of the Council of Chalcedon)*. The challenge for writers of the Gospels in emerging Christianity, however, was either to portray Jesus with certain kinds of "emptiness" while he was on earth or to present his struggles as he tried to "deal with" life on earth while he was actually "full" of divinity. The many Gospels that early Christians wrote, both inside and outside the New Testament, show how early Christian writers worked with these two alternatives in their storytelling.

One of the features of this book, then, is interpretation of Gospels outside the New Testament as part of the story of "who people say Jesus is." There is a special approach to these Gospels in this book, however. In each instance, my goal is to help the reader more fully understand the Gospels *in* the New Testament as the reader is learning about a Gospel *outside* the New Testament. In the chapter on the Coptic *Gospel of Thomas*, therefore, there is significant discussion about the nature of God the Father and Jesus the Son in the Gospel of John. In the chapter on the *Infancy Gospel of Thomas*, there is significant discussion of how scenes especially from the Gospel of Luke are reworked on the basis of the understanding of Jesus as the Logos/Word in the Gospel of John as InfThomas tells the story of Jesus' boyhood from age five to age twelve. In the chapter on the *Infancy Gospel of James*, often called the Protevangelium of James, there is significant attention to the manner in which the story reworks scenes from the Gospel of Luke by bringing the Gospel of John topics of Jesus as the Logos/Word and as the light that became flesh and dwelled among us into them. But there is also significant discussion of the way InfJames interweaves a Gospel of Luke way of telling about births with a Gospel of Matthew way of telling about births. In the chapter on the *Gospel of Mary*, there is significant discussion of the way Mary Magdalene is singled out in the Gospel of John as the only woman to whom Jesus appeared after his resurrection. Also, however, the way in which the disciples do not believe Mary in the Gospel of Mary is like the disciples' unwillingness to believe the women in the Gospel of Luke. In the chapter on the *Gospel of Judas,* there is significant attention to the way in which Jesus criticizes many Jewish rituals, especially in the Gospel of Luke but also in the Gospel of Mark. Likewise, the ascension of Jesus, which is only present in the Gospel of Luke and in Acts in the New Testament, looks very different in the Gospel of Judas. In the chapter on the *Acts of John,* again there is significant attention to reworking of scenes and topics in the Gospel of John. In a remarkable way, however, scenes only in the Gospel of Luke, including the ascension of Jesus, also play an important role as John "retells" the story of Jesus' time on earth in the *Acts of John.*

Some readers of this book will know that I approach texts from the perspective of Sociorhetorical Interpretation (SRI). I have introduced sociorhetorical strategies of interpretation especially in two books that first appeared in 1996: *Exploring the Texture of Texts: A Guide to Socio-Rhetorical Interpretation* and *The Tapestry of Early Christian Discourse: Rhetoric, Society and Ideology.* Then recently I have developed those strategies further in volume 1 of *The Invention of Christian Discourse,* which focuses on wisdom, prophetic, and apocalyptic aspects of emerging Christian discourse.

Rarely in this present book do I use specific language from sociorhetorical strategies of interpretation. Readers who are "in the know," however, will recognize that many SRI strategies guide and inform me as I proceed. I pay considerable attention to the "inner texture" of each text I interpret. In addition, throughout the book I am actively working with "intertexture" between the Gospel I am interpreting, other Gospels early Christians wrote, and in some instances writings in the Old Testament/ Hebrew Bible. I pay some attention, but not much, to the "social and cultural texture" of each text. Often, however, the "ideological texture" of a text stands strongly in the forefront of my interpretation of a Gospel.

In addition to the role of SRI "textures" in my approach to each Gospel I interpret in this book, I am guided by SRI insights into the function of "rhetography" in texts, namely how the rhetoric of texts (and of all discourse) prompts images and pictures in the mind. A second aspect of this is how these pictures are "emergent." Once a certain picture of Jesus was created in the minds of early Christians, this picture created the context for a new dimension of "that picture" to emerge, or for another picture to emerge "out of that earlier picture." In other words, it may be helpful for the reader of this book to know that I think of this book as "a moving picture" from the beginning to the end. Or, I could say I understand the entire book to be like a movie, in which each chapter is part of the unfolding sequence of the movie. In other words, this book is one way to tell a particular story about emerging Christianity during the first three centuries of its presence in the Mediterranean world. I will be waiting for Hollywood to call!

My wife Deanna, who has read all the chapters in this book, has encouraged me to add a final paragraph that warns readers that as the chapters unfold they encounter pictures of Jesus that may be unusual, unbelievable, or even frightening to them. She suggests that I encourage readers to keep an open mind as they read. The reason is that the overall story tells us many things about Christianity that may be very strange to us, but many of the things that are strange to us may be very meaningful for some other people as they attempt to understand who Jesus is.

From my perspective, the different pictures of Jesus people encounter as they read this book are related to many things they see in the world today. Many people may be accustomed to stories about Jesus that present him rather like a divine Superman, 007, or Spiderman: in other words, someone who can walk on water, whose face and body can change, who can appear and disappear, and who can even ride on a cloud from heaven to earth. It is possible to read the Gospels of Mark, Matthew, and Luke pretty much in this way. Some of these chapters present Jesus more like a divine alien from another world. The Gospel of John is more like this, where Jesus comes to earth as light and then becomes flesh. This kind of being can remind a person of E.T., the little extraterrestrial being who was left on earth and did wonderful things for a number of children and adults before a spaceship came and took him away. In the final chapters in this book, we see Jesus both as an interplanetary being and as a "cosmic" being who is able to be present everywhere at all the times. Again, this may be frightening to some people. In this book, however, I do not analyze and interpret any literature that is like horror stories or "action" movies filled with violence, destruction, and death. Some other writers during the last two decades have written such "action" fiction, guided by apocalyptic thinking, but this book does not take this approach.

There is no portrayal of "action" violence, destruction, and death in this volume, since the pathway I am following here moves from prophetic-apocalyptic to pre-creation imagery, namely imagery of Jesus existing prior to the creation of the world. In some Gospels, already starting with the Gospel of John, Jesus is with God before the world is created and then the agent (in John called the Logos/Word) through whom the world is created. This kind of "pre-creation" literature moves toward cosmic, mystical encounter of the believer with Jesus rather than into violent, destructive encounter. Those who "do not believe" simply do not experience that special encounter with Jesus. Many Christian leaders have turned away from this Gnostic "pre-creation" journey for Christian belief, calling it "heretical." Instead, they have opted for an "apocalyptic" view of Jesus that features violent destruction at "the end of time" for those who are unrighteous in the eyes of God and Jesus. Perhaps it is the "milder sorts" who like to explore the cosmic Jesus whose goal is to unite the earthly realm with the eternal realm. If so, I find myself among the milder sorts, rather than among those who prefer violence and destruction as the "reward" for those do not "properly believe" in Jesus.

For me, Jesus should help us learn how to live with one another, no matter how strange we may seem to one another. Indeed, my vision of Jesus is as a courageous being who accepted "strangeness" within himself as well as strangeness within others. I hope this volume will help many readers to think about the possibility that "being like Jesus" means being willing to accept and celebrate, without fear, all kinds of strange things and people in the world in which we live "without feeling the need to destroy them." So, perhaps the "more strange" Jesus becomes as this book proceeds, the closer we get to the "innermost nature" of Jesus. A number of readers will know that in 1906 Albert Schweitzer concluded his *The Quest of the Historical Jesus* with these sentences:

> He comes to us as One unknown, without a name, as of old, by the lake-side, He came to those men who knew Him not. He speaks to us the same word: "Follow thou me!" and sets us to the tasks which He has to fulfil for our time. He commands. And to those who obey Him, whether they be wise or simple, He will reveal Himself in the toils, the conflicts, the sufferings which they shall pass through in His fellowship, and, as an ineffable mystery, they shall learn in their own experience Who He is. (Schweitzer 403)

In this little book, which I have written more than 100 years later, I am proposing that it is not simply that Jesus is a person unknown to us because the time and culture in which he lived are strange to us. And I am not entirely sure that people "shall learn in their own experience Who He is." Rather, I have come to believe that Jesus accepted strangeness within himself, and the strangeness he accepted gives him a close relation to all "the strangeness" in our world today. And what is the nature of the strangeness today? The strangeness is found not only in people who live on the fringes of society, and people of every color, creed, nationality, and religious belief. The strangeness is found also in the highly unusual, even "totally weird" images, pictures, and, can we say, "beliefs," that some people create today. In other words, if we really could believe that Jesus accepted a role of being "strange," then it may help us accept not only many of the strange things that happen in our world today, but also how strange some of the things we say and think may seem to other people, even as the things they say and believe seem strange to us.

VERNON K. ROBBINS
Emory University

LEARNING ACTIVITIES

1. Read about how King David was designated God's "son" by virtue of his kingship in 2 Samuel 7:11-14.
2. Read Mark 8:35 to see how the Markan Jesus confronts self-involvement. Consider what this portraiture may reveal about how the Gospel and its author/editor "use" Jesus.
3. Read and compare Philippians 2:9-11 and Colossians 1:15-20. Observe how these separate passages represent two different ways early Christ groups presented Jesus in the context of emerging Christianity.

BIBLIOGRAPHY

Brown, Dan. 2003. *The DaVinci Code: A Novel.* New York: Doubleday. Film (2006) produced by John Calley and Brian Grazer, directed by Ron Howard. Sony Pictures Releasing.

Cameron, Ron (ed.). 1982. *The Other Gospels: Non-Canonical Gospel Texts.* Philadelphia: Westminster.

Carroll, James. 2001. *Constantine's Sword: The Church and the Jews — A History.* New York: Houghton Mifflin.

The Definition of the Council of Chalcedon (451 A.D.): http://www.reformed.org/ documents/index.html?mainframe=http://www.reformed.org/documents/ chalcedon.html

Early Christian Writings online: http://www.earlychristianwritings.com/.

Ehrman, Bart D., and Zlatko Pleše (eds.). 2011. *The Apocryphal Gospels: Texts and Translations.* New York: Oxford University Press.

Elliott, J. K. (ed.). 1993. *The Apocryphal New Testament: A Collection of Apocryphal Christian Literature in an English Translation Based on M. R. James*. Oxford: Clarendon.

Foster, Paul. 2009. *The Apocryphal Gospels: A Very Short Introduction*. New York: Oxford University Press.

———— (ed.). 2008. *The Non-Canonical Gospels*. New York: T & T Clark.

Hennecke, Edgar. 1964. *New Testament Apocrypha*. Volumes I-II. Edited by W. Schneemelcher; translated by R. McL. Wilson. Philadelphia: Westminster.

James, M. R. (ed.). ©1924; 2004. *The New Testament Apocrypha*. Oxford: Oxford University Press; Berkeley: Apocryphile.

Klauck, Hans-Josef. 2003. *Apocryphal Gospels: An Introduction*. New York: T & T Clark.

Miller, Robert J. (ed.). © 1992; 2010. *The Complete Gospels*. Fourth edition. Salem: Polebridge.

Perrin, Norman. 1967. *Rediscovering the Teaching of Jesus*. New York: Harper & Row.

Robbins, Vernon K. 1996. *Exploring the Texture of Texts: A Guide to Socio-Rhetorical Interpretation*. New York: Continuum.

————. 1996. *The Tapestry of Early Christian Discourse: Rhetoric, Society and Ideology*. London: Routledge.

————. 2008. "Rhetography: A New Way of Seeing the Familiar Text," in C. Clifton Black and Duane F. Watson (eds.). *Words Well Spoken: George Kennedy's Rhetoric of the New Testament*. Studies in Rhetoric and Religion 8; Waco: Baylor University Press. 81-106.

————. 2009. *The Invention of Christian Discourse*. Volume 1. Blandford Forum: Deo.

Schweitzer, Albert. 1998. *The Quest of the Historical Jesus: A Critical Study of the Progress from Reimarus to Wrede*. Baltimore: Johns Hopkins University Press.

Wesley Center Online. *Noncanonical Literature-Gospels:* http://wesley.nnu.edu/sermons-essays-books/noncanonical-literature/noncanonical-literature-gospels/

1

Are You the One to Come?

Are you the one to come? This question must have been important for people who thought Jesus of Nazareth brought decisive changes into the world. And if you are the one to come, then exactly who are you and how can we understand who you are? Are you more than a teacher of wisdom? Are you more than a prophet of God? Are you more than a king? Indeed, are we headed on the right track when we think of you as "more than" something we already know? Or must we decisively change our way of thinking? Are you something different from what anyone has ever expected? And if you are something different, then how is there any possibility that we can know that you are, in fact, the one people have expected to come?

An Early Gospel Containing Only Sayings?

Many scholars think some early followers of Jesus of Nazareth became so convinced that Jesus was the one people had expected to come that they committed to memory many of the things he said. They repeated these sayings over and over again to others, and soon they began to write them down into a longer and longer list of sayings. They wrote on wax tablets, pieces of wood, sheets of papyrus, or rolls made of skin of sheep or goats (Lee and Scott 2010). Gradually such a long list of sayings of Jesus existed that it became the first Gospel, namely written words people read aloud to others to present "good news" that God had done something special in the world through a person named Jesus of Nazareth. Some scholars think

there is not sufficient evidence to describe exactly how Jesus' sayings began to be collected together and written down. But other scholars think
there is substantial evidence in some long paragraphs of sayings in the
Gospels of Matthew and Luke that are not present in either the Gospel of
Mark or the Gospel of John. This evidence began to emerge at the beginning of the 20th century after a large number of scholars became convinced that the Gospel of Mark, rather than the Gospel of Matthew, was
the earliest Gospel in the New Testament.

If Mark is the earliest Gospel, written around 70 C.E., then there is extensive evidence to suggest that both Matthew and Luke used the basic
outline of Mark's sixteen chapters as a beginning place for expanding the
story of Jesus into more than twenty chapters of stories and sayings. But
where did Matthew find twelve more chapters of material and Luke eight
more? The answer is not so clear about the sources for the extra stories, but
many scholars think there is a good answer about the source for many of
the additional sayings. There are more than sixty units of sayings in Matthew and Luke that agree closely with one another and are not in Mark or
John (Mack 1993; Kloppenborg 2008). When scholars have printed those
parallel sayings in Matthew and Luke out by themselves, following the order in which they appear in Luke, a Sayings Gospel appears in the form of
five major speeches or sermons (Mack 1993; Allison 1997; Kloppenborg
2008). In other words, sayings in common between Luke and Matthew,
where there is no parallel in Mark or John, together look like an early Sayings Gospel both Matthew and Luke used when they expanded Mark.
Since this Sayings Gospel was a "source" for sayings now present in Matthew and Luke and some of the earliest people who discovered this Gospel
were German, this Gospel is regularly called "Q," which is shorthand for
the German word "Quelle," which means "source." During the earliest
stage, this collection contained only sayings attributed to Jesus, and Paul
seems to have known some of these sayings (during the 50s C.E.).[1] But it
was common in antiquity for collections of sayings to grow longer as they
were copied and recopied.

---

1. Cf. 1 Cor 9:14 with Luke 10:7//Matt 10:10; Rom 12:14 with Luke 6:27//Matt 5:44; Rom
12:17//1 Thess 5:15 with Luke 6:29//Matt 5:39-40; 1 Thess 5:2 with Luke 12:39//Matt 24:43; and
Rom 14:10 with Luke 6:37//Matt 7:1-2.

John the Baptist at the Beginning of the Q Sayings Gospel

By the time Matthew and Luke used the "Q" Sayings Gospel around 80 C.E., it contained sayings of John the Baptist at the beginning. This created a framework in the Q Sayings Gospel where Jesus came as "a greater one" after John.[2] In this context, one of the most famous scenes features John the Baptist sending two of his disciples to ask Jesus if He is the One to Come, or if they should wait for another. The Lukan version presents the question twice, once when John instructs his disciples and once when the disciples put the question to Jesus. Notice that when the words agree exactly between Luke and Matthew, the display will present the wording only once in boldface, in the middle underneath wording that varies slightly between the QLuke and QMatthew versions of the Q Sayings Gospel:

John the Baptist Sends Disciples to Jesus

QLuke 7	QMatthew 11
[18]. . . **John** summoned two of **his disciples** [19]and **sent** them . . . to ask, . . . [20]When the men had come to him [Jesus], they said, "John the Baptist has sent us to you to ask,	[2]. . . [John] **sent** word by **his disciples** [3]and said to him [Jesus],

'Are you the one who is to come, or are we to wait for another?'"

. . . [22]And he **answered them, "Go and tell John what you** have seen and heard:	[4]Jesus **answered them, "Go and tell John what you** hear and see:

the blind receive their sight, the lame walk, the lepers are cleansed, the deaf hear, the dead are raised, the poor have good news brought to them. [23]And blessed is anyone who takes no offense at me."

Hebrew Bible/Old Testament

When questions arise concerning the importance and role of both John the Baptist and Jesus in the Q Sayings Gospel, people who played an important role in the Hebrew Bible/Old Testament are very important in the background. The most important people are Moses, Elijah, and Elisha: people called by God in one way or another to perform special tasks to advance God's will among the people of Israel. In addition to these people,

---

2. No writing attributed to the Apostle Paul refers to John the Baptist.

the writings attributed to the prophets Isaiah and Malachi in the HB/OT[3] contain sayings early followers of Jesus interpreted as pointing to the coming of both John the Baptist and Jesus. Some Jews before the emergence of Christianity thought God would send Elijah back to earth from heaven, where God had taken him on a chariot of fire with horses of fire in a whirlwind (2 Kgs 2:11). Once back on earth, they thought, Elijah would perform special tasks to prepare for God's coming to the Jerusalem Temple, from which God would rule over all nations. In particular, Jewish people expected Elijah to "turn the hearts of parents to their children and the hearts of children to their parents" (Mal 4:6) before the Day of the Lord, when God would come to the Jerusalem Temple, which would become the center of worship for all people in the world (Mal 3:1-2; 4:5). The early followers of Jesus applied these prophetic biblical sayings and expectations about Elijah to John the Baptist, who, in their experience, had been sent by God to fulfill tasks that extended the story of God's interactions with Israel beyond the earlier events in the HB/OT to the story of Jesus.

Looking beyond sayings in Malachi, early followers of Jesus found a number of sayings in the prophetic book of Isaiah they considered to apply either to John the Baptist or to Jesus. The best-known saying is Isaiah 40:3: "A voice cries out: 'In the wilderness prepare the way of the LORD.'" When early followers of Jesus applied the verse to John the Baptist, they changed the punctuation to read: "the voice of one crying out in the wilderness, 'Prepare the way of the Lord.'"[4] For them, the voice did not cry out that people should go into the wilderness to prepare the way of the Lord, as the people at the Qumran community, who produced the Dead Sea Scrolls, thought.[5] Rather, for early followers of Jesus the verse referred to a man who cried out while he himself lived in the wilderness, namely John the Baptist. Then, indeed, this man prepared the way for Jesus by himself being killed and buried (Mark 6:17-29). These early followers also found verses beyond Isaiah 40:3 they considered to apply to Jesus and his activities on earth. In particular, they found verses in chapters 6, 26, 35, 58, and 60 of Isaiah, which we will discuss below.

---

3. HB/OT refers to Hebrew Bible, which for Christians is the Old Testament.
4. Mark 1:3; Matt 3:3; Luke 3:4; John 1:23.
5. 1QS on Isa 40:3.

Teacher and Disciple

One of the most natural places for questions to arise about people's identities is interaction between a teacher and his disciples. In the Q Gospel as well as in Matthew, Mark, Luke, and John, John the Baptist had disciples before Jesus started his activities (see Mark 2:18; 6:29; Matt 9:14; Luke 11:1; John 1:35). Early attempts to describe the inner character and identity of Jesus and John the Baptist arise in the Q Gospel in the context of questions raised by John and his disciples about Jesus. When John hears about Jesus' activity either through his disciples (Luke 7:18) or through general circulation of information (Matt 11:2), he sends his disciples to ask Jesus if he is "the one who is to come" or if they should "wait for another" (Luke 7:19// Matt 11:3). The formulation of the question locates the inquiry about Jesus in a context of prophetic belief. According to biblical tradition, God started a practice beginning with Abraham of choosing specific people to confront leaders with a message that they must change their practices to fulfill God's will (Robbins 2009: 1:219-328). This activity continued through Moses, Elijah, and Elisha before major prophets like Amos, Isaiah, and Jeremiah arose in the story of Israel's struggle to remain a nation in the context of attacks from Assyria and Babylonia that led to the destruction of the Jerusalem Temple and a later return to rebuild the Temple during the time of Nehemiah and Ezra.

Miracles of Healing

In the Q Gospel, when John the Baptist sends his disciples to find out if Jesus is "the one who is to come," Jesus answers with comments that blend activities of Elijah, Elisha, and Isaiah with his own (Luke 7:22//Matt 11:5). Jesus tells John's disciples to report to John what they have seen and heard: with "the blind receive their sight, the lame walk, the lepers are cleansed, the deaf hear, the dead are raised" he is reciting language from Isa 35:5-6; "the lepers are cleansed" continues the tradition of Elisha with Naaman the leper; and "the dead are raised" continues the tradition of Elijah with the son of the widow of Zarephath (1 Kgs 17:17-24) and Elisha with the son of the Shunammite woman (2 Kgs 4:32-37). Beyond this, Isaiah brought a message of good news to the poor (Isa 61:1).

Healing the Blind, Lame, and Deaf

1-2 Kings, Isaiah	QLuke 7	QMatthew 11
	[22]And he answered them, "Go and tell John what you have seen and heard:	[4]Jesus answered them, "Go and tell John what you hear and see:
Isaiah 35:5: Then the eyes of **the blind** shall be opened,	the blind receive their sight,	
Isaiah 35:6: then **the lame** shall leap like a deer,	the lame walk,	
2 Kings 5:14: So he [Naaman the **leper**] went down and immersed himself seven times in the Jordan, according to the word of the man of God [Elisha]; his flesh was restored like the flesh of a young boy, and he **was clean**.	the lepers **are cleansed**,	
Isaiah 35:5, 6: and the ears of **the deaf** unstopped . . . and the tongue of the speechless sing for joy.	the deaf hear,	
1 Kings 17:22: The LORD listened to the voice of Elijah; the life of the child came into him again, and he **revived**.[6] 2 Kings 4:32, 35: When Elisha came into the house, he saw the child lying **dead** on his bed . . . the child sneezed seven times, and the child opened his eyes.	the dead are **raised**,	
Isaiah 61:1: he has sent me to **bring good news to the oppressed**.[7]	the poor have good news brought to them."	

---

6. Cf. Luke 7:11-17; Isa 26:19: "Your dead shall live, their corpses shall rise."

7. Cf. Luke 4:18.

Perhaps the greatest surprise about the episode in the Q Gospel that features an inquiry into the identity of Jesus is the absence of focus on Jesus' relation to messianic power in relation to the kingship of David. There is no reference to Jesus as the Son of David in the Q Gospel. This is one of the differences between this earliest Gospel and the later Gospels that now stand at the beginning of the New Testament.

The focus in the Q Sayings Gospel is on a blend of prophetic traditions concerned with restoring human bodies to normal physical function. This physical well-being, in the mode of prophetic hopefulness, allows people to participate fully in society and nurtures the entire community's well-being. Indeed, the goal is to restore well-being in the form of justice for an entire nation.

This focus on restoration is expressed in four ways. First, there is emphasis on healing two major openings in people's heads, namely their eyes and ears, to allow them to receive information that guides them toward a productive and righteous life. One of the views of people in antiquity was that people who could not see and hear had obstructions over their eyes and in their ears.[8] Since seeing and hearing are the primary means by which people are able to receive wisdom, people with their eyelids stuck over their eyes and with their ears blocked are unable to grow in wisdom and knowledge of God and God's ways. Since wisdom is the means by which people become producers of good things, including righteousness, malfunctioning of people's eyes and ears prevents their potential for participating in good and righteous activities. Second, there is a focus on being raised from the dead or being enabled to walk and thus to join with others in community activities and to work purposefully with others. All this creates well-being not only in the people who are healed but also in the people around them. Third, there is an emphasis on removing the stigma of uncleanness or unholiness so a person can be thoroughly integrated into social community with other people. Fourth, there is a focus on the poor receiving honor through a message of good news from God. This message reasserts the necessity within biblical tradition to welcome the stranger, feed the hungry, and serve the needs of the widow.[9] One might say these four points were cornerstones of Jesus' ministry.

---

8. Application of honey, saliva, salve, beef suet boiled with oil, warm water, or soft cheese made from goat's milk, fumigation with steam from goat's liver, and forcing the eyelids open with one's fingers are common for healing of eye fluxes (incrustations) in antiquity: Cotter 1999: 18, 41, 188, 214-15; Mark 8:23; John 9:6-7. Jesus digs in the ears of a deaf man to remove wax in Mark 7:33.

9. See Deut 24:19-21; 27:19; Isa 1:17; Jer 22:3; Zech 7:10; cf. Matt 25:31-46.

Comparing John the Baptist and Jesus

In the context of the Q Sayings Gospel, inquiry into the identity of Jesus leads to a comparison of Jesus not only with Elijah, Elisha, and sayings in Isaiah, but also with John the Baptist. After the disciples of John leave Jesus, Jesus asks the crowds what they expected when they came out into the wilderness to see John. Did they come out to see a prophet? (Luke 7:26// Matt 11:9). Indeed they did, he says. Yet w.1at they saw was someone more than a prophet.

In the Q Gospel, the "more than" aspect of John is a continuation of activity that began in a message to Moses that a prophet like Moses would arise at a later time. This indeed is how prophetic tradition pushes history forward. People reconfigure promises made in one context so that they apply to later contexts. Emerging Christian tradition blends words from these earlier contexts together through recitation attributed to Jesus. To put it another way, words of God to Moses, which become words of the prophet Malachi, become in emerging Christian tradition a saying of Jesus about John the Baptist, who came with speech and action that prepared the way for Jesus!

Jesus Describes John the Baptist as More than a Prophet

Deuteronomy 18:15, 18	QLuke 7	QMatthew 11
	²⁴When John's messengers had gone,	⁷As they went away,
	JESUS BEGAN TO SPEAK TO THE CROWDS ABOUT JOHN: "What did you go out into the wilderness to look at? A reed shaken by the wind? ²⁵What then did you go out to see? Someone dressed in soft robes?	
	Look, those who put on fine clothing and live in luxury are in royal palaces."	⁸ . . . Look, those who wear soft robes are in royal palaces.
¹⁵The LORD your God will raise up for you **a prophet** like me from among your own people; you shall heed such **a prophet**. ¹⁸I will raise up for them **a prophet** like		⁹What then did you go out to see? **A prophet**? Yes, I tell you, and **MORE THAN a prophet**."

Deuteronomy 18:15, 18	QLuke 7	QMatthew 11
you from among their own people; I will put my words in the mouth of the **prophet,** who shall speak to them everything that I command.[10]		

In the Q Gospel, Jesus himself discusses with crowds who he considers John the Baptist to be. Yes, John is a prophet. This means John could be that prophet God spoke about to Moses. John could be that prophet "like Moses" who would arise and go into the wilderness to lead people forward according to God's will. But John is more than a prophet, Jesus says. Jesus' description of John as more than a prophet creates an opening for Jesus to interpret John in relation to himself. Jesus goes on to say that John's special role as a prophet is to be a "messenger," and here Jesus interprets words God spoke to Moses as though they were words God spoke to himself.

Angel/Messengers and John the Baptist

Jesus Describes John the Baptist in Relation to an Angel/Messenger

Exodus 23:20; Malachi 3:1	QLuke 7:27; QMatthew 11:10
Exodus 23:20: I am going to <u>send</u> an angel[/**messenger**] in front of YOU [Moses], to guard YOU on the way and to bring YOU to the place that I have <u>prepared</u>.	[27]This is the one about whom it is written, "See, I [God] am sending my messenger ahead of <u>YOU [Jesus]</u>,
Malachi 3:1: **See, I [God] am sending my messenger** to **prepare** the **way before** me, and the Lord [God] whom you seek will suddenly come to his temple.	who will **prepare** <u>YOUR</u> **way before** <u>YOU</u>."

In the book of Exodus in the Torah, God had told Moses that He would send an angel/messenger ahead of him to lead the way toward the land of Canaan. In the Q Gospel, Jesus recites these words as though God had spoken them to himself about John the Baptist. Jesus says that God told him that he was sending a messenger before him not to the place God had al-

10. Cf. Acts 3:22; 7:37.

ready prepared, namely Canaan (Exod 23:20), but "to prepare the way" before him. Malachi had already changed the phrase to "to prepare the way"
(Mal 3:1), that is, the way for the Lord God of Hosts to come to the Jerusalem Temple. When Jesus speaks in the Q Gospel, he uses the pronoun "you"
from Exodus, but the phrase "to prepare the way" from Malachi, arranging
them so that they say that God had told him that John the Baptist would
come as a messenger who would prepare the way before Jesus himself.

Kingdom of God

After speaking about John as a prophetic messenger, Jesus continues by explaining John's relation to the kingdom of God, which Jesus himself announces as coming soon. From the perspective of the Q Gospel, Jesus
viewed John as part of the biblical story prior to the coming of the kingdom, as the one who prepared the way for the coming of Jesus. But John
himself was not a participant in the kingdom of God! Jesus says this in
very clear terms in the Q Gospel, but in a mode of highest praise of John
the Baptist and the work he is doing.

Jesus Describes John the Baptist in Relation to the Kingdom of God/Kingdom of Heaven

QLuke 7	QMatthew 11
[28]I tell you, among those born of women no one is greater than John; yet the least in the kingdom of God is greater than he."	[11]Truly I tell you, among those born of women no one has arisen greater than John the Baptist; yet the least in the kingdom of heaven is greater than he.

John, Jesus says, is unsurpassed by anyone else born of women. What an
amazing compliment! John was a prophet who confronted people with
God's will and a messenger who prepared the way for Jesus' coming and Jesus' proclamation of the coming of the kingdom of God. But John himself
was not a participant in the coming of the kingdom. This is a very puzzling
statement. One would think Jesus would have included John the Baptist in
the coming of the kingdom. This seems, however, to be one more way of
presenting Jesus as "the coming one" who is "more than" anyone who came
before him. When Luke writes his Gospel toward the end of the first century, he creates a schema in which John the Baptist was the last person of
the time of the prophets, Jesus' activity brought the kingdom of God into

the people's lives, and the time of the church began after Jesus ascended into heaven. The Q Gospel has the beginnings of such an idea, but the idea is not yet fully developed. Instead, it simply asserts that no one born of women was a greater prophet and messenger than John, but "the least in the kingdom of God" is greater than he!

Funerals and Weddings

After Jesus' amazing claim that John is not part of the kingdom of God, he shifts abruptly into a parable about children playing weddings and funerals. With this parable he compares the people to whom he is speaking to people who refuse either to play funerals or to play weddings with children in the marketplace.

Jesus Describes People in Relation to Funerals and Weddings

QLuke 7	QMatthew 11
[31]To what then will I compare the people of this generation, and what are they like?	[16]But to what will I compare this generation?

[32]**They are like children sitting in the marketplace and calling to one another, "We played the flute for you, and you did not dance; we wailed, and you did not weep."**

When children play the flute and expect people to dance to the music, like at a wedding, they refuse to dance. So they change to wailing, like at a funeral, and expect people to weep. But people refuse also to weep! So, whether the children want to be joyous or sad, the people in the marketplace refuse to participate happily or with grief in their game. This way of telling a little parable to confront people is characteristic of Jesus as Mark, Matthew, and Luke present him. The Q Gospel also presents Jesus in this way. But why, one wonders, is Jesus talking about children in this way? The reason emerges in the next part of the scene, where Jesus compares the activity of John the Baptist and Jesus. John, Jesus says, came in a very serious mode denying himself special pleasures of food and drink, and people did not respond positively to him. Jesus, in contrast, came with joy and celebration, eating and drinking, but people did not respond positively to him either.

Comparing John the Baptist and the Son of Man

Jesus Describes John the Baptist in Relation to the Son of Man

QLuke 7	QMatthew 11
³³**For John** the Baptist <u>has come</u> **eating** <u>no</u> bread and **drinking** <u>no</u> wine, **and** you **say,**	¹⁸**For John** <u>came neither</u> **eating** <u>nor</u> **drinking, and** they say,
	"He has a demon";
³⁴**the Son of Man** <u>has come</u> **eating and drinking, and** you **say,**	¹⁹**the Son of Man** <u>came</u> **eating and drinking, and** they say,
"Look, a glutton and a drunkard, a friend of tax-collectors and sinners!"	

When Jesus refers to John, it is very clear about whom he is speaking. When he refers to himself, he refers to "the Son of Man." Jesus' assertion is that John came with an ascetic lifestyle, neither eating ordinary food nor drinking wine. Here Jesus might be interpreting John's style of life in relation to people like Samson or Samuel, whose mothers were told that their sons were not to drink strong drink or wine or eat anything unclean, or the son made a Nazirite vow (Num 6:1-4; Judg 13:4-5, 7; 1 Sam 1:11). When the angel Gabriel tells Zechariah that he and his wife Elizabeth will have a son, he tells them that "He [John the Baptist] must never drink wine or strong drink" (Luke 1:15). An alternative meaning of Jesus' statement could be a traditional view of the austere lifestyle of the prophet Elijah, who ate only locusts and wild honey (Mark 1:6//Matt 3:4). Still another possibility could be that John's diet echoed the diet of the people in Israel during their time of wandering in the desert (Bock 1994: 682), where God tells the people of Israel: "you have not eaten bread, and you have not drunk wine or strong drink — so that you may know that I am the LORD your God" (Deut 29:6). Whether the Q portrayal of Jesus' view refers to John as having taken a Nazirite vow, having adopted a lifestyle associated with Elijah, or having adopted a diet that reenacts the life of the people of Israel in the wilderness, Jesus presents the lifestyle of John as austere and severe, in contrast to his own lifestyle.

When Jesus refers to his own lifestyle in the Q Gospel, he uses the phrase "the Son of Man." Scholars have spent much time investigating this phrase, and there is disagreement over many aspects of its usage. It is important to know at the beginning that the phrase "the Son of Man" never occurs in any writing attributed to Paul or in any of the other letters in the

New Testament. This means that the phrase is found only in Gospels, Acts, and Revelation. In the Gospels the phrase virtually always occurs on the lips of Jesus rather than in the narrative. In other words, the Gospel writers considered "the Son of Man" to be characteristic of Jesus' speech, alongside his emphasis on the coming of the kingdom of God. A scholar named Geza Vermes did extensive research throughout Aramaic literature to analyze the occurrences of the phrase "the Son of Man" in ancient Jewish literature and became convinced that presence of this phrase on Jesus' lips in contexts like the one we are discussing reflects a usage especially in the northern Galilean dialect of the Aramaic language, which most scholars think Jesus spoke (Vermes 1973; Perrin 1967). In this dialect, "the Son of Man" could refer, perhaps in an especially authoritative way, to the person who is speaking. This mode of speaking is still present among some males today who, instead of referring to themselves as "I," will refer to themselves as "the Man." In other words, if you ask them how they are today, they may say, "The man is doing okay, thank you." When Jesus refers to himself as "the Son of Man," then, he is adopting a mode of speech that refers to himself with "a bearing of importance," one might say.

Referring to himself as the Son of Man, Jesus describes his lifestyle as though he were continually at a wedding. A description of the joyous activity at a wedding is present in a scene in the Gospels where John's disciples are fasting and people come to Jesus and ask him why his own disciples are not fasting. Jesus' response is: "The wedding guests cannot fast while the bridegroom is with them, can they?" (Mark 2:19; cf. Matt 9:15// Luke 5:34; John 3:29). Then as Jesus continues, he includes statements about wine: "And no one puts new wine into old wineskins; otherwise, the wine will burst the skins, and the wine is lost, and so are the skins; but one puts new wine into fresh wineskins" (Mark 2:22//Matt 9:17//Luke 5:37-39).

Jesus' Table Fellowship

Scholars consider the joyous atmosphere of Jesus' life to be characteristic of his "table fellowship" with marginalized people on his itinerant travels throughout Galilee. In contrast to Jews who were instructed to eat only certain "clean" foods and to associate only with certain "acceptable" people when eating, Jesus was accused of eating practices that did not follow these guidelines. Most scholars think this lifestyle reflects Jesus' "celebration" of the coming of the kingdom of God into the midst of people through his own activity of enacting God's acceptance of marginalized people. These people were traditionally excluded from religious rites that renewed and confirmed the forgiveness and salvation/shalom of Jewish people. In the context of Jesus' table fellowship, he enacts God's acceptance of them as members of the kingdom of God.

Conclusion

In summary, the Q Gospel presents Jesus as superior to his messenger, John the Baptist. A major way in which he is superior is his actual enactment of the kingdom of God, rather than simply announcing it and preparing people for it by calling them to repent and be baptized. Jesus especially enacts the kingdom in the Q Gospel through his restoration of malfunctioning human bodies through healing. Also, Jesus' demeanor and activity are joyous, characterized by the joy at weddings, in contrast to the activity of John the Baptist, which is likened to weeping and mourning at funerals. In Q, Jesus is known for his table fellowship with tax collectors and sinners, which appears to be a context in which he celebrates their inclusion in God's kingdom.

As Jesus speaks in the Q Gospel, he moves beyond prophetic modes of understanding to a reference to "wisdom." Indeed, he refers to wisdom as a special feminine personage who is shown to be wise either by her children or by her deeds.

Jesus Describes Himself and John the Baptist in Relation to Wisdom

QLuke 7:35	QMatthew 11:19
[35]Nevertheless, **wisdom** is vindicated by all her children."	Yet **wisdom** is vindicated by her deeds."

Wisdom appears as a feminine personage in Proverbs 8, which begins by speaking about wisdom (8:1-3). Then in v. 4, Wisdom herself begins to speak. As she tells her story, she describes how she cries out to people to learn prudence and acquire intelligence (v. 5) and how she came into being as God's first act of creation (v. 22). This allowed her to work alongside God as "a master worker" while God was creating the world, daily bringing him joy and delight (v. 30). In vv. 32-33 she begins speaking to "her children," telling them to listen carefully to her and follow her ways:

And now, my children, listen to me:
  happy are those who keep my ways.
Hear instruction and be wise,
  and do not neglect it.

Approximately two hundred years before the emergence of Christianity, another "wisdom" book was written, called Ben Sira or Sirach. Ben Sira 4 explains the work of Wisdom with her children in some detail. One of the amazing statements in Ben Sira occurs in 4:15: "Those who obey her [Wisdom] will judge the nations." This view of Wisdom leads us to another important topic in the Q Gospel, namely the range of meanings associated with the phrase "the Son of Man" in the Q Sayings Gospel. This is the topic of the next chapter.

LEARNING ACTIVITIES

1. Read Isaiah 35:1-10; 61:1-11 in relation to healing and the focus on the poor in the Q Gospel.
2. Read the stories of Elijah and Elisha raising the dead in 1 Kings 17:17-24; 2 Kings 4:17-37.
3. Read the story of Elijah's ascent to heaven in a chariot of fire in 2 Kings 2:1-14.
4. Read the story of Elisha's cleansing of the leper Naaman in 2 Kings 5:1-27.
5. Read the message of God to Moses about an angel/messenger who would go in front of the Israelites to lead the way (Exod 23:20-32).
6. Read the prophetic message in Malachi 3 and 4 about a messenger who will come to prepare the way before the Lord of hosts comes to the Jerusalem Temple. Emerging Christianity applied these verses to the coming of John the Baptist before Jesus (Mal 3:1; 4:5-6).
7. Read the promise of comfort given to the people of Israel in Isaiah 40:1-5. Early followers of Jesus applied v. 3 to the wilderness activity of John the Baptist, the forerunner of Jesus. Compare this interpretation in Mark 1:3//Matt 3:3//Luke 3:4//John 1:23 with the Qumran community's application of the same passage in 1QS 8:12-16 (cf. 9:14-22).
8. Read about Nazirite vows in Numbers 6:1-21; Judges 13:2-25; 1 Samuel 1:1-28; and Luke 1:5-25.
9. Read about wisdom in Proverbs 8:1-36. Compare it with Sirach 4:1-31. If you do not have a Study Bible that includes Sirach, search for it online under "NRSV Apocrypha online."

BIBLIOGRAPHY

Allison, Dale C. 1997. *The Jesus Tradition in Q.* Harrisburg: Trinity.

Bock, Darrell L. 1994. *Luke 1:1–9:50.* Baker Exegetical Commentary on the New Testament. Grand Rapids: Baker.

Cotter, Wendy. 1999. *Miracles in Greco-Roman Antiquity: A Sourcebook.* New York: Routledge.

Jacobson, Arland D. 1992. *The First Gospel: An Introduction to Q.* Sonoma: Polebridge.

Kloppenborg, John S. 2008. *Q, the Earliest Gospel: An Introduction to the Original Stories and Sayings of Jesus.* Louisville: Westminster John Knox.

Kloppenborg, John S., Marvin W. Meyer, Stephen J. Patterson, and Michael G. Steinhauser. 1990. *Q-Thomas Reader.* Sonoma: Polebridge.

Lee, Margaret, and Bernard Brandon Scott. 2010. *Sound Mapping the New Testament.* Eugene: Polebridge.

The Lost Sayings Gospel Q: http://www.earlychristianwritings.com/q.html.

Mack, Burton L. 1993. *The Lost Gospel: The Book of Q and Christian Origins.* San Francisco: HarperCollins.

Perrin, Norman. 1967. *Rediscovering the Teaching of Jesus.* New York: Harper & Row.

Robbins, Vernon K. 2009. *The Invention of Christian Discourse,* vol. 1. Blandford Forum: Deo.

Robinson, James M. 2007. *Jesus According to the Earliest Witness.* Minneapolis: Fortress.

Robinson, James M., Paul Hoffmann, and John S. Kloppenborg. 2000. *The Critical Edition of Q.* Hermeneia. Minneapolis: Fortress.

Tuckett, Christopher M. 1996. *Q and the History of Early Christianity: Studies on Q.* Edinburgh: T & T Clark.

Vermes, Geza. 1973. *Jesus the Jew: A Historian's Reading of the Gospels.* New York: Macmillan.

2

Who Is the Son of Man?

What kind of person is the Son of Man? Could people understand the phrase or title in different ways? The use of the phrase "the Son of Man" in the New Testament is highly unusual. One can see a change in usage from the Q Gospel to the Gospels of Mark, Matthew, Luke, and John. Again we should remind ourselves that "the Son of Man" does not occur in any of Paul's letters or in any other letter in the New Testament.[1] In fact, in the Gospels "the Son of Man" occurs only in sayings spoken by Jesus. As a result of the different meanings related to "the Son of Man" in different writings, most scholars think we can see how the earliest followers of Jesus moved from significant puzzlement about the meaning of the phrase to certainty that it referred to Jesus. Even though they decided it referred to Jesus, however, they had significantly different views about what the phrase meant when it referred to Jesus. In other words, once they were certain "the Son of Man" referred to Jesus, they began to apply the phrase to different dimensions of Jesus' life and activities.

In this chapter we will learn about two types of Son of Man sayings in the Q Gospel: (1) "earthly" sayings, namely sayings where Jesus uses the phrase "the Son of Man" to refer to things he is doing on earth, and (2) "heavenly" sayings, in which Jesus refers to "the Son of Man" as a personage who comes from heaven to earth. In chapter 3, we will learn about a third type of Son of Man saying, namely sayings in Mark where Jesus states that it is "necessary" that "the Son of Man" be rejected, suffer, die, and rise

---

1. Outside the Gospels, "the Son of Man" occurs in Acts 7:56 and "like a son of man," obviously reciting the phrase from Dan 7:13, occurs in Rev 1:13; 14:14.

up. We will start with Jesus' earthly Son of Man sayings in the Q Sayings Gospel.

The Earthly Son of Man

There are three sayings in the Q Gospel where Jesus refers to his activity on earth with the unusual phrase "the Son of Man." One of them is the saying we discussed in the previous chapter where he compares himself to John the Baptist. There, we must recall, he describes the Son of Man as one who "has come eating and drinking" in such a way that people call him "a glutton and a drunkard"! This is not a very positive picture of Jesus. What could lie behind it? What exactly did he do that called forth this kind of description of him and his activities, and why did he do it? And why would it be that Jesus uses the phrase "the Son of Man" to describe himself doing these things?

As we look more closely at this saying, let us recall that both Luke and Matthew present Jesus as saying that when he acts as he does "wisdom is vindicated" either "by all her children" or "by her deeds."

QLuke 7	QMatthew 11
[34]**the Son of Man** <u>has come</u> **eating and drinking, and** you **say,**	[19]**the Son of Man** <u>came</u> **eating and drinking, and** they **say,**

"**Look, a glutton and a drunkard, a friend of tax-collectors and sinners!**"

[35]Nevertheless, **wisdom** is vindicated by all **her** children.	Yet **wisdom** is vindicated by **her** deeds.

First, when Jesus applies "the Son of Man" to himself in this context, he does not say he is rejected as a glutton and a drunkard because he is acting as a prophet. Here, in other words, Jesus describes himself as somehow different from a prophet. Instead of a prophet commissioned by God to confront people and their leaders with a message concerning their disobedience to God's will, he is a person acting according to the wisdom that "Wisdom" herself has taught him. But who is "Wisdom"? The answer lies in the book of Proverbs in the Hebrew Bible/Old Testament and in "wisdom" books in the deuterocanonical books of the Old Testament Apocrypha.

Proverbs 8 presents Wisdom as a personified feminine being who helped God create the earth and then came down on earth to instruct people how to act in accordance with God's will. In Proverbs 8:4 she says, "To you, O people, I call, and my cry is to all that live." Then in 9:5-6 she says, "Come, eat of my bread and drink of the wine I have mixed. Lay aside immaturity, and live, and walk in the way of insight." The Q Sayings Gospel presents Jesus as a person who acts according to the guidelines of Wisdom, who authoritatively embodies and enacts the wisdom she has taught. In fact, the happiness and rejoicing Jesus exhibits seem to be an embodiment of Wisdom's assertions: "Happy are those who keep my ways" (Prov 8:32), and "Happy is the one who listens to me" (v. 34).[2] This means that some of the early followers of Jesus extended the list of people whom wisdom "instructs" in Sirach 44–48 to include Jesus (Robbins 2009: 180-183). In other words, in the Q Gospel Jesus embodies, enacts, and teaches "wisdom" that has come from Wisdom herself, that female personage who helped God create the world and then came down to earth to instruct important people in the history of Israel. In the Q Gospel, this special embodiment of wisdom is "the Son of Man."

One of the special characteristics of wisdom tradition is its focus not only on regular activities in life like weddings and funerals but also on plants and animals in God's "created world," those things which came into being with Wisdom's help. Proverbs 30:24-28, for example, refers to four things on earth that are small yet exceedingly wise: "the ants are a people without strength, yet they provide their food in the summer; the badgers are a people without power, yet they make their homes in the rocks; the locusts have no king, yet all of them march in rank; the lizard can be grasped in the hand, yet it is found in kings' palaces." The relation of "the Son of Man" to God's created world is in the foreground in a second earthly Son of Man saying that describes the nature of discipleship in relation to Jesus' itinerant life:

QLuke 9	QMatt 8
[57]As they were going along the road, someone **said** to him,	[19]A scribe then approached and **said**, "Teacher,"

"I will follow you wherever you go." [58]**And Jesus said to him, "Foxes have holes, and birds of the air have nests; but the Son of Man has nowhere to lay his head."**

In this saying, Jesus describes his life as "in the midst of God's created world." Its special emphasis is that, in contrast to the rest of God's living

---

2. Cf. the way Wisdom brings joy to God in Prov 8:30-31: "I was daily his delight, rejoicing before him always, rejoicing in his inhabited world and delighting in the human race."

creatures, Jesus himself has no comfortable home. In other words, the "wisdom" that guides him drives him away from his home out into God's world, where he has "nowhere to lay his head." Anyone who wishes to become his disciple, therefore, must face a life of wandering to and fro from village to village without the support and comfort of family, friends, and home.

In relation to this, a number of scholars have noticed similarities between Jesus and traveling Cynic philosophers during Jesus' time. One of the most famous was Diogenes, of whom Seneca the Younger (4 B.C.E.–65 C.E.) said: "on seeing a boy drink water from the hollow of his hand, forthwith he took his cup from his wallet and broke it," calling himself a fool for carrying around such unneeded baggage. Then praising this sage to whom people should listen, Seneca concludes with "Follow nature, and you will need no skilled craftsman" (Crossan 1995: 116).

This leads to the next earthly Son of Man saying, which Jesus forms as a beatitude, a special blessing on those who are willing to accept a life of discipleship to the Son of Man, who is guided by God's Wisdom.

QLuke 6	QMatt 5
[22]Blessed are you when people hate you, and when they exclude you, revile you, and defame you on account of **THE SON OF MAN**.	[11]Blessed are you when people revile you and persecute you and utter all kinds of evil against you falsely on **MY** account.

Matthew's version has Jesus refer explicitly to himself rather than obliquely to himself as "the Son of Man," as in Luke. Here we see special activity among the Gospel writers of changing "the Son of Man" to "my" or "I" to emphasize in their storytelling that the Son of Man is really Jesus and not some other personage named "the Son of Man." This issue becomes very important when we discuss the second type of Son of Man saying in the Q Gospel, namely "heavenly" Son of Man sayings in which Jesus refers to "the Son of Man" who comes from heaven to earth rather than "the Son of Man" who is already on earth acting in accord with guidance from God's Wisdom.

The Heavenly Son of Man

A special feature of the Q Sayings Gospel is the presence of four "heavenly" Son of Man sayings by Jesus in addition to the three "earthly" Son of Man sayings. Already at the beginning of the 20th century, scholars like Albert Schweitzer observed that in these "heavenly" Son of Man sayings Jesus refers to a personage different from himself! On the basis of this startling discovery, Schweitzer argued that there was a period during Jesus' life on earth when he thought a heavenly personage other than himself, whom he called "the Son of Man," would come from heaven to earth. Indeed, a major activity of this Son of Man would be to judge people on the basis of their positive or negative response to Jesus' words and deeds. Schweitzer found the key verse that presented Jesus' expectation in Matthew 10:23, where Jesus tells the twelve disciples that the heavenly Son of Man will come before they have gone through all the towns of Israel and have returned to Jesus.

The Heavenly Son of Man as Someone Different from Jesus

Matthew 10:5-6, 23

⁵THESE TWELVE [DISCIPLES] JESUS SENT OUT with the following instructions: "Go nowhere among the Gentiles, and enter no town of the Samaritans, ⁶but go rather to the lost sheep of the house of Israel. . . .

²³"When they persecute you in one town, flee to the next; for truly I tell you, YOU WILL NOT HAVE GONE THROUGH ALL THE TOWNS OF ISRAEL BEFORE THE SON OF MAN COMES."

Once a person entertains the possibility of a period of time in Jesus' life on earth when Jesus talked about the Son of Man as a heavenly being other than himself, the question becomes: "Who would this heavenly Son of Man be?" This brings us to the topic of apocalyptic beliefs, which intensified both prophetic and wisdom beliefs by emphasizing God's judgment of the world at the end of time. One of the special aspects of apocalyptic literature is a presentation of many kinds of "heavenly assistants" of God. Many of these assistants were angels, but some were humans like Enoch or Elijah, whom God had taken directly from earth into heaven without making them die first.

One Like a Son of Man in Daniel

In Daniel 7:13-14 the major assistant of God is called "one like a son of man." This scene became highly important for emerging Christianity, so we should look carefully at it for a moment:

¹³As I watched in the night visions,
I saw one like a son of man [NRSV mg.]
    coming with the clouds of heaven.
And he came to the Ancient One
    and was presented before him.
¹⁴To him was given dominion
    and glory and kingship,
that all peoples, nations, and languages
    should serve him.
His dominion is an everlasting dominion
    that shall not pass away,
and his kingship is one
    that shall never be destroyed.

The scene opens with one like a son of man coming on clouds "to God,"
who is called "the Ancient One" or in some translations "the Ancient of
Days." In the middle of the scene, God gives this son of man glory and
kingship over all people. Then the scene closes with an assertion that the
kingship of this son of man will be eternal, that it will never pass away or
be destroyed.

Various phrases from this scene occur in many places in the New Testament. But 1st-century Christians changed the scene in one very important way as they applied it to Jesus as "the heavenly Son of Man." Instead of
Jesus the Son of Man "coming to God on a cloud," they changed it to Jesus
the Son of Man "coming on a cloud from God to earth." In other words,
once followers of Jesus became convinced that Jesus had been resurrected
from earth to heaven after his death, they began to apply Daniel 7:13-14 to
Jesus. However, they used the words of the verses to talk about Jesus' "return to earth" as the heavenly Son of Man, rather than his "going to God"
to receive glory and the kingship he would exercise when he returned to
earth. With 1st-century Christian recitation of phrases from Daniel 7:13-14,
then, we see some of the earliest theological interpretation of Jesus by his
followers.

The Heavenly Son of Man in 1 Enoch

Scholars have discovered passages in Jewish apocalyptic writings written
prior to and during the time of the emergence of Christianity that talked

about the coming of a heavenly Son of Man, and a haunting question is who this heavenly "Son of Man" might be. Some have thought he might be "Original Man," namely "the Man" created in the image of God in Genesis 1:26-27, rather than "Adam, the man of dust" God created in Genesis 2:7. Others considered the possibility that this Son of Man might be Enoch, who was so righteous that God simply took him up into heaven rather than let him die on earth (Gen 5:24). The identity of the heavenly Son of Man as Enoch is presented at the end of the Book of Parables[3] in 1 Enoch, a writing that was started during the 2nd century B.C.E. but expanded over a period of many years into the 1st century C.E.. The Book of Parables in 1 Enoch ends by identifying Enoch as the heavenly Son of Man and telling the things that will happen around him in the new world that is to come.

> [14]Then an angel came to me [**Enoch**] and greeted me and said to me, "You, Son of Man, who art born in righteousness and upon whom righteousness has dwelled, the righteousness of the Antecedent of Time [**God**: cf. Dan 7:13] will not forsake you."
>
> [15]He added and said to me, "He shall proclaim peace to you in the name of the world that is to become. For from here proceeds peace since the creation of the world, and so it shall be unto you forever and ever and ever.
>
> [16]Everyone that will come to exist and walk shall (follow) your path, since righteousness never forsakes you. Together with you shall be their dwelling places; and together with you shall be their portion. **THEY SHALL NOT BE SEPARATED FROM YOU FOREVER AND EVER AND EVER."**
>
> [17]So **THERE SHALL BE LENGTH OF DAYS WITH THE SON OF MAN**, and peace to the righteous ones; his path is upright for the righteous, in the name of the Lord of the Spirits forever and ever."
> (1 Enoch 71:14-17, Charlesworth 1983: 50)

In apocalyptic literature written before and during the emergence of early Christian literature, then, many Jewish people believed that God would select and empower "one like a son of man" from a personage already in heaven to come to earth, rule over people, and judge people on the basis of their righteousness or unrighteousness. Perhaps surprisingly, Elijah never seems to have been a major candidate to be named as "the Son of Man." As

---

3. The Book of Parables, commonly called The Similitudes: 1 Enoch 37:1–71:16.

mentioned above, "Original Man" was a candidate in some apocalyptic literature. But some of the most productive apocalyptic literature was "Enochic." This means that it focused on Enoch, the great-grandfather of Noah, who was so righteous God had taken him directly into heaven rather than requiring that he die and be buried on earth. In the view of Enochic literature, Enoch had special status because he was "prediluvian," which meant that he was taken into heaven before the Great Flood by which God destroyed everything in the time of Noah. Since Enoch was in heaven prior to the flood, he was able to see and hear everything that happened during that time, both in the heavens and on earth. This meant that Enoch had special information about the ways of God and about God's plans that people on earth could learn about only if this information was "revealed." This is the key to Enochic literature as apocalyptic literature. The word *apokalypsis* in Greek means "revelation," and information in Enochic literature "reveals" the "apocalyptic wisdom" of Enoch to people who are privileged to read the Enochic literature.

Jesus Expects the Coming of the Heavenly Son of Man

Since the earliest followers of Jesus were informed not only by prophetic and wisdom literature but also by apocalyptic literature, they were especially interested in the possibility that Jesus would return as "the Son of Man." In fact, the concept of "resurrection from the dead" became a central topic in apocalyptic literature, and during the time of Jesus the Pharisees accepted it but the Sadducees did not.[4] Jesus also believed in resurrection from the dead, and this belief guided early followers of Jesus as they wrestled with the issue of what God had been doing through the life and then the death of Jesus. The Q Sayings Gospel presented Jesus talking about the Son of Man in a way that could allow people to think he was referring to someone other than himself. But after Jesus' followers began to believe that God had resurrected Jesus from death into heaven, they began to believe that Jesus himself was this heavenly Son of Man who would come to earth and do all the things Jewish writers had written about the heavenly Son of Man, such as judge people on the basis of whether they had or had not led a righteous life in relation to the teachings of Jesus.

---

4. Cf. Mark 12:18-27; Acts 23:6-10; Josephus, *Jewish Antiquities* 18.16; *Avot de Rabbi Nathan* 5.2.

The first heavenly Son of Man saying in the Q Gospel focuses on a public occasion either before the angels of God or before God in heaven when the heavenly Son of Man will present to the angels and to God those people who have accepted Jesus' proclamation of the coming of the kingdom of God. In contrast, the heavenly Son of Man will deny before God and the angels any acceptance of those who have refused to accept Jesus' proclamation and enactment of the coming of the kingdom of God.

The Heavenly Son of Man's Public Acceptance or Denial of People before God's Angels and God

QLuke 12	QMatthew 10
[8]And I tell you, **everyone who acknowledges me before others, THE SON OF MAN also will acknowledge before** the angels of God;	[32]**Everyone** therefore **who acknowledges me before others, I** also **will acknowledge before** my Father in heaven;
[9]**but whoever denies me before others will** be <u>denied</u> **before** the angels of God.	[33]**but whoever denies me before others**, I also **will** <u>deny</u> **before** my Father in heaven.

This saying depicts what scholars call an "apocalyptic" event. The event occurs at the end of time, when the Son of Man will come from heaven to earth and "present" people to God on the basis of their righteousness or unrighteousness. In this version of the event in the Q Gospel, the heavenly Son of Man will present people to God's angels and to God on the basis of their acceptance or denial of Jesus and his message when he was on earth.

Matthew's version changes "the Son of Man" to "I," thus giving Jesus the honor of acknowledging before God those who have responded favorably to him and of denying before God those who have denied him, rather than giving it to the heavenly Son of Man, who would come to earth before Jesus finished his earthly work. In other words, the Gospel of Matthew gives Jesus himself the functions of this heavenly Son of Man. Jesus could not perform these functions, of course, unless he were first in heaven. This means that the followers of Jesus had to believe that Jesus had been raised from death into heaven before he could be a candidate to be the Son of Man who would come from heaven to earth. The Q Gospel shows the transition in emerging Christianity from a time when Jesus' speech referred to the heavenly Son of Man as a person other than Jesus to the belief that this Son of Man was Jesus himself.

The Day of the Son of Man

In addition to the saying about the Son of Man's acknowledgment or denial of people on the basis of their response to Jesus' sayings and actions on earth, there are three heavenly "Son of Man" sayings in the Q Gospel that describe what it will be like on the day when the Son of Man comes to earth. In these sayings, Jesus says that lightning will flash over the entire sky to signal that the Son of Man is coming. The dramatic effect of the coming of this heavenly Son of Man, Jesus says, will be like the terrible things that happened during the time of Noah.

Separation on the Day of the Heavenly Son of Man

QLuke 17	QMatthew 24
[23]They will say to you, "Look there!" or "Look here!" Do not go, do not set off in pursuit.	[23]Then if anyone says to you, "Look! Here is the Messiah!" or "There he is!" — do not believe it. . . .
[24]For as the lightning flashes and lights up the sky from one side to the other, so will the Son of Man be in his day. . . .	[27]For as the lightning comes from the east and flashes as far as the west, so will be the coming of the Son of Man. . . .
[26]Just as it was in the days of Noah, so too it will be in the days of the Son of Man. [27]They were eating and drinking, and marrying and being given in marriage, until the day Noah entered the ark, and the flood came and destroyed all of them. . . .	[37]For as the days of Noah were, so will be the coming of the Son of Man. [38]For as in those days before the flood they were eating and drinking, marrying and giving in marriage, until the day Noah entered the ark, [39]and they knew nothing until the flood came and swept them all away,
[30]it will be like that on the day that the Son of Man is revealed. . . .	so too will be the coming of the Son of Man.
[34]I tell you, on that night there will be two in one bed; one will be taken and the other left. [35]There will be two women grinding meal together; one will be taken and the other left.	[40]Then two will be in the field; one will be taken and one will be left. [41]Two women will be grinding meal together; one will be taken and one will be left.
[37]. . . He said to them, Where the corpse is, there the vultures will gather.	[28]Wherever the corpse is, there the vultures will gather.

When the Q Gospel presents Jesus' sayings about the coming Son of Man, it emphasizes that certain people will be "taken" and others will be "left." Surely the understanding is that the people who are taken "will not be separated from" the Son of Man "forever and ever and ever," as it asserts in 1 Enoch 71:16, presented above. Those who are left, in contrast, will become corpses around whom vultures will gather!

The Twelve Will Sit on Thrones

But there is yet one more promise by Jesus. In the view of the Q Gospel, God will not destroy the entire earth when the heavenly Son of Man comes. Rather, God will renew the earth, making it the kingdom of God. The final verse of the Q Gospel presents Jesus telling the twelve disciples about their role: they will sit on thrones over the twelve tribes of Israel!

Jesus' Promise That the Twelve Will Sit on Thrones over the Tribes of Israel

QLuke 22	QMatt 19
[28] "**You** are those **who have** <u>stood by</u> **me** in my trials; . . .	[28]Jesus said to them, ". . . **you who have** <u>followed</u> **me**
[30]. . . and **you will sit on thrones judging the twelve tribes of Israel.**"	will also **sit on twelve thrones, judging the twelve tribes of Israel.**"

Many readers will be surprised at the statement by Jesus in these verses that the twelve disciples will sit on thrones judging the people of Israel. The next chapter, on the Gospel of Mark, will explain why we may be so surprised by it. In Mark, Jesus tells James and John that they must not think that Jesus will allow them to sit on his right and left hand in his glory (Mark 10:37-40). We can see from the Q Gospel why followers of Jesus might think Jesus' special disciples will have such a position of power. We will learn in the next chapter how the Gospel of Mark confronted followers of Jesus with the necessity to rethink many of their prophetic and apocalyptic expectations surrounding John the Baptist and Jesus.

Conclusion

In the previous chapter we saw how early followers of Jesus naturally began with prophetic expectations they had from traditions about Moses, Elijah, and Elisha, and from sayings they knew in the prophetic writings of Isaiah and Malachi. We also saw how Jesus' use of the phrase "the Son of Man" in

the Q Gospel presented Jesus' joyous lifestyle as a dramatic contrast to
John the Baptist's severe, ascetic lifestyle. In this chapter, we have seen how
the phrase "the Son of Man" could refer to a heavenly being who would
come in the future to verify the truth of Jesus' proclamation of the coming
of the kingdom of God. Moreover, we have seen that as soon as followers of
Jesus believed that Jesus had been raised from death into heaven they were
convinced that the heavenly Son of Man who would come in the future
would be Jesus himself. This Jesus, they also believed, would establish the
twelve disciples of Jesus on thrones judging the twelve tribes of Israel.

LEARNING ACTIVITIES

1. Read (or reread) Proverbs 8:1-36. Compare it with Sirach 4:1-31. If you
   do not have a Study Bible that includes Sirach, search for it online under "NRSV Apocrypha online."
2. Find Sirach either in a Study Bible or online and read the account of
   Wisdom singing the praise of famous men in chs. 44–50.
3. Read all of Matthew 10 to see the context in which it is said that the
   heavenly Son of Man will come as a personage different from Jesus before the disciples have gone through all the towns of Israel with their
   message of good news about the coming of the kingdom of heaven (vv.
   7) and their activity of healing people (vv. 8-9). See how the disciples
   are to adopt the lifestyle of "the Son of Man" who "has nowhere to lay
   his head" as they take no money, food bag, tunic to sleep in, or sandals
   as they travel (vv. 9-15). Notice also how Matthew's account presents
   the disciples as prophets sent out in the same way that God sent Jesus
   (vv. 40-42).
4. Read the brief reference in Genesis 5:21-24 about God's taking of Enoch
   directly into heaven in response to his righteous life. Also read in
   2 Kings 2:6-14 how Elisha saw Elijah's ascent into heaven.
5. Resurrection from the dead became a central concern in apocalyptic
   literature around the time of Jesus. Read Mark 12:18-27; Acts 23:6-10;
   Josephus, *Jewish Antiquities* 18.16; *Avot de Rabbi Nathan* 5.2, and compare how these early traditions frame one strand of debate about this
   issue.
6. Read all of Daniel 7 to see the context of the four beasts who are the
   four terrible, violent kingdoms on earth before God chooses "one like a
   son of man" to rule eternally over "all peoples, nations, and languages"
   (vv. 13-14). Notice how in Daniel the kingship and dominion is given

"to the people of the holy ones of the Most High" (vv. 22, 27), rather than to the Messiah Jesus. In other words, in Daniel itself the "one like the son of man (human being)" is understood to be a group of holy people who have lived righteous lives rather than a single person. This changes in 1 Enoch 71, discussed briefly above, where "one like a son of man" is understood to be one person.

7. In relation to QLuke 22:28-30/QMatthew 19:28, read Judges 2:6–3:6 in the HB/OT to see how the era of the judges began in Israel. Read Judges 3:7-11 to see how Othniel served as an ideal judge over Israel until he died. Then read Judges 17:6; 18:1; 19:1; and 21:25 to see how disappointment over how the judges ruled led to hopes that a king could lead Israel into righteous ways of living.

BIBLIOGRAPHY

Allison, Dale C. 1997. *The Jesus Tradition in Q.* Harrisburg: Trinity.

Charlesworth, James H. (ed.). 1983. *The Old Testament Pseudepigrapha,* Volume 1: *Apocalyptic Literature and Testaments.* Garden City: Doubleday.

Collins, John J. 1992. "The Son of Man in First-Century Judaism." *New Testament Studies* 38: 448-66.

Crossan, John Dominic. 1995. *Jesus: A Revolutionary Biography.* San Francisco: HarperSanFrancisco.

Jacobson, Arland D. 1992. *The First Gospel: An Introduction to Q.* Sonoma: Polebridge.

Kloppenborg, John S., Marvin W. Meyer, Stephen J. Patterson, and Michael G. Steinhauser. 1990. *Q-Thomas Reader.* Sonoma: Polebridge.

The Lost Sayings Gospel Q: http://www.earlychristianwritings.com/q.html

Luz, Ulrich. 1992. "The Son of Man in Matthew: Heavenly Judge or Human Christ." *Journal for the Study of the New Testament* 48: 3-21.

Mack, Burton L. 1993. *The Lost Gospel: The Book of Q and Christian Origins.* San Francisco: HarperCollins.

Robbins, Vernon K. 2009. *The Invention of Christian Discourse,* Volume 1. Blandford Forum: Deo.

Tuckett, Christopher M. 1996. *Q and the History of Early Christianity: Studies on Q.* Edinburgh: T & T Clark.

3

You Cannot Be the Suffering-Dying Son of Man!

In the middle of the Gospel of Mark, Jesus asks his disciples who people say he is (8:27). The disciples respond with points of view related to prophetic expectations like those in the Q Sayings Gospel. When Jesus responds to the disciples in Mark, he uses the term "the Son of Man," again a similarity with the Q Gospel. But this time Jesus introduces a whole new scenario: the Son of Man must suffer, be rejected, be killed, and after three days rise again (8:31). In the Q Sayings Gospel, Jesus says nothing about death and resurrection as events in the career of the Son of Man. But in Mark these events become a major topic, and thus a remarkable feature of Mark emerges. Jesus' disciples make it clear that they are not willing to think that God's Messiah must be killed and rise again. This leads us to the scene, which regularly is called the Caesarea Philippi story, in the center of this sixteen-chapter Gospel.

King Herod's Opinion about Jesus

The disciples' answer to Jesus' question about his identity has been known to the reader since ch. 6, where King Herod Antipas, son of Herod the Great,[1] oversees the killing of John the Baptist. Antipas heard about Jesus' ability to heal people when Jesus' disciples were traveling around Galilee curing people in Jesus' name.

---

1. Herod Antipas, officially a tetrarch but popularly known as "King Herod," ruled Galilee and part of Transjordan from 4 B.C.E. to 39 C.E. See Josephus, *Jewish Wars* 1.14.4, where Antony persuades the senate to make Herod "king."

42

Mark 6

What King Herod Heard

¹³They [the twelve disciples] cast out many demons, and anointed with oil many who were sick and cured them. ¹⁴King Herod heard of it, for **Jesus' name had become known**.

People's Opinions about Jesus and His Disciples

Some were saying, "**John the baptizer HAS BEEN RAISED** from the dead; and for this reason these powers are at work in him." ¹⁵But others said, "It is **Elijah**." And others said, "It is a prophet, like **one of the prophets** of old."

King Herod's Opinion about Jesus

¹⁶But when Herod heard of it, he said, "**John**, whom I beheaded, **HAS BEEN RAISED**."

When Jesus' disciples respond to Jesus' question concerning who people say he is, they include "John the Baptist" but omit the assertion that John was raised from the dead:

Mark 6	Mark 8
¹³They cast out many demons, and anointed with oil many who were sick and cured them. ¹⁴King Herod heard of it, for **Jesus' name had become known**.	²⁷Jesus went on with his disciples to the villages of Caesarea Philippi; and on the way he asked his disciples, "**Who do people say that I am?**"
Some were saying, "**JOHN THE BAPTIZER HAS BEEN RAISED from the dead**; and for this reason these powers are at work in him."	²⁸And they answered him, "**JOHN THE BAPTIST**,"
¹⁵But others said, "It is **ELIJAH**." And others said, "It is a prophet, like **ONE OF THE PROPHETS** of old." ¹⁶But when Herod heard of it, he said, '**JOHN**, whom I beheaded, **HAS BEEN RAISED**.'	and others, "**ELIJAH**," and still others, "**ONE OF THE PROPHETS**."

As in the earlier discussion of King Herod, however, Jesus' disciples tell Jesus that some think he is Elijah. Then they change the earlier statement from Jesus being "a prophet like one of the prophets of old" simply to "one of the prophets." There are two similarities here with the approach we saw in a previous chapter about the Q Sayings Gospel. In order to understand Jesus, people begin with concepts with which they are familiar in relation to the biblical prophets. Second, they correlate these concepts in some way with events surrounding John the Baptist.

Jesus as the Suffering Son of Man

The special features of Mark emerge when Jesus shifts the question from "Who do people say I am?" to "Who do you (as disciples) think I am?" Here is the issue. Who Jesus is affects the life of a disciple of Jesus. Therefore, disciples have a much keener interest in "exactly who Jesus might be" than most people would have. The interchange between Jesus and his disciples unfolds in 8:29-31 as follows:

> [29]He asked them, "**BUT WHO DO YOU SAY THAT I AM?**"
>
> **PETER** answered him, "**YOU ARE THE MESSIAH.**" [30]And he sternly ordered them not to tell anyone about him.
>
> [31]Then he **began to teach** them that
> **THE SON OF MAN MUST UNDERGO**
> great **SUFFERING,**
> and **BE REJECTED** by the elders, the chief priests, and the scribes,
> and **BE KILLED,**
> and **AFTER THREE DAYS RISE AGAIN.**

When there was discussion of Jesus as "the coming One" in the Q Sayings Gospel, no one spoke explicitly about the possibility that Jesus might be the Messiah of Israel. Rather, the discussion stayed within the bounds of Jesus as somehow more than a prophet both by the ways he was different from John the Baptist and by the way his joyous activities as "the Son of Man" brought forth accusations that he was a glutton and a drunkard. In contrast to the way in which the scene unfolds in the Q Gospel, in Mark Peter openly asserts that Jesus is the Messiah. When Peter says Jesus is the Messiah, Jesus does not openly agree or disagree with him. Rather, Jesus tells the disciples not to say to anyone that he is the Messiah and teaches them a new definition of "the Son of Man." This new definition describes the Son of Man as a person who "must accept" events of suffering, being rejected, being killed, and on the third day rising again.

But then a remarkable exchange occurs in vv. 32 and 33. Peter refuses to accept this "new" definition of the Son of Man:

> [32]He said all this quite openly.
>
> And **PETER** took him aside and **BEGAN TO REBUKE HIM.**
>
> [33]But turning and looking at his disciples, **HE REBUKED PETER** and said, "Get behind me, **SATAN!**

For you are **SETTING YOUR MIND
NOT ON DIVINE THINGS
BUT ON HUMAN THINGS."**

After Jesus teaches this new definition of the Son of Man, Peter takes Jesus aside and "rebukes" him as if he is trying to cast a demonic spirit out of Jesus' mind (8:32).[2] In turn, Jesus rebukes Peter, calling him Satan and telling him he has human thoughts rather than divine thoughts in his mind (v. 33). Why this sharp interchange between Jesus and Peter? The answer to this question has many dimensions, and they are central to understanding the role of the Gospel of Mark in emerging Christianity. As Christianity was still working at defining itself in the midst of events in the Mediterranean world four decades after the death and resurrection of Jesus, followers of Jesus were living in the midst of a terrible war between Rome and Jews in the region of Galilee and Judea. The war not only destroyed many villages and cities, but it led to wholesale destruction of Jerusalem and its Temple in 70 C.E. and to the bombardment of Masada that led to wholesale suicide in 73 C.E. In the context of the onslaught and devastation produced by the Roman army, suffering, rejection, and death were acquiring special meaning for the followers of Jesus.

As the Jewish-Roman War of 66-73 C.E. progressed, followers of Jesus had to decide if they would participate in military resistance against the Romans and/or action against Jewish sympathizers with the Romans. Ched Myers led the way in 1989 in arguing that Christians who were allied to the story of Jesus as it is told in Mark were unwilling to participate in military violence (Myers 2008). For them Jesus of Nazareth served as a model of a person who accepted suffering, rejection, and death rather than fighting back with swords or some other kind of attack. Jesus was willing to lose his life for the sake of the gospel, and in his losing life his life was saved (8:35). From their point of view, Jesus died with a false charge against him as a king with the intention of ruling over Israel. Mark argues this point of view especially by the way it presents the disciples of Jesus struggling with this "new" concept of king-Messiah.

---

2. See "rebuke" in Mark 1:25-26.

The Disciples Cannot Understand Jesus

In relation to the point of view in the Q Sayings Gospel, the belief in Mark that Jesus had no intention of setting up a political situation where the disciples would have power over the tribes of Israel presents a new, and perhaps disturbing, alternative. As we saw in the two previous chapters, the Q Sayings Gospel ends with a promise to the twelve disciples that they will sit on thrones judging the twelve tribes of Israel. Mark, in contrast, presents Jesus as a person who denies any such status for the disciples. This view about the disciples emerges in the progressive texture of Mark 8–10 as Jesus teaches his disciples a second and third time that the Son of Man must suffer, be rejected, be killed, and on the third day rise again.

Jesus Repeatedly Teaches about Himself as the Suffering, Dying, Rising Son of Man

8	9	10
[31]Then he **began to teach** them that **THE SON OF MAN** must undergo great suffering, and be rejected by the elders, the chief priests, and the scribes,	[31]for he was **teaching** his disciples, saying to them, "**THE SON OF MAN** is to be betrayed into human hands,	[33]saying, "See, we are going up to Jerusalem, and **THE SON OF MAN** will be handed over to the chief priests and the scribes, and they will condemn him to death; then they will hand him over to the Gentiles; [34]they will mock him, and spit upon him, and flog him,
and **BE KILLED**,	and **THEY WILL KILL HIM**,	and **KILL HIM**;
and **AFTER THREE DAYS RISE AGAIN**.	and **THREE DAYS AFTER BEING KILLED, HE WILL RISE AGAIN**."	and **AFTER THREE DAYS HE WILL RISE AGAIN**."

The third time Jesus teaches this new definition of the Son of Man (10:33-34), James and John come to Jesus with a request that presupposes a view of Jesus' establishment of the kingdom of God in a manner related to the Q Sayings Gospel, but now with a decidedly different response from Jesus. Indeed, the elaborate response of Jesus creates the dramatic ending of ch. 10.

James and John Misunderstand

[35]James and John, the sons of Zebedee, came forward to him and said to him, "Teacher, we want you to do for us whatever we ask of you." [36]And he said to them, "What is it you want me to do for you?" [37]And they said to him, "Grant us to sit, one at your right hand and one at your left, in your glory."

Jesus Teaches Proper Markan Understanding

[38]But Jesus said to them, "You do not know what you are asking. Are you able to drink the cup that I drink, or be baptized with the baptism that I am baptized with?" [39]They replied, "We are able." Then Jesus said to them, "The cup that I drink you will drink; and with the baptism with which I am baptized, you will be baptized; [40]but to sit at my right hand or at my left is not mine to grant, but it is for those for whom it has been prepared."

When James and John come to Jesus asking him to do whatever they ask of him, Jesus begins by asking them what they want him to do for them (10:36). They answer that they want him to grant them a place at his right and left hand in his glory (v. 37). Jesus tells them they do not know what they are asking and asks if they are able to accept the drink and the baptism he faces (v. 38). When they say they are able, Jesus tells them they will indeed face the drink and the baptism he faces, but it is not his to grant who will sit at his right and left hand in his glory (vv. 39-40). Much as in the Caesarea Philippi story where Jesus talks with all the disciples after an interchange with one disciple (8:31-32, 34–9:1), Jesus speaks to all the disciples after speaking to James and John. But here the other ten have heard the discussion and are angry with James and John (10:41). Presumably their anger concerns the privileged position James and John have sought. Instead of wanting to be at Jesus' right and left hands, they should be willing to take an equal position alongside the rest of the disciples judging the twelve tribes of Israel! But Jesus has still another point of view, and he explains this view to all of them together as a group (vv. 41-45):

[41]When the ten heard this, they began to be angry with James and John. [42]So Jesus called them and said to them,

Commonly Accepted Knowledge:

"You know that **AMONG THE GENTILES THOSE WHOM THEY RECOGNIZE AS THEIR RULERS LORD IT OVER THEM, AND THEIR GREAT ONES ARE TYRANTS OVER THEM.**"

Argument from the Opposite:

[43]But it is **NOT SO AMONG YOU;**

Thesis:

but **WHOEVER WISHES TO BECOME GREAT AMONG YOU MUST BE YOUR SERVANT,**
[44]and **WHOEVER WISHES TO BE FIRST AMONG YOU MUST BE SLAVE OF ALL.**

Rationale:

[45]For **THE SON OF MAN CAME NOT TO BE SERVED BUT TO SERVE, AND TO GIVE HIS LIFE A RANSOM FOR MANY."**

Jesus Calls His Disciples to Serve Others

The narrator of this scene in Mark presents Jesus' argument to his disciples as a special "call." Calling to them, he presents to them a tightly constructed argument that begins with something commonly known and then presents an opposite point of view in the form of a thesis supported by reasoning that uses "the Son of Man" as a model for their own action. This argument provides a conclusion to two chapters of teaching and events that started with the question and answer scene at Caesarea Philippi. The teaching about the Son of Man that Jesus presented in that Caesarea Philippi scene introduced the model of the Son of Man Jesus uses to support his argument concerning how his disciples must act toward one another and toward all people. Since the Son of Man did not come to rule but to serve and give his life for others, so they, his disciples, must be willing to be servants to one another and slaves to all people.

"True Kings" Serve Their People

This argument by Jesus may seem to be totally unheard of in the context of the common point of view about rulers with which Jesus starts his argument. In fact, however, there was considerable discussion among moral philosophers of the time about the way a "true king" should rule. It was widely accepted, of course, that soldiers should be willing to die as a benefit to the society in which they lived. For instance, there was a well-known poetic verse of Horace (65-68 B.C.E.): "sweet and fitting it is to die for one's fatherland" (Robbins 2009: 188). But this was also applied to kings. Probably the most well-known example was King Codrus of Athens who, following the guidance of a prophetic oracle, went out among the troops in slave's clothing, unrecognized, and was killed, but by doing so he saved Athens (Hengel 1981: 13-14, 82). Clement of Rome, who wrote a couple of decades after Mark's Gospel was written, shows knowledge of this tradition of kings dying for their people when he writes:

> Many kings and rulers, when a time of pestilence has set in, have followed the counsel of oracles, and given themselves up to death, that they might rescue their subjects through their own blood. (*1 Clement* 55:1)

In addition to the tradition that a king should, in certain extreme times, be willing to die for the people over whom he rules, a writer named Dio Chrysostom (ca. 40–after 112 C.E.) wrote four essays on kingship to teach that a king should at all times focus on the needs of his people. A true king is willing to endure hardship (3.2) and to serve others (4.66). In addition, the true king is a shepherd of people (3.41; 4.43; cf. Mark 6:34; 14:27). Since the king considers himself to be appointed to his work by the greatest God (Zeus), he believes he is only obeying the god who gave him this task as he attends to the needs of those over whom he rules (3.55). As the king does this, he depends on the faithfulness of his friends, whom he needs as co-workers (3.86). Indeed, his greatest suffering arises when he is wronged by his friends, who he thought could never be his enemies (3.114). In the fourth discourse, where Dio presents his view of true kingship through a scene in which the Cynic philosopher Diogenes teaches Alexander the Great, some of the teaching gets even closer to some of the points of view in the Gospel of Mark. Diogenes teaches Alexander that if a king is a son of Zeus (4.21) he will know the foolishness of attempting to gain money and possessions (4.6; cf. Mark 8:36) and of clamoring after wealth (4.10; cf. Mark 10:25; 12:41). Indeed, the instruction in kingship is of two opposing kinds: divine and human (4.29). Here we see a distinction very close to the assertion Jesus makes to Peter about being on the side of God or on the side of humans (Mark 8:33). In fact, Dio even says that the king who has received divine instruction as a son of Zeus at once recognizes the way (4.33; cf. Mark 1:2-3; 8:27; 9:33-34; 10:17, 32, 52; 12:14). If the king follows human rather than divine instruction, this leads to seduction by wealth and other desires, to weakness, and to cowardice (4.29). It is important that the king live according to divine instruction. In this way he can fulfill both the tasks he has been appointed to fulfill and his responsibility to present a model by which people should live on a daily basis.

The reasoning Jesus presents about the right way to be great and first in Mark 10:41-45, then, was not so unusual in the Mediterranean world. What was unusual, it appears, was the argument that this is how the Messiah of Israel should act.[3] The Gospel presents Jesus arguing this point of view by using the phrase "the Son of Man" in relation to a suffering, rejected, dying, and rising Messiah. As Jesus brings his teaching to a close about the effect of his role as the suffering, rejected, dying, and rising Son of Man on those who follow him as disciples, he presents both what is well-known about living under powerful rulers who function as tyrants (10:42) and about how to live according to a model of "true kingship." Those who want to be truly great must be servants, and, if they wish to be truly first, they must be slaves (vv. 43-44). Mark presents Jesus teaching this view of being great and first in a context where the Roman emperor is using violence and destruction throughout Galilee and Judea to bring peace and salvation to the Roman Empire! The emperor's way is not true kingship. It can never be the way in which God brings in the kingdom of God through actions of the Son of Man. Rather, true kingship where people who are first and great live like servants of one another and slaves of all people gives a preview of the kingly rule of God over all people. In Mark, Jesus presents this reasoning through an argument that the Son of Man did not come to be served but to serve. Indeed, he came to give his life as a benefit for many (v. 45). If this was something known about "true kings" in Roman society, it was a view rarely followed by Roman emperors and not a view regularly associated with the Messiah of Israel. The writer of the Gospel, allying himself with discussions of "true kingship" in the Roman world, presents Jesus teaching that the Messiah of Israel would not "lord it over" everyone as tyrants do (v. 42), but would be a suffering, rejected, dying, and rising Son of Man. Mark presents the struggle of this change in point of view among emerging Christianity as a messianic Jewish movement through the inability of Jesus' disciples to understand and accept this argument prior to Jesus' actual enactment of this way of life in his own death on the cross.

---

3. It was common understanding during the 1st century C.E. that the Messiah of Israel would sit on the throne of Zion in triumph over Israel's enemies; see the Dead Sea Scrolls text 4QFlorilegium 1.10-13: "*And YHWH declares to you that He will build you a house; and I will raise up your seed after you, and I will establish his royal throne forever. I will be a father to him and he shall be My son* [2 Sam 7:11c-14a]. This is 'the branch of David' who will stand with the interpreter of the Law, who will sit on the throne in Zion at the end of days; as it is written, *I will raise up the tent of David which is fallen* [Amos 9:11]."

The Son of Man Rises Up and Comes Again

But if the "dying" part is clear, what about the "rising" part? The startling conclusion to the Gospel of Mark is an empty tomb, where a young man in a white robe tells women who come to the tomb that he "has risen" and "is not here." The women are to tell "the disciples and Peter" that Jesus is going ahead of them to Galilee. There they will see him, just as he told them (16:6-7; cf. 14:28). The question is how Jesus will appear to the disciples in Galilee. There is no account of an appearance of Jesus to his disciples at the end of the Gospel.[4] Will he appear to them as the heavenly Son of Man after his resurrection? In 8:38 Jesus said that the Son of Man will come "in the glory of his Father with the holy angels." Then later Jesus describes the coming of the Son of Man after many wars, earthquakes, and famines in various places (13:7-8) and also after the disciples have been handed over to councils, beaten in synagogues, and made to stand before governors and kings while they are proclaiming the gospel to all nations (vv. 9-10). After these things, Jesus says, the Son of Man will come "in clouds with great power and glory" (v. 26). The amazing thing is the single action the Son of Man will take at this time: "Then he will send out the angels, and gather his elect from the four winds, from the ends of the earth to the end of heaven" (v. 27). In Mark there is no description of the Son of Man destroying any enemies. In 8:38 Jesus says that when the Son of Man comes he will be "ashamed" of those who "are ashamed" of Jesus and his words. But in Mark there is no description of the Son of Man's public shaming of these people by sending them to a place of punishment or destruction, or anything like that. Rather, the Son of Man simply sends angels out to all corners of the earth to gather together "his elect."

Indeed, the absence of any punishment or destruction of anyone or anything in Mark 13:26-27 is similar to Paul's description of the descent from heaven of "the Lord himself" in 1 Thessalonians 4:16-17. In Paul's account also there is no destruction of anyone or anything. But Paul's account differs by presenting a two-step process of "rising." First the dead in Christ will rise (1 Thess 4:16), then believers who are alive "will be caught up in the clouds together with them to meet the Lord in the air" (v. 17). Then, as Paul says, "We will be with the Lord forever," surely meaning that

---

4. The earliest manuscripts end with the story of the empty tomb (16:8). Scribes who could not accept such an ending added endings of varying length asserting that Jesus appeared to the disciples later.

they will be with "the Lord Messiah" forever. The focus both in Mark and
1 Thessalonians, then, is on the descent of either "the Son of Man" (Mark
13:26) or "the Lord himself" (1 Thess 4:16) to gather to himself "his elect"
(Mark 13:27) or both "the dead in Christ" and "we who are alive" (1 Thess
4:16-17). The view seems to be that the elect ones have "given their life"
abundantly on earth, so that when the Son of Man (or the Lord himself)
comes, the total focus of the one who comes will be to gather them "to
himself" so they may be with him forever. It is as though there is no need
for the Son of Man to punish or destroy anyone or anything, because "rulers" cause so much violence and destruction that it is not necessary for any
emissary of God also to destroy!

Conclusion

The Gospel of Mark presents Jesus' disciples as people who added Messianic expectations to prophetic expectations in order to understand Jesus'
actions. In other words, they expected the Messiah to come as a king who
would rule over God's kingdom. According to Mark, Jesus disappoints the
disciples by arguing that "the Son of Man" must suffer, be rejected, be
killed, and after three days rise up.

An amazing thing about Mark is that the disciples never do accept Jesus' view of a suffering-dying-rising Son of Man/Messiah. They flee when
Jesus is arrested (14:50), and Peter even denies that he ever was with Jesus
(vv. 66-72). The result is that none of Jesus' disciples either see Jesus die on
the cross or see the empty tomb. None of them participates in the burial of
Jesus, in contrast to disciples of John the Baptist, who take John's body and
bury it in a tomb (6:29)! Rather, Mary Magdalene, Mary the mother of
James the younger, and Salome see Jesus die on the cross (15:40), and they
see the empty tomb when they bring spices on the first day of the week to
anoint Jesus' body (16:1-2). But the narrator of Mark says that the women
did not tell the disciples or anyone else about the tomb, because they were
afraid (v. 8)! This is a remarkable ending, since all hearers/readers will actually know, on the basis of Mark 13:9-11, that the disciples accepted a life of
derision and punishment after Jesus' death to "proclaim the gospel to all
nations." Surely a major reason for this ending is to build within the
hearer/reader a feeling of necessity to tell the story, since the women did
not tell it! And the hearer/reader knows the story was told, because the
story now exists as a public story in the Gospel.

But there is yet one more thing the reader should know before ending this chapter. The Gospel of Mark also uses the term "Son of God" to describe Jesus, the suffering, rejected, dying, rising Son of Man Messiah. By the time we receive the written form of the Gospel, the opening verse announces "The beginning of the gospel of Jesus Messiah, the Son of God" (1:1). When Jesus is baptized, the heavens split apart when Jesus is coming out of the water, the Spirit descends like a dove onto him, and a voice from heaven says, "You are my Son, the Beloved; with you I am well pleased" (v. 11). At various points in the story, unclean spirits shout out to Jesus, "You are the Son of God" (cf. 3:11; 5:7). When Jesus is transfigured on a high mountain so that his clothes become dazzling white, a voice comes out of the cloud saying, "This is my Son, the Beloved, listen to him" (9:7). After Jesus is arrested and the high priest asks Jesus if he is "the Son of the Blessed One," Jesus says, "I am, and you will see the Son of Man seated at the right hand of the Power, and coming with the clouds of heaven" (14:62). Then when Jesus gives a loud cry and breathes his last on the cross, the Roman centurion, seeing that he died in this way, said, "Truly this man was God's Son!" (15:39). In the end, then, a person outside Jesus' inner circle of disciples sees and understands the true nature of Jesus' messiahship. The Messiah of the Judeans, which is the title above the cross where Jesus is hanging (15:26), is a suffering, rejected, dying Messiah. When the Roman centurion sees Jesus' death, he calls Jesus God's Son, but when Jesus talked about suffering, rejection, and death he used the title "the Son of Man." For the early messianic Jewish followers of Jesus, the term "Son of Man" had become a special way to think through belief in Jesus as a suffering, rejected, dying Messiah of Israel. But this would not be a phrase a Roman centurion would understand. Also, there is no evidence that the centurion entertains any possibility that as God's Son Jesus will rise from the dead. In contrast, some women are told about Jesus' resurrection when they find an empty tomb instead of a tomb with Jesus' corpse in it. But they do not tell anyone! The hearers/readers of the Gospel of Mark also hear about the resurrection of Jesus. And everyone should know about it, right? Jesus spoke of it over and over again in Mark 8–10.

Why do Jesus' disciples resist Jesus' teaching about a suffering-dying-rising Messiah in Mark? Scholars think this reflects puzzlement within the early decades of the early Christian movement itself. First and foremost, the earliest followers of Jesus were a messianic Jewish movement. They agreed that somehow Jesus of Nazareth was bringing in the kingdom of God, and this meant that Jesus was somehow a Messiah-king. But how was he "kingly"? Mark presents a narrative argument that Jesus was a king-Messiah who accepted suffering, rejection and death for his people. The story also contains a promise that this king-Messiah would "rise up" from death. But instead of showing his resurrection, it shows an empty tomb where a young man says Jesus has risen up from death (16:6). The young man also says Jesus' disciples will see him in Galilee (v. 7). Will they see him in Galilee when he comes in clouds as the heavenly Son of Man? Or will they see him earlier, in some special appearance to them before his more glorious return when the sun becomes dark, the moon does not give light, the stars fall from heaven, and the powers in heaven are shaken (13:24)? The Gospel does not make this entirely clear, so scholars debate whether or not the Markan story presupposes a penultimate appearance of Jesus to his disciples in Galilee before he appears in his glorious form at a later date. This is another "mysterious" aspect of Mark. In fact, one of the characteristics of the Markan story is that even though the disciples (and the reader) are told the secret mystery of the kingdom of God (4:11), the disciples never really understand it, and a hearer/reader cannot be sure they understand all aspects of it either! But isn't this the nature of mystery?

The final message is that the Son of Man will come in clouds accompanied by angels and gather together his elect. But when exactly will he come (Mark 13:32-33)? And who exactly will be the elect (v. 27)? The writers of Matthew and Luke thought some, if not all, of these uncertainties should be addressed more fully. Matthew expands Mark's sixteen chapters into twenty-eight and Luke expands them to twenty-four chapters so that the story about Jesus' life, death, and resurrection can give clearer guidance concerning how a follower of Jesus should think and act. So we will turn to these two Gospels in the next chapters of this book.

LEARNING ACTIVITIES

1. Read the story of John the Baptist's death in Mark 6:14-29. Notice how John's disciples take John's body and bury it in a tomb, in contrast to the absence of Jesus' disciples when Jesus is buried.

2. Read all of Mark 13:1-37 to see how Jesus tells Peter, James, John, and Andrew about the end of time and the coming of the Son of Man in the context of the destruction of the Jerusalem Temple.

3. Compare Mark 10:35-40 with QLuke 22:28-30/QMatthew 19:28 to see how the Markan Jesus rejects political aspirations for himself and his disciples.

4. Read Paul's description of the Lord's coming in 1 Thessalonians 4:16-17 alongside Mark 13:26-27. Observe how neither passage focuses on punishment or destruction. Note as well, however, that Paul's description of the future event has believers rising in a two-step process that differs from what one finds in Mark.

5. Compare Jesus' post-resurrection appearances in Matthew 28 and Luke 24 to the empty tomb ending in Mark 16:1-8.

6. Read further about the nature of true kingship in biblical tradition and the Mediterranean world in Robbins, *Jesus the Teacher*, 180-94.

BIBLIOGRAPHY

Beavis, Mary Ann. 2011. *Mark*. Paideia Commentaries on the New Testament. Grand Rapids: Baker Academic.

Black, C. Clifton. 2011. *Mark*. Abingdon New Testament Commentaries. Nashville: Abingdon.

Collins, Adela Yarbro. 2007. *Mark: A Commentary*. Hermeneia. Minneapolis: Fortress.

Donahue, John R., and Daniel J. Harrington. 2002. *The Gospel of Mark*. Sacra Pagina. Collegeville: Liturgical.

Dowd, Sharyn. 2000. *Reading Mark: A Literary and Theological Commentary on the Second Gospel*. Macon: Smyth & Helwys.

Gospel of Mark: http://www.earlychristianwritings.com/mark.html

Hengel, Martin. 1981. *The Atonement: The Origins of the Doctrine in the New Testament*. Philadelphia: Fortress.

Myers, Ched. 2008. *Binding the Strong Man: A Political Reading of Mark's Story of Jesus*. Maryknoll: Orbis.

Robbins, Vernon K. 2009. *Jesus the Teacher: A Socio-Rhetorical Interpretation of Mark*. Minneapolis: Augsburg Fortress.

Waetjen, Herman C. 1989. *A Reordering of Power: A Socio-Political Reading of Mark's Gospel*. Minneapolis: Fortress.

4

You Are the Messiah, the Son of the Living God!

The Gospel of Matthew has a longer version than Mark of the scene at Caesarea Philippi where Jesus asks his disciples about who he is. In Matthew Peter replies with "You are the Messiah, the Son of the Living God." Instead of immediately responding with a statement not to tell anyone, Jesus blesses Peter and tells him he is the rock on which he will build his church. Matthew is the only Gospel in the New Testament in which the word "church" appears. Jesus' use of the Greek word *ekklēsia*, regularly translated in English as "church," gives Peter a special position of authority and leadership in God's "assembly" of people. In Greek, this word refers to those who are "called" *(kaleō)* "out from" *(ek)* the total population of people to be an assembly that decides "political" issues. In Greece, political issues were *"polis"* issues, from the Greek word meaning "city." In other words, to Greek hearers, Jesus is putting Peter in charge of the political assembly that makes major decisions about actions associated with a city or city-state. Peter is to be the leader of those who are Messiah "citizens."

Peter's Authority over a Messiah Torah Assembly

As soon as we introduce the term "Messiah," which transliterates the Hebrew noun *māšiaḥ*, "Anointed One," we know the heritage of the concept of assembly in Matthew is biblical. And here we encounter the Hebrew concept of the *qahal*, translated into Greek as *ekklēsia*, the assembly of people that God "called out" from the total population in Egypt under the leadership of Moses to be the people of Israel.[1] In Matthew's Gospel, Jesus is giving Peter a status of authority in a line of leaders that begins in the story of God's establishment of Israel as a "priestly kingdom and holy nation" (Exod 19:6). The result is a blending of biblical heritage with Greek heritage to define followers of Jesus as an "assembly" of God's people.

Why would Matthew contain such a change in tone concerning Peter and concerning discipleship? The answer lies in the challenges before emerging Christian communities in the decades following the destruction in 70 C.E. of the Jerusalem Temple as the center of Jewish worship. As long as the Temple existed, priestly families and Sadducees had the most official positions of authority among the Jewish people. For them, the Torah was most important as a guide for practices and rituals that created holiness in the Temple. In the decades following the destruction of the Temple, Pharisees became the authoritative leaders in Jewish communities. Pharisees established their power by adapting and relocating the Torah so it could guide practices and rituals in households, synagogues, and Jewish communities throughout the Mediterranean world. Within time Rabbis, who were the successors of the Pharisees, decided on the basis of the Torah and other Jewish literature they considered authoritative that there were 613 commandments that showed Jewish people how to live in a mode of *halakhah,* a way to walk *(halakh)* daily in gratitude to God when the Jerusalem Temple no longer existed. In the midst of these emerging *halakhic* "Torah" communities within Judaism, the Gospel of Matthew presented an emerging Christianity that featured Messiah Jesus with a *halakhic* Jewish heritage in the tradition of Abraham, David, Moses, and Solomon. The Matthean version of emerging Christianity presented Jewish heritage in its own special way, of course, as a result of its own particular way of blending emerging Jewish *halakhic* commandments with stories and sayings attributed to Jesus of Nazareth.

Matthew begins with: "An account of the genealogy of Jesus the Messiah, the son of David, the son of Abraham" (1:1). This beginning does not put any terminology concerning Moses in the foreground. Rather it emphasizes the role of the patriarch Abraham and the famous King David in a storyline that moves from Abraham through David to the deportation or exile of Israel to Babylon before the coming of Jesus as the Messiah. The

---

1. Deut 4:10 contains the first occurrence of the word *ekklēsia* in the Greek Septuagint: ". . . in the day of the assembly *(ekklēsia)* when the Lord said to me [Moses], 'Assemble *(ekklēsiason)* to me the people and let them hear my word. . . .'"

last line of the genealogy refers to "Joseph the husband of Mary, of whom Jesus was born, who is called the Messiah" (v. 16). Immediately after the genealogy, when Joseph discovers that Mary is pregnant before they have lived together, an angel of the Lord appears to him in a dream (vv. 18-20). For those who know the Old Testament/Hebrew Bible (OT/HB), Joseph's dream in Matthew could call to mind Joseph in Genesis, who had dreams that caused his brothers to sell him to people who took him to Egypt, and who had additional dreams once he was in Egypt.[2]

After Jesus is born in Matthew 2:1, New Testament Joseph has a second dream in which an angel of the Lord tells him to take the child and his mother to Egypt, because King Herod is making plans to destroy him (v. 13). Again, for those who know the OT/HB, King Herod's plan to kill the children calls to mind the command of the king of Egypt for midwives to kill newborn Hebrew children because the Hebrew people were becoming too numerous and powerful (Exod 1:9, 16). The purpose for going to Egypt, the narrator of the Gospel tells the hearer/reader, is "to fulfill what had been spoken by the Lord through the prophet, 'Out of Egypt I have called my son'" (Matt 2:15). With Egypt in focus in this manner, even though the narrator does not refer specifically to Moses, people who know the biblical story will know that Moses led the people of Israel out of Egypt.

In Matthew, after Herod dies an angel of the Lord again appears to Joseph in a dream, telling him to take Jesus and Mary to the land of Israel (2:19-20). After Joseph has another dream that causes him to make his home in Nazareth (vv. 22-23), the narrator focuses on the wilderness of Judea (3:1), where Jesus comes to John to be baptized (v. 13). After this, Jesus is led by the Spirit into the wilderness, where he is tested by the devil after fasting forty days and forty nights (4:1-2).

Jesus as a New Moses

With the movement of the story in Matthew from Egypt to the wilderness in the land of Israel, Jesus, God's Son, emerges as a new Moses "who has been called out of Egypt" (2:15) and whose fasting forty days and nights in the wilderness is like Moses' fasting after he went through the wilderness to Mount Sinai (Exod 34:28). When the Matthean story presents the devil

2. Genesis 37–41.

testing Jesus in the wilderness, Jesus responds to the devil's temptations from memory, reciting reasons from the Torah of Moses why he should not do what the devil asks him to do. In other words, instead of forgetting God and failing the "test in the wilderness" as Israel often did, Jesus is guided by chs. 6–8 of Deuteronomy, the last book of the Torah, in which Moses teaches Israel the final things they need to know as they travel through the wilderness toward the land of Israel:

> **Matthew 4:3-4:** The tempter came and said to him, "If you are the Son of God, command these stones to become loaves of bread." But he answered, "It is written, 'One does not live by bread alone, but by every word that comes from the mouth of God'" (Deut 8:3).

> **Matthew 4:5-7:** Then the devil took him to the holy city and placed him on the pinnacle of the temple, saying to him, "If you are the Son of God, throw yourself down. . . ." Jesus said to him, "Again it is written, 'Do not put the Lord your God to the test'" (Deut 6:16).

After these two tests, the devil takes Jesus to "a very high mountain," where he shows Jesus "all the kingdoms of the world and their splendor" and tells him that if he falls down and worships him the devil will give all of them to him (Matt 4:8-9). This movement to a very high mountain, of course, reconfigures the journey of Moses and Israel to Mount Sinai/Horeb in the wilderness, where Moses receives the Ten Commandments and the book of the covenant. Jesus responds to the devil's test on the mountain with:

> **Matthew 4:10:** "Away with you, Satan! for it is written, 'Worship the Lord your God, and serve only him'" (Deut 6:13).

This final response by Jesus calls to mind his response to Peter in Mark 8:33, where Jesus tells Peter, "Get behind me, Satan," when Peter is unable to accept Jesus' teaching about the Son of Man who had to suffer, be rejected, killed, and rise again. Matthew 16:23 keeps this response to Peter by Jesus, but by this time in the storyline of Matthew the major issues of following Jesus have focused on living in an environment of "Torah culture" rather than an environment that is questioning whether the Messiah of Israel could suffer, be rejected, killed, and rise again. In Matthew 4:10 Jesus' statement about worshipping the Lord your God and serving only him recalls verses in Deuteronomy where Moses is interpreting the meaning of the Shema, which stands at the center of Jewish monotheistic belief: "Hear, O Israel: The Lord is your God, the Lord alone. You shall love the Lord your God with all your heart, and with all your soul and with all your might. Keep these words that I am commanding you today in your heart" (Deut 6:4-6). It is obvious that Jesus, the "new Moses" in Matthew's presentation, has learned by heart not only the Shema but also Moses' three-chapter sermon interpreting the Shema in Deuteronomy 6–8.[3]

After Jesus passes the devil's test on the "very high mountain" in Matthew 4:8-11, he returns to "the mountain" (5:1) to teach his disciples after he travels throughout Galilee "proclaiming the good news of the kingdom and curing every disease and every sickness among the people" (4:23). This focus on "the mountain" signals Jesus' function as a new Moses who provides teaching that will function as a "new Torah" to guide the new "assembly" of God's people around God's Messiah. At this point Jesus presents a three-chapter sermon (Matt 5:1–7:29) in which he reinterprets Moses' teaching on two of the Ten Commandments and on four other topics Moses interprets for the people of Israel:

The Ten Commandments:

Matthew 5:21: "You shall not murder"; "Whoever murders shall be liable to judgment" (Exod 20:13; Deut 5:17).

v. 27: "You shall not commit adultery" (Exod 20:14; Deut 5:18).

Other Torah Commandments:

v. 31: "Whoever divorces his wife, let him give her a certificate of divorce" (Deut 24:1-4).

v. 33: "You shall not swear falsely, but carry out the vows you have made to the Lord" (Lev 19:12; Num 30:2; Deut 23:21; cf. Exod 20:16: "You shall not bear false witness against your neighbor").

v. 38: "An eye for an eye and a tooth for a tooth" (Exod 21:23-24; Lev. 24:19-20; Deut 19:21).

v. 43: "Love your neighbor" (Lev 19:18) and "Do not hate your enemy" (cf. Exod 23:4-5).

The three-chapter Sermon on the Mount is the first of five sermons Jesus preaches in Matthew, and these five sermons present detailed guidelines for living in "the church" of Messiah Jesus:

---

3. After Moses' three-chapter sermon on the Shema ends in Deut 8:20, his discussion of Israel's crossing of the Jordan begins with, "Hear, O Israel!" (9:1), which harks back to the Shema in Deut 6:4.

1. The Sermon on the Mount (5:1–7:28)
2. The Sermon on Mission (9:35–10:42)
3. The Parable Sermon on the Kingdom (13:1-52)
4. The Sermon on Church Discipline (18:1-35)
5. The Sermon against the Pharisees (23:1-36), on the End (24:1-51), and on the Son of Man's Judging (25:1-46)

It is possible that the hearer/reader of these five sermons should understand them as Jesus' reconfiguration of the five books of Torah. We cannot be certain about this, but the effect of these five sermons, embedded in the Matthean story, is to present a messianic "new Torah" Judaism in the context of the story of Jesus' birth, life, death, and resurrection.

Jesus' Disciples Understand Jesus' Messianic Teaching

It is noticeable in the context of Matthew's presentation of Jesus as a new Moses that Jesus' disciples exhibit significant understanding of Jesus and his messiahship. As the writer of Matthew was using the Gospel of Mark as a source, he expanded it from sixteen chapters to twenty-eight. This new version often keeps Markan scenes and statements where Jesus' disciples have difficulty understanding Jesus, but overall Matthew presents Jesus' disciples in a much more positive manner than Mark does. Thus, for example, Jesus' conversation with his disciples at the end of the Matthean Parable Sermon on the Kingdom ends with a highly favorable view of the disciples' understanding of what Jesus is teaching them (Matt 13:51-52):

> [51]"Have you understood all this?"
> They answered, "Yes."
> [52]And he said to them, "Therefore every scribe who has been trained for the kingdom of heaven is like the master of a household who brings out of his treasure what is new and what is old."

In this scene, Matthew depicts Jesus' disciples not only as followers who understand what Jesus teaches them but also as scribes who write Jesus' teaching down so others can hear it read to them. Indeed, the greatest disciples of Jesus are scribes who are "trained for the kingdom of heaven," like the scribe who has written the Gospel of Matthew! Jesus' disciples are those who understand what Jesus taught them and write it down so other later followers may teach others by reading the story to them.

A few episodes after the Parable Sermon on the Kingdom, Jesus walks on the sea to his disciples in a boat, and when he reaches out his hand to Peter, who has begun to sink while walking on the water himself (14:25-31), Jesus' disciples in the boat "worship" Jesus, saying, "Truly you are God's Son" (v. 33). In Matthew, therefore, it is not necessary for the hearer/reader to wait until Jesus' crucifixion for someone other than unclean spirits to recognize that Jesus is God's Son. Not only did the devil recognize Jesus' identity during the testing in the wilderness (4:1-11), but in the middle of Matthew's twenty-eight-chapter story (14:33), Jesus' disciples understand that Jesus is "truly" God's Son, and they worship him.

Peter Properly Understands Jesus' Messiahship

The hearer/reader of Matthew, then, is prepared by chapter sixteen for Simon Peter's intelligent response to Jesus' question about who they think he is. Perhaps, in fact, the hearer/reader anticipates a positive response by Jesus to Simon Peter's knowledge. Let us look more closely at Matthew's version of the Caesarea Philippi story to see more details in Jesus' response.

The author of Matthew changes Mark's version of the Caesarea Philippi story very little in the opening scene.

Matthew 16	Mark 8
[13]Now when **Jesus** came into <u>the district of</u> **Caesarea Philippi, he asked his disciples, "Who do people say that THE SON OF MAN** is?"	[27]**Jesus** went on with his disciples to <u>the villages of</u> **Caesarea Philippi**; and on the way he asked his disciples, "**Who do people say that I am?**"
[14]**And they** <u>said</u>, "Some say **John the Baptist**, but **others Elijah**, and still **others JEREMIAH or one of the prophets.**"	[28]**And they** <u>answered</u> him, "**John the Baptist**; and **others, Elijah**; and still **others, one of the prophets.**"

Matthew changes Mark's "villages" to "the district" of Caesarea Philippi, a phrase that more accurately describes the geographical location as a Gentile region during the 1st century C.E. decade of the 80s. Then Matthew changes Jesus' "I" to "the Son of Man," something which occurs frequently in Matthew and which shows how the Markan presentation of Jesus as the Son of Man established an undisputed framework for the presentation of

Jesus in later Gospels. In the final part of the disciples' response to Jesus, the Matthean version adds "Jeremiah" to one of the prophets people might have thought Jesus to be. Perhaps this is because Jeremiah was known for having been severely rejected by the leaders of Israel in Jerusalem, or perhaps simply because some people expected Jeremiah to return during difficult times.[4]

Matthew's account of the second scene in the Caesarea Philippi story adds many things to Mark's account.

Matthew 16	Mark 8
[15]**He** <u>said</u> to **them, "But who do you say that I am?"**	[29]**He** <u>asked</u> **them, "But who do you say that I am?"**
[16]Simon **Peter answered, "You are the Messiah,**	**Peter answered** him, **"You are the Messiah."**
the Son of the living God."	
[17]And Jesus answered him, **"Blessed are you, Simon son of Jonah!** For flesh and blood has not revealed this to you, but **my Father in heaven.** [18]And I tell you, **you are Peter, and on this rock I will build my church,** and the gates of Hades will not prevail against it. [19]I will give you the **keys of the kingdom of heaven,** and **whatever you bind on earth will be bound in heaven, and whatever you loose on earth will be loosed in heaven."**	
[20]Then **he sternly ordered** <u>the disciples</u> **not to tell anyone that he was the Messiah.**	[30]And **he sternly ordered** <u>them</u> **not to tell anyone** about him.

When Peter responds to Jesus' question, he describes the Messiah as "the Son of the Living God" (16:16). Peter's response with "Messiah" repeats a title for Jesus the author introduced in 1:1, repeated three times at the end of the genealogy and the beginning of the account of Jesus' birth (1:16-18), and used when King Herod inquired where the Messiah would be born (2:4). In addition, Matthew adds to the Q Gospel that John the Baptist in prison heard "what the Messiah was doing" (11:2; cf. Luke 7:18) before he sent two of his disciples to Jesus to ask if he was "the one who is to come."

---

4. 2 Maccabees 15:13-16; Matthew refers specifically to Jeremiah in 2:17; 27:9.

When Peter adds the description "Son of God" to "Messiah" he is repeating, as we have seen above, what the devil called Jesus in the wilderness testing story (4:3, 6) and what the disciples have called Jesus when
they worship him at the end of the sea story in 14:33. In addition, in 8:29
two demoniacs in the country of the Gadarenes meet Jesus and call out to
him, "What have you to do with us, Son of God . . . ?" So again the hearer/
reader is prepared for Peter's response to Jesus.

When Peter adds the word "living" to his description of God, saying Jesus is the Son of the "living" God, he anticipates the question of the high
priest Caiaphas in the Matthean version of the scene. In Matthew's account, the high priest says, "I put you under oath before the living God, tell
us if you are the Messiah, the Son of God" (26:63). Reference to the "living"
God was especially representative of Greek-speaking Judaism, where the
God of Israel was presented in contrast to dead Gentile idols (Luz 2001:
361). The importance of this description among 1st-century followers of Jesus is obvious from 1 Thessalonians 1:9; Acts 14:15; 2 Corinthians 6:16; Hebrews 3:12; 9:14; and 1 Timothy 4:10.

Jesus' response contains argumentative texture that emphasizes Peter's
close relation to God, heaven, and the kingdom of heaven. Jesus' reasoning
presents a thesis that Simon is especially blessed by God. Then Jesus sup-
ports this thesis with an assertion that Peter has received a special revelation of knowledge from Jesus' "Father in heaven." But Jesus continues even
beyond this!

Jesus' statement that "flesh and blood has not revealed this to you" but
"my Father in heaven" reminds a person familiar with the New Testament
of Paul's assertion that he did not receive the gospel from any human
source but "received it through a revelation of Jesus Messiah" (Gal 1:12).
There is no evidence that the author of Matthew knows this statement in
Paul's letter, but its similarity is noticeable.

Jesus' statement builds on statements he made earlier in the story. After
John's disciples had come to Jesus asking him if he was the coming one or
they should look for another (Matt 11:2), Jesus gave thanks to God for those
"infants," which include his disciples (Luz 2001: 362), to whom God has revealed "hidden things" (v. 25). Then in the midst of his Parable Sermon on
the Kingdom, referred to above, Jesus pronounces a blessing on his disciples: "But blessed are your eyes, for they see, and your ears, for they hear.
Truly I tell you, many prophets and righteous people longed to see what
you see, but did not see it, and to hear what you hear, but did not hear it"
(13:16-17). Now in the Caesarea Philippi story Jesus blesses Peter in a spe-

cial way. He will be the rock, a special play on his name *petros,* which in Greek means "rock," on which Jesus will "build" his assembly.

For a hearer/reader of the New Testament, Jesus' language in the Matthean version of this scene calls to mind the special language Paul uses in his letters when he refers to "building" communities of people who work together for their common good. On the basis of our best information, even though Paul's letters were written more than two decades earlier than the Gospel of Matthew, it is not clear that Matthew was influenced by Paul's letters. But the emphasis in both Paul's letters and Matthew on communities of believers in Jesus as "assemblies" is noticeable, even though many of the emphases are different. Paul's letters emphasize the importance of "building up" the assembly (1 Cor 14:4-5, 12). His guide for this is love, "which does not rejoice in wrongdoing, but rejoices in the truth" (1 Cor 13:6). Matthew calls the guideline "righteousness" that even exceeds the righteousness of the scribes and Pharisees (5:20).

Righteousness as a Guide for God's Church

But how can there be an understanding of righteousness that guides people in these positive ways? For Matthew, the answer lies in the teachings of Jesus Messiah, the new Moses. Jesus presents these teachings especially in his five sermons as the story emerges. Jesus starts the Sermon on the Mount with nine "blessings" on his disciples. In Deuteronomy, the final book of the Torah, Moses presents six "blessings" on the people of Israel if they walk in the way of God's commandments.

> [1]If you will only obey the LORD your God, by diligently observing all his commandments that I am commanding you today, the LORD your God will set you high above all the nations of the earth; [2]all these blessings shall come upon you and overtake you, if you obey the LORD your God.
> [3]**BLESSED** shall you be in **the city,** and
> **BLESSED** shall you be in **the field.**
> [4]**BLESSED** shall be the fruit of your womb, the **fruit of your ground,** and the fruit of your livestock, both the increase of your cattle and the issue of your flock.
> [5]**BLESSED** shall be **your basket and your kneading-bowl.**
> [6]**BLESSED** shall you be when you come in, and

BLESSED shall you be **when you go out**.
. . .
[7]The LORD will **CAUSE YOUR ENEMIES** who rise against you **TO BE DEFEATED** before you; . . .
[8]The LORD . . . will **BLESS YOU IN THE LAND THAT THE LORD YOUR GOD IS GIVING YOU.**
[9]The LORD will **ESTABLISH YOU AS HIS HOLY PEOPLE,**
as he has sworn to you,
if you **KEEP THE COMMANDMENTS** of the LORD your God and **WALK IN HIS WAYS** (Deut 28:1-9)

Moses' blessings focus on Israel's living in the land God gives to them. Thus, they will be blessed in the city and in the field. Blessings will come in the form of "fruit," from the womb, the ground, and livestock. This means they will be blessed both when they are in their homes and when they are out in public. Beyond this, God will protect them from enemies who may come to destroy them, which will allow them to enjoy the blessings God gives them in the land. God's overall goal with these blessings is to make Israel a holy people, and this can be accomplished through Israel's "walking" in the ways of God's commandments, that is, living according to *halakhah*.

In Matthew, Jesus teaches a way of walking according to God's commandments that blends the goal of holiness with topics and statements from the biblical prophets, the psalms of David, and wisdom teachings especially associated with Solomon the son of David. Putting verses from the Hebrew Bible and the wisdom book of Sirach alongside the blessings, commonly called beatitudes, at the beginning of the Sermon on the Mount provides initial insight into the nature of the new Torah Jesus teaches in Matthew.

Opening Blessings in Matthew's Sermon on the Mount (Matt 5:3-12)	Topics in Prophetic Writings, Wisdom, and Psalms of David
[3]Blessed are the **poor in spirit**, for theirs is the kingdom of heaven.	For thus says the high and lofty one who inhabits eternity, whose name is Holy: I dwell in the high and holy place, and also with those who are **contrite and humble in spirit**, to revive the **spirit of the humble**, and to revive the heart of the contrite (Isa 57:15).
[4]Blessed are **those who mourn**, for they will be **comforted**.	In Isaiah's days . . . by his dauntless spirit he saw the future, and **comforted the mourners** in Zion (Sir 48:23-24).

[5]Blessed are **the meek**, for they **will inherit the earth**.	But **the meek shall inherit the land**, and delight in abundant prosperity (Ps 37:11).
[6]Blessed are those who **hunger** and **thirst** for righteousness, for they will be **filled**.	For He satisfies the **thirsty**, and the **hungry** He **fills** with good things (Ps 107:9).
[7]**Blessed are the merciful**, for they will receive mercy.	Those who dishonor the destitute sin, but **those who are merciful** to the poor **are blessed** (Prov 14:21 LXX).
[8]Blessed are the **pure in heart**, for they will see **God**.	Truly **God** is good to the upright, to those who are **pure in heart** (Ps 73:1).[5]
[9]Blessed are the **peacemakers**, for they will be called children of God.	These are the things that you shall do: "Speak the truth to one another, render in your gates judgments that are true, and **make for peace**" (Zech 8:16).[6]
[10]Blessed are those who are persecuted for **righteousness**' sake, for theirs is the kingdom of heaven.	Listen to me, you who know **righteousness**, you people who have my teaching in your hearts;
[11]Blessed are you when people **revile you** and persecute you and utter all kinds of evil against you falsely on my account. [12]Rejoice and be glad, for **your reward is great in heaven**, for in the same way they persecuted the prophets who were before you.	do not fear the **reproach of others**, and do not be dismayed when they **revile you**. [8]For the moth will eat them up like a garment, and the worm will eat them like wool; but **my deliverance will be forever**, and my salvation to all generations (Isa 51:7-8).

Without discussing each verse individually, one can readily see that topics in the prophetic writings, wisdom writings, and Psalms are present in the blessings or beatitudes with which Jesus opens the Sermon on the Mount. The new topics focus the blessings on people whose attributes show a special orientation toward God's will for humans, the poor in spirit, those who mourn, etc. The location is changed from the city, the field, and the land to the kingdom of heaven. Instead of emphasizing that God will establish them as holy people, Jesus' beatitudes speak of people seeing God and being called children of God. Likewise, the focus on defeat of enemies in Deuteronomy is reconfigured in Matthew into acceptance of persecution.

Overall, the beatitudes on the lips of Jesus in Matthew move a step be-

---

5. Cf. Ps 24:4-5.

6. In Mishnah *Aboth* 1.12 Hillel says: "Be of the disciples of Aaron, loving peace and pursuing peace, loving mankind and bringing them near to the Law"; in 1.18 Rabban Simeon B. Gamaliel says: "By three things is the world sustained: by truth, by judgment, and by peace, as it is written, 'Execute the judgment of truth and peace'" (Zech 8:16).

yond using the biblical prophets as a model for understanding Jesus, as we saw earlier in both the Q Sayings Gospel and Mark. Moving beyond the approach of Q and Mark, Matthew develops the tradition of the biblical prophets as a model for understanding both the spiritual commitment and the daily practice of followers of Jesus. In Matthew, Jesus is a "new Moses" who teaches a new Torah-prophet model for living in the world.

The final topic of focus in the beatitudes, therefore, is not abuse and persecution of Jesus in the tradition of the prophets but abuse and persecution of Jesus' followers. The Matthean Jesus becomes a teacher of the inner principles and practices that guided the Mark Son of Man, who suffered, was rejected, killed, and rose up. Jesus' "new prophetic Torah," therefore, is "gospel Torah." The inner beliefs and outward actions of Jesus Messiah as presented in Mark become the inner fabric of Jesus' prophetic Torah teaching and preaching in Matthew.

The Church of God and God's Messiah Built on a Rock

Now that we have seen that righteousness is central to the inner nature of the blessings with which Jesus as the "new Moses" begins the Sermon on the Mount, let us return to Jesus' words to Peter that expand the Markan version of the Caesarea Philippi story. As we return, let us compare each verse of Matthew's expansion with verses that occur in other places in Matthew. Jesus begins, as we saw above, with a blessing on Peter that is motivated by the insight that Jesus' "Father in heaven" has revealed special knowledge to Peter about Jesus' messiahship.

Revelation to Peter from Jesus' Father in Heaven

Matthew 16	Matthew 11
[17]And Jesus answered him, "Blessed are you, Simon son of Jonah! For flesh and blood has not revealed this to you, but **my Father in heaven**."	[25]At that time Jesus said, "I thank you, **Father, Lord of heaven and earth**, because you have hidden these things from the wise and the intelligent and have **revealed** them to infants; [26]yes, **Father**, for such was your gracious will."

When we place Matthew 11:25-26, which comes soon after John's disciples ask Jesus if he is the coming one, alongside Jesus' response to Peter, we notice Jesus' emphasis in the earlier scene that God's revelation regularly comes to many "infants." This means that Peter's insight into the nature of Jesus' messiahship can potentially be shared by anyone who becomes an "infant in learning God's ways." A person becomes this "infant" by listening carefully to the teaching and preaching of Jesus in Matthew. Jesus' teaching in the Gospel of Matthew, then, is teaching for "all" of God's children under heaven and on earth.

When we look at the next verse in the Matthean expansion, we see an emphasis by Jesus on building his church on a rock so that the forces of Hades cannot destroy it.

Building Jesus Messiah's Church

Matthew 16	Matthew 7
[18]And I tell you, you are Peter, and **on this rock I will build my church**, and the gates of Hades **will not prevail against it**.	[24]Everyone then who hears these words of mine and acts on them will be like a wise man who **built his house on rock**. [25]The rain fell, the floods came, and the winds blew and beat on that house, but **it did not fall**, because it had been founded **on rock**.

Jesus' words to Peter about his church thus have a fascinating relation to the final image Jesus uses in his Sermon on the Mount.

In the middle of the Sermon on Mission (9:35–10:42), Jesus talks specifically about the relation of a disciple to his teacher, explaining that a disciple is not "above the teacher" but "like the teacher." Then he says, "If they have called the master of the house Beelzebul, how much more will they malign those of the household" (10:25). People in the household of the Messiah, therefore, can expect that they will be spoken against and even acted against.

Thus, after Jesus spoke in the Sermon on the Mount about his followers being "blessed" in the tradition of the prophets when they are reviled and persecuted for righteousness' sake (5:10-11), he asserted in the Sermon on Mission that people should not fear "those who kill the body but cannot kill the soul," but rather "fear him who can destroy both soul and body in hell" (10:28). Then as Jesus is ending the sermon he says, "Whoever welcomes a prophet in the name of a prophet will receive a prophet's reward; and whoever welcomes a righteous person in the name of a righteous person will receive the reward of the righteous" (v. 41). Then he concludes with the image of a person who "gives even a cup of cold water to one of these little ones in the name of a disciple," and asserts that "none of these will lose their reward" (v. 42).

We will see below how Jesus addresses "receiving the reward of the righteous" in his final sermon. At present we want to see that in the Caesarea Philippi scene Jesus asserts that "the gates of Hades will not prevail" against his "assembly" of God's people built on the rock, Peter (16:18). This language prepares the way for the statement about receiving the keys of the kingdom Jesus makes to Peter next in the scene.

Keys for Binding and Loosing on Earth and in Heaven

Matthew 16	Matthew 18
	[15]If another member of the **church** sins against you, go and point out the fault when the **two** of you are alone. . . . [16]. . . if you are not listened to, take **one or two others along with you**, so that every word may be confirmed by the evidence of **two or three witnesses**. [17]If the member refuses to listen to them, tell it to the **church**; and if the offender refuses to listen even to the **church**, let such a **one** be to you as a Gentile and a tax-collector.
[19]I will give you the keys of the kingdom of heaven, and **whatever you bind on earth will be bound in heaven, and whatever you loose on earth will be loosed in heaven**.	[18]Truly I tell you, **whatever you bind on earth will be bound in heaven, and whatever you loose on earth will be loosed in heaven**. [19]Again, truly I tell you, if **two** of you agree on earth about anything you ask, **it will be done for you by my Father in heaven**. [20]For where **two or three** are gathered in my name, I am there among them. [21]Then Peter came and said to him, "Lord, if another member of the **church** sins against me, **how often should I forgive**? As many as seven times?" [22]Jesus said to him, "Not seven times, but, I tell you, **seventy-seven [or: seventy times seven] times**."

After referring to his "church" built on the rock, Jesus talks to Peter about "the keys of the kingdom of heaven" (16:19). This imagery calls to mind a real building, an actual house, which may have an open door that allows people to enter or a door that is locked so people cannot enter it. In the Sermon on the Mount Jesus teaches his disciples that if they knock the door will be opened to them (7:7-8). But what if someone locks the door? Near the beginning of Jesus' final three-chapter sermon on Judgment and Reward when the Son of Man comes (Matthew 23–25) Jesus says that the scribes and Pharisees lock people out of the kingdom of heaven rather than using the keys of the kingdom so that they themselves and others may go in (23:13-14). In contrast, in the Caesarea Philippi story Jesus tells Peter he is giving him "the keys of the kingdom of heaven," and then he explains that these keys create a context where what is bound on earth is bound in heaven and whatever is loosed in heaven will be loosed on earth.

Negotiating Wrongs in the Church

In Jesus' Sermon on Church Discipline, which follows soon after the Caesarea Philippi story, Jesus explains the process by which this binding and loosing should occur (18:15-20). According to Jesus, the process begins when someone has been wronged by another member in the assembly. The first step should be a conversation between the person who has been wronged and the person who performed the improper act (v. 15). If this conversation does not yield good results, then the wronged person should take one or two others along to talk with the person a second time. The additional people create a context where there are two or three witnesses (v. 16). In contrast to teaching in the Torah where two or more witnesses make a statement in the context of a religious court (Deut 19:15), Jesus asserts that if two members agree on what they will ask, then it will be done by Jesus' Father in heaven, since "where two or three are gathered in my name, I am there among them" (Matt 18:20).

While the two or more witnesses procedure might seem to be an "asking system" in which only two, rather than a larger "jury," function in the manner of a Torah court, Peter asks Jesus about a hypothetical case that allows Jesus to explain his view of the process. How many times, Peter asks Jesus, should he forgive a member of the assembly who sins against him? Seven times? Since seven is a traditional number of perfection within Judaism, based on the seven days in which God created the world, it appears that Peter is asking Jesus if he is expected to offer "perfect forgiveness" rather than limited forgiveness (Luz 2001: 465). Jesus responds to him, "Not seven times but, I tell you, seventy-seven [or: 'seventy times seven'] times" (18:22). Jesus' answer is that "the most perfect" is demanded of Peter.

Just as Jesus introduced the other topics we discussed above in the Sermon on the Mount, so he also introduced there the topics of forgiveness and perfection. In the Sermon on the Mount Jesus emphasized the importance of forgiving others in the following words: "For if you forgive others their trespasses, your heavenly Father will also forgive you; but if you do not forgive others, neither will your Father forgive your trespasses" (6:14-15). Already in Jesus' first sermon, therefore, he introduced the concept of action on earth "binding or loosing" action in heaven. In that context Jesus had also said, "Be perfect, even as your heavenly Father is perfect" (5:48), as well as asserting that "unless your righteousness exceeds that of the scribes and Pharisees, you will never enter the kingdom of heaven" (5:20). But how can a person live in the context of these kinds of expectations?

How Is It Possible to Walk according to the Messiah's New Gospel Torah?

This leads us to Jesus' final sermon, which is also three chapters long (Matt 23:1–25:46). He begins this sermon with the amazing assertion "to the crowds and to his disciples" that they should do whatever the scribes and Pharisees teach, since they "sit on Moses' seat" (23:2). This statement by Jesus, which is not in any of the other Gospels, exhibits the orientation toward what we have called "gospel Torah" in this chapter. According to Jesus in this Gospel, the scribes and Pharisees teach the proper things; the issue is how a person acts in the context of the teaching. To clarify how a person must act to fulfill gospel Torah, Jesus presents lengthy criticism of the actions of the scribes and Pharisees in seven "woes" in the opening of the sermon (23:13-36). These woes update the curses that came before and after the blessings Moses presented in Deuteronomy 27:14-26; 28:15-46.

Then Jesus tells how the system of blessings and curses will work "when the Son of Man comes in his glory, and all the angels with him," and he sits on the throne of his glory and all nations gather before him (Matt 25:31-32).[7] As the scene unfolds, people either "inherit the kingdom" and

---

7. In the context of the Son of Man's judging of the nations, Matthew retains Jesus' statement in the Q Sayings Gospel that those who have followed him "will also sit on twelve thrones, judging the twelve tribes of Israel" (19:28).

go into eternal life (vv. 34, 46) or depart "into the eternal fire" to receive eternal punishment (vv. 41, 46) on the basis of caring for people. A distinctive part of the emphasis in Matthew is that the people who either fulfilled or did not fulfill this righteousness of caring for people "did not realize" (vv. 37-45) they were doing or not doing what they should do. The goal in Matthew is for believers to develop a way of life in which actions exceed the righteousness even of scribes and Pharisees (5:20) on the basis of an internalized disposition toward justice, mercy, and faith (23:23). Thus, in Matthew 25, people do not realize they have been fulfilling righteousness because their actions have become a natural part of their inner spiritual nature as righteous people.

Conclusion

In conclusion, then, Matthew expands Mark into a twenty-eight-chapter Gospel containing five major sermons of Jesus, with the first and last sermon being three chapters long. In these five sermons, Jesus presents "gospel Torah" that blends topics from prophets, wisdom, and Psalms in the Old Testament/Hebrew Bible. The end result is a focus on attributes that guide individual people's inner spirituality and outward practices on a daily basis. Matthew 16:13-20 contains an expanded version of the Markan Caesarea Philippi story in which Jesus establishes Peter as the rock on which he will build his Messiah "assembly," commonly called "church." Where two or three gather in Jesus' name, this church functions as a community on earth whose actions are embedded in the will and action of Jesus' "Father in heaven." Guided by gospel Torah, this community is instructed by Jesus to practice forgiveness that exceeds "perfect forgiveness" and to nurture actions by its members that fulfill God's righteousness on a daily basis without realizing they are doing so. Perhaps we should have little surprise that Christian writers during the second and third centuries c.e. repeated in their writings more words from Matthew, which is the longest Gospel in the New Testament, than any other New Testament Gospel. In addition, we should observe that this amazingly rich and complex Gospel moved into a position of preeminence during the first four centuries c.e. as the first Gospel in the New Testament. If a person opens the New Testament to read it from beginning to end, the first book they read will be Matthew.

LEARNING ACTIVITIES

1. Read Deuteronomy 4:9-14, where Moses tells the people of Israel how God told him to assemble (Greek *ekklēsiason*) the people into an assembly *(ekklēsia).*

2. Read Genesis 37–41, where dreams play a central role in the life of Joseph.

3. Read 2 Maccabees 15:12-16 to see an account of the return of Jeremiah to assist the Maccabees in their confrontation of the Hellenistic rulers who were forbidding them to follow their Jewish practices.

4. Read 1 Thessalonians 1:9; Acts 14:15; 2 Corinthians 6:16; Hebrews 3:12; 9:14; and 1 Timothy 4:10 in the New Testament to see the importance of the phrase "the living God" for followers of Jesus during the first century C.E.

5. Read the blessings Moses presents to the people of Israel in Deuteronomy 28:1-14 and the curses that come before and after the blessings in Deuteronomy 27:14-26 and 28:15-46.

6. When you can find the time, read programmatically through all of Jesus' five sermons in Matthew: chs. 5–7; 9:35–11:1; 13:1-53; ch. 18; and chs. 23-25.

BIBLIOGRAPHY

Allison, Dale C. 1993. *The New Moses: A Matthean Typology.* Minneapolis: Fortress.

Crosby, Michael. 1988. *House of Disciples: Church, Economics, and Justice in Matthew.* Maryknoll: Orbis.

Davies, W. D., and Dale C. Allison. 1988, 1991, 1997. International Critical Commentary. *Matthew.* 3 volumes. Edinburgh: T & T Clark.

Donaldson, Terence L. 1985. *Jesus on the Mountain: A Study in Matthean Theology.* Journal for the Study of the New Testament Supplement Series 8. Sheffield: JSOT.

Garland, David E. 1993. *Reading Matthew: A Literary and Theological Commentary on the First Gospel.* New York: Crossroad.

Gospel of Matthew: http://www.earlychristianwritings.com/matthew.html

Harrington, Daniel J. 1991. *The Gospel of Matthew.* Sacra Pagina. Collegeville: Liturgical.

Luz, Ulrich. 2001. *Matthew 8–10.* Hermeneia. Minneapolis: Fortress.

Overman, J. Andrew. 1996. *Church and Community in Crisis: The Gospel According to Matthew.* The New Testament in Its Context. Valley Forge: Trinity.

Senior, Donald. 1998. *Matthew.* Abingdon New Testament Commentaries. Nashville: Abingdon.

5

The Spirit of the Lord "Anointed" Me!

Unlike the Gospels of Mark and Matthew, the Gospel of Luke does not open with a statement about Jesus Messiah. Rather, it starts with an introduction where the author talks about other people who have written about "events that have been fulfilled among us" (1:1). After the introduction (1:1-4), the narrator locates the story first during the reign of King Herod of Judea (1:5) and then during the reign of the Roman emperor Caesar Augustus (2:1). The specific reference to Caesar Augustus introduces a focus on the broader Roman Empire that is not present in Mark or Matthew. As Luke begins, it establishes an interplay between the kingdom of Judea and the Roman Empire that sets the stage for the births of John the Baptist and Jesus as the angel Gabriel first visits the priest Zechariah in the Jerusalem Temple and then visits a virgin girl named Mary in the Galilean town of Nazareth (1:5-38).

Jesus the Prophetic Anointed One

As the story unfolds, Luke 7 presents the Q Gospel scene in which two of John the Baptist's disciples ask Jesus if he is the one who is to come (7:18-23). The scene occurs just after people call Jesus "a great prophet" in response to his raising of a dead boy to life (vv. 11-17).

Then Luke 9 presents a version of the well-known story in which Jesus asks the disciples who they think he is. In 9:18-22, Peter replies that Jesus is "the Messiah of God," and Peter does not rebuke Jesus for teaching that he is the Son of Man who must die, nor does Jesus rebuke Peter and call him

75

Satan as in Mark and Matthew. According to Luke, the relation of Jesus to his followers unfolded slowly and surely, deepening and enriching Jesus' identity as he was traveling slowly toward Jerusalem, telling various stories and encountering different people, speaking throughout the events that led to his crucifixion and even during his crucifixion and then appearing on various occasions after his resurrection, until he leads the eleven and those with them out from Jerusalem to Bethany, where he ascends into heaven (24:33, 50-53).

So who was Jesus, according to the Gospel of Luke? If Jesus was the Messiah of God, how did he receive this status and what specific tasks was he to achieve with this status? The following pages should help to clarify Luke's view of Jesus. The word "Messiah" means "the Anointed One," and a good question is "Was Jesus ever anointed?" The major letters in the noun Messiah transliterate letters in the Hebrew word *māšîaḥ*, which means a person on whom oil has been poured or rubbed in a public ceremony.

The word plays a major role in the Hebrew Bible when the priest-prophet Samuel, following directions from YHWH, makes Saul the first "anointed" king of Israel by pouring oil on him and kissing him (1 Sam 9:15-17; 10:1-2). Before Saul started his duties as king, however, a band of prophets came to him with harp, tambourine, flute, and lyre, and the Spirit of YHWH/God possessed him (10:5-11). When the people who knew Saul saw him prophesy with the prophets, they said, "Is Saul also among the prophets?" Later when Samuel anointed David with oil to make him king in the presence of his brothers, the Spirit of YHWH came "mightily upon David from that day forward" (16:13) and departed from Saul (v. 14).

Around four hundred years after King Saul and King David had reigned as kings of Israel, the prophetic book of Isaiah presented Isaiah saying, "The Spirit of YHWH God is upon me, because YHWH has anointed me . . ." (Isa 61:1). Does this mean that the prophet Isaiah was anointed with oil? It is not clear that Israelite prophets were ever anointed with oil in public ceremonies. Rather, it appears that the anointing of the kings Saul and David with both oil and Spirit had blended together so that presence of the Spirit could be referred to as "having been anointed."

There is also another dimension to kingship in the Hebrew Bible. After David was king, the prophet Nathan explained to him that when he became king YHWH had become his father, so that David himself was YHWH's son (2 Sam 7:14). In a Psalm of David associated with the enthronement of the king of Israel, YHWH tells the king "You are my son; today I have begotten you" (Ps 2:7). This means that in Israelite/Jewish tradition God's son was fully human but had received special tasks to perform from "his Father" when God adopted him.

So how does anointment with oil, anointment with Spirit, and becoming God's Son function in relation to Jesus in Luke? The answer is that Jesus is a special blend of messianic king and messianic prophet. The special way Luke presents the birth, life, death, and resurrection of Jesus as a messianic prophet-king is highly informative for the emergence of Christianity during the first century c.e.. In Luke, the term "Messiah" does not appear when the angel Gabriel comes to Mary to tell her she will have a son named Jesus. Instead, he tells her that her son will be called "the Son of the Most High," that "the Lord God will give to him the throne of his ancestor David," that "he will reign over the house of Jacob forever," and that "his kingdom will have no end" (1:32-33). This sounds to the hearer/reader as though Jesus will be a fully human being who is an anointed king. But instead of "anointed" the angel uses "Son of God," a title that people in the Roman Empire could easily recognize as an alternative to the son of the divine Roman emperor. So now the issue could become the power of Jesus as anointed king of the Judeans versus an emperor who is the son of a previous emperor whom the Roman Senate has declared to be a divine god.

Anointment by the Holy Spirit

But let us go back to the issue of Jesus' anointing, because it tells us so much about how the story unfolds in Luke's Gospel. If Jesus is the Son of God in Luke, did he become Son of God through a process of anointment? If so, then what kind of process was it? The answer, as in Mark and Matthew, seems to be that Holy Spirit first anoints Jesus at his baptism, and only later does someone anoint Jesus with oil. This is a reversal of the order of anointing when people were made kings over Israel. In Mark, "the Spirit" descends "like a dove" on Jesus at his baptism. In this context, a voice from heaven tells Jesus he is God's beloved Son (1:10-11). The hearer/reader of Mark will, on the basis of the Hebrew Bible, understand that this language has a close relation to promises associated with David's "eternal" kingship. After Peter's disagreement with Jesus in Mark over the meaning of Jesus' messiahship (8:32-33), none of Jesus' disciples clearly understand and accept Jesus' teaching about his messiahship. Three days before Jesus is crucified, however, an unnamed woman brings an alabaster jar of oil to the house of Simon the leper at Bethany and pours ointment on Jesus' head

(14:3-4). When Jesus interprets the woman's act as anointment of his body for burial (v. 8), it would seem that the disciples should understand that Jesus' messiahship will include his death. As Mark unfolds, it becomes clear that Jesus' disciples never do accept Jesus' death as an integral part of his messiahship. The reader understands, however, and this is an important achievement of the Gospel of Mark in emerging Christianity.

While the Gospel of Luke accepts the Markan view that Jesus' messiahship includes his death, it presents some important changes in the story. It does not include the story of the woman's anointing of Jesus before his death and burial. Instead, Luke has a story in the middle of Jesus' Galilean ministry where an unnamed sinful woman comes without invitation to a dinner party in a Pharisee's house[1] and kisses and anoints Jesus' feet with oil and her tears (7:36-38). In this setting, Jesus does not interpret her actions as anointing for burial. And there is no other anointment of Jesus before his burial in the Lukan account.[2] An interesting question, then, can be: Exactly how does the Lukan story present the anointing of Jesus with Spirit and oil, and what do these anointings mean? Since there seems to be no special anointing of Jesus' body with oil in preparation for his burial, do anointings with both Spirit and oil have some other meaning in Luke? And if they do have some other meaning, what are those meanings?

In order to answer these questions, it is important to go back to the beginning of the Lukan story, which contains events focused on the birth of both John the Baptist and Jesus before it turns to their adult activity. In the accounts of these events, the Holy Spirit is active in some of the earliest verses. An angel tells Zechariah that he and his wife Elizabeth will have a son named John, who "even before his birth will be filled with the Holy Spirit" (1:15). A bit later the angel Gabriel tells Mary, "The Holy Spirit will come upon you, and the power of the Most High will overshadow you; therefore the child to be born [Jesus] will be holy; he will be called God's son" (v. 35). When Mary visits Elizabeth, John leaps in Elizabeth's womb and Elizabeth is "filled with the Holy Spirit" (v. 41). Then after John is born, his father Zechariah, "filled with the Holy Spirit" (v. 67), speaks a prophetic hymn that identifies John as "the prophet of the Most High" who

1. There is no clear location for the Pharisee's house in Luke. Before this event, Jesus has visited Nain (7:11), which is in southern Galilee.

2. When Joseph of Arimathea takes Jesus' body down from the cross, he simply wraps it in a linen cloth and lays it in a rock-hewn tomb (Luke 23:53). Women who see Joseph bury Jesus' body prepare spices and ointments and come to the tomb on the first day of the week, but Jesus' body is not there, so they cannot anoint it (23:56–24:3).

will go before the Lord to prepare his ways (v. 76). At this point in the story it looks as though John the Baptist's special identity is as God's prophet and Jesus' special identity is as God's Son.

After Jesus is born, further clarification concerning the identities of John and Jesus emerges. Jesus' birth in Bethlehem creates the setting for the first occurrence of the word "Messiah" in Luke. When Jesus is born, an angel of the Lord appears to shepherds living in the fields and tells them that "in the city of David a Savior, who is the Messiah, the Lord," has been born (2:11). The shepherds respond by going to Bethlehem and finding Mary and Joseph and the child lying in a manger (v. 16). After Jesus has been circumcised, his parents take him to the Jerusalem Temple for their purification (vv. 21-22). While they are there a man named Simeon, "upon whom the Holy Spirit rested," comes to the Temple because it "had been revealed to him by the Holy Spirit that he would not see death before he had seen the Lord's Messiah" (vv. 25-26). So, "guided by the Spirit," he comes to the Temple, takes Jesus in his arms, praises God for the salvation God is bringing to all people, and blesses Jesus and his parents (vv. 27-34).

The Holy Spirit is thus exceptionally present and active in the context of the births of both John the Baptist and Jesus, and the term "Messiah" emerges for Jesus when he is born in Bethlehem, the city of David. Was Jesus, then, already anointed by the Holy Spirit before he was born? Is this how we are to understand the announcement of the angels? Probably not. The presence of the Holy Spirit with John the Baptist in the womb of his mother Elizabeth does not make him Messiah. Rather, in the Gospel of Luke the Holy Spirit is present with many people as they participate in the story of the coming forth of God's Messiah.

The Hungry, Praying, Spirit-Anointed Jesus

Things begin to be sorted out further in Luke when John and Jesus grow up and start their adult activity. When John begins his "baptism of repentance" (3:3) and people wonder if perhaps he is the Messiah, he tells them that someone "more powerful than he" is coming, who will baptize them "with Holy Spirit and fire" (vv. 15-16). Then when the Lukan story presents Jesus' baptism by John, there is a special sequence of events that is not present either in Mark or Matthew, two events rather than simply one.[3]

3. In both Mark and Matthew Jesus' baptism is one continuous event containing the splitting apart of the heavens, the descent of the Spirit, and the voice from heaven.

The first is Jesus' baptism with water (v. 21a). Then, after the baptism, Jesus begins to pray. While he is praying, the heavens open, the Holy Spirit descends on him in bodily form like a dove, and a voice from heaven says, "You are my Son, the Beloved; with you I am well pleased" (vv. 21b-22). This coming of the Holy Spirit while Jesus is praying appears to be Jesus' special "anointing by the Spirit" in Luke.

This special event sets the stage for the later coming of the Holy Spirit upon Jesus' followers in Acts while they are gathered together in the Jerusalem Temple. In that later context, there is special reference to prayer by the believers[4] and once to their "constant devotion to prayer" (Acts 1:14) before the coming of the Holy Spirit upon them. And when the Holy Spirit does come, it comes in the form of "divided tongues, as of fire" (2:3-4) to equip them for their tasks now that Jesus has ascended into heaven. This coming "as of fire" appears to be Jesus' baptism of the people with fire, according to John's prediction in Luke 3:16, and it also fulfills Joel's anticipation that not only God's Spirit but also "fire" would appear as a sign on the earth below "before the coming of the Lord's great and glorious day" (Acts 2:17-21).

The coming of the Holy Spirit on Jesus while he is praying establishes a regular practice of prayer by the Lukan Jesus that brings about special events in the story. In other words, the Spirit-anointed Jesus is a praying Jesus. After the Holy Spirit descends on Jesus while he is praying, Jesus returns from the Jordan "full of holy spirit" and is guided "by the Spirit" in the wilderness while he is tested by the devil for forty days (4:1-2). In Luke, the devil's testing of Jesus reveals that an internal part of the Spirit-anointing within Jesus is remembering, knowing, and acting according to Deuteronomic Torah, namely Torah as Moses taught it in Deuteronomy, the final book of Torah in the Hebrew Bible. When the devil tests Jesus, Jesus responds by reciting verses from Deuteronomy 6 and 8.[5] The Matthean and Lukan versions both present the first temptation as a setting where the devil tells Jesus to turn stone to bread.[6] In Luke 4:4, Jesus responds with, "One does not live by bread alone," while Matthew 4:4 includes an additional clause of the verse, "but by every word that proceeds out of the mouth of God." While the Lukan Jesus does not recite the clause about living by every word that proceeds from the mouth of God, it becomes obvi-

4. Acts 1:14, 24; 2:42; 3:1.
5. Deut 8:3; 6:13, 16.
6. Matt 4:3; Luke 4:3.

ous that Spirit-anointed Jesus lives according to words of Torah from the mouth of God. In particular, Jesus embodies the words of God through Moses in Deuteronomy 8:2-3:

> ²Remember the long way that the LORD your God has led you these forty years in the wilderness, in order to humble you, testing you to know what was in your heart, whether or not you would keep his commandments. ³He humbled you by letting you hunger, then by feeding you with manna, which you did not know, nor did your fathers know; that he might make you know that one does not live by bread alone, but that one lives by everything that proceeds out of the mouth of the LORD.

This means that anointed Jesus in Luke is a remembering Jesus. He has learned the story of Israel during his childhood and now knows the things he is supposed to remember from that story as he is tested at the beginning of his public adult life. He is tested through a process of eating nothing for forty days so that "when they were ended, he was hungry" (Luke 4:2).[7] In Deuteronomy 8:3 this is an experience designed to "humble" a person. The purpose of this humbling process is to teach a person that "one lives by everything that proceeds out of the mouth of the LORD." As the testing story proceeds, Jesus responds appropriately to the devil on the basis of statements "from the mouth of the LORD" as they are present in Deuteronomy 6–8, which Jewish interpreters understand to be God's interpretation of the Shema (Deut 6:4-6) in the Torah. Jesus' appropriate responses show that he remembers "by heart" God's commandments and keeps them when he is tested. He knows in humility that God not only provides bread but also provides guidance from "his mouth" for every circumstance in life.[8]

In the Lukan testing story Jesus is being disciplined as a father disciplines his son (Deut 8:5). The devil refers to Jesus as "the Son of God" in the first and last tests (Luke 4:3, 9), evoking the concept of God the Father disciplining his Son.[9] In addition, the testing enacts the importance of remembering, so a person remembers to be humble rather than "forgetting" God, which leads one to exalt oneself (Deut 8:11-14). Later in the

---

7. Cf. Moses in Exod 34:28; Deut 9:9, 18 and Elijah in 1 Kgs 19:8.

8. Cf. the testing in Deut 6:16; 8:2, 16 and the learning and remembering in Deut 6:1-3, 6, 17, 24-25; 7:9, 11-12; 8:1-2, 6, 11, 18.

9. Cf. Heb 12:5-11.

story, while Jesus is dining in the house of a ruling Pharisee, Jesus discusses the importance of humbling oneself rather than exalting oneself
(Luke 14:7-11). Then on a later occasion, as a direct challenge to Pharisees, Jesus says: "You are those who justify yourselves in the sight of others; but God knows your hearts; for what is exalted by human beings is
an abomination in the sight of God" (16:15). On a still later occasion, Jesus tells a parable about a Pharisee and a tax collector to people "who
trusted in themselves that they were righteous and regarded others with
contempt" (18:9-14). The parable ends with the premise that "all who exalt themselves will be humbled, but all who humble themselves will be
exalted." In the Lukan story, when people become "exalted," they have
"forgotten" the commandments of the Lord (Deut 8:2-3, 6). Deuteronomy 8:17-18 refers specifically to the problem that, when the people of Israel became rich, they easily forgot that God gave them the power to get
their wealth, rather than them obtaining their wealth through their own
power and the power of their hands. This tradition informs the story in
Luke so that already in the first chapter Mary says it is necessary for God
to bring down the powerful and lift up the lowly (1:52).

The Jewish Shema in Jesus' Memory

Even beyond these things, there is one more important aspect of the testing story. In the second and third tests, Jesus responds to the devil from the
chapter in Deuteronomy where Moses teaches the people of Israel the famous Jewish Shema: "Hear, O Israel: The LORD our God is one LORD; and
you shall love the LORD your God with all your heart, and with all your
soul, and with all your might" (Deut 6:4-5). In the second and third tests
Jesus responds to the devil with verses that interpret the Shema. First,
when he says, "Worship the Lord your God, and serve only him" (Luke
4:8), this is an oral version of Deuteronomy 6:13,[10] which interprets the
topic in the Shema, "The LORD our God is one LORD" (6:4). Second, when
Jesus says, "Do not put the Lord your God to the test" (Luke 4:12), this is
the first part of the verse (Deut 6:16) that begins the interpretation of "You
shall love the LORD your God with all your heart, soul, and might" in the
Shema (6:5). This means that in the final two tests Jesus introduces topics

---

10. The written version of this portion of Deut 6:13 is "The Lord your God you shall fear;
him you shall serve."

that are conventionally associated in the biblical story with interpretation of the Jewish Shema, which many Jews repeat a number of times each day, and which all Jews then and now certainly know by heart.

As the story unfolds in Luke, the anointed Jesus knows the Shema and tests if others know it, and this becomes important in later scenes. Luke 10:27 features the Shema in the response of the lawyer to Jesus before Jesus tells the parable of the Good Samaritan (10:30-37). At the end of the lawyer's recitation of the Shema, he adds Leviticus 19:18: "and [you shall love] your neighbor as yourself" (Luke 10:27). These statements by the lawyer show that he not only knows the Shema "by heart" but also "knows" that the broader meaning of "love" for God means "love" for one's neighbor also. The lawyer's knowledge about the expansion of this love creates a context in which Jesus is able to teach the lawyer about mercy (10:37), but we will also see that this broader understanding of love is an integral part of the program of activity that guides the Spirit-anointed Messiah of God in the Gospel of Luke toward those who are poor, oppressed, and marginalized.

From Torah Memory to Prophetic Tasks

After the devil's testing of Jesus, Jesus begins to perform the special tasks his anointing by the Spirit has given him to perform. He returns to Galilee "in the power" of the Spirit, and a report about powerful activities spreads through all the surrounding country (4:14). He returns to his home town of Nazareth, where he gets up to read on the Sabbath in the synagogue. When Jesus' speech in the synagogue brings forth Isaiah 61, there is a shift from special topics in Deuteronomic Torah to special topics in the prophets, from the scriptural topics of remembering God's commandments in a context where one has become rich (Deuteronomy 6–8) to confronting God's people with special responsibilities for the poor, the captive, the blind, and the oppressed (Isa 61:1-2; 58:6).

When the attendant gives the scroll to Jesus, Jesus turns to Isaiah 61:1,[11] which says:

> [18]"The Spirit of the Lord is upon me,
>   because he has anointed me

11. The text as present in Luke actually blends words from Isa 58:6 with Isa 61:1.

to bring good news to the poor.
He has sent me to proclaim release to the captives
   and recovery of sight to the blind,
    to let the oppressed go free,
[19]to proclaim the year of the Lord's favor."
[20]And he rolled up the scroll, gave it back to the attendant, and sat down. The eyes of all in the synagogue were fixed on him. [21]Then he began to say to them, "Today this scripture has been fulfilled in your hearing."

This scene in Luke establishes a special program of tasks for Jesus, the one Anointed by the Spirit of the Lord. In contrast to Mark's Gospel, anointment by the Spirit in Luke does not focus specifically on equipping Jesus with the ability to cast out unclean spirits. Rather, Jesus' anointment equips him first and foremost with a message of good news to the poor. This message includes casting out unclean spirits and demons (e.g., 4:31-41; 6:18), but Jesus' special focus on the poor becomes clear at the beginning of his Sermon on the Plain (6:20-21):

[20]Then he looked up at his disciples and said:
"Blessed are you who are poor,
   for yours is the kingdom of God.
[21]Blessed are you who are hungry now,
   for you will be filled.
Blessed are you who weep now,
   for you will laugh."

In the Lukan story, instead of Jesus presenting a Sermon on the Mount as in Matthew, Jesus spends a night in prayer to God on the mountain (6:12) and then comes down to a level place, where he heals many people and then preaches the Sermon on the Plain (vv. 17-49). This sermon begins not with blessings that emphasize attributes of the heart that change the meaning of the Ten Commandments, as in Matthew 5:1-12, but with Jesus blessing the poor and pronouncing woes on the rich (Luke 6:20-25). This sets the stage for special teaching about lending without expecting anything in return (vv. 34-35) and giving that brings abundance (v. 38). With his Sermon on the Plain, then, Spirit-anointed Jesus clearly brings good news to the poor and brings a strong prophetic challenge to the rich to be generous to the poor. Here, then, the reader begins to see how Spirit-anointed Jesus blends Deuteronomic Torah's focus on love of God with Isaiah's prophetic message of good news to the poor.

Soon after the Sermon on the Plain, when John the Baptist sends two of his disciples to ask Jesus if he is the one to come, Jesus' answer blends his "anointment by the Spirit" activity with a full program of healing and raising the dead (7:21-23):

> [21]Jesus had just then cured many people of diseases, plagues, and evil spirits, and had given sight to many who were blind. [22]And he answered them, "Go and tell John what you have seen and heard:
> the blind receive their sight,
> the lame walk,
> the lepers are cleansed,
> the deaf hear,
> the dead are raised,
> the poor have good news brought to them.
> [23]And blessed is anyone who takes no offense at me."

As we have seen in the first chapter, on the Q Sayings Gospel, all the topics in this healing program are from the prophetic book of Isaiah. Now it is important for us to see that Jesus' statement in 7:22 is a restatement of the program of activity he introduced when he recited Isaiah 61:1 in the Nazareth synagogue at the beginning of his adult ministry (4:18-19). In Luke, Jesus is a Spirit-anointed prophetic Messiah whose speech and action not only bring good news to the poor but also heal the afflicted and even raise the dead.

Jesus the Prophetic Messiah of Social Responsibility

But now let us notice that Jesus ends his statement with an additional beatitude: "Blessed is anyone who takes no offense at me" (7:23). The importance of this blessing appears to be enacted in the next event in the Gospel. When the scene with the two disciples of John comes to an end, a Pharisee who invites Jesus to dine with him is offended that Jesus does not speak a prophetic rebuke against a sinful woman in the city who kisses Jesus' feet as she anoints them with oil and her tears (7:39). This dinner begins a sequence of three times when Jesus dines in the house of a Pharisee (7:36-50; 11:37-54; 14:1-24). At these dinners, Jesus introduces topics either from

Deuteronomy or from Isaiah in a manner that transforms traditional "religious" issues into issues that concern social responsibility. Jesus' activity in these settings reconfigures emphases at the beginning of the prophetic book of Isaiah. In Isaiah 1:16-17, the prophet summarizes what the LORD says to the people with an emphasis on social responsibility:

> [16]Wash yourselves; make yourselves clean, [17]learn to do good; seek justice, rescue the oppressed, defend the orphan, plead for the widow.

At the three dinners in a Pharisee's house in Luke 7:36–14:24, Jesus especially confronts people in a manner similar to Isaiah's confrontation of the people of Israel. In each instance, Jesus criticizes a focus on traditional "religious" issues that bypasses "social responsibilities." When the sinful woman anoints Jesus in the house of Simon the Pharisee, Simon raises a traditional religious issue concerning the association of a holy prophet with a sinner (7:39). In 7:41-43, Jesus transforms the "religious" issue into a prophetic challenge to "forgive a financial debt" (v. 41). Forgiveness, then, concerns wealth, which is an issue that goes back to Deuteronomy 6, which Jesus recited to the devil in response to two of the tests (Luke 4:5-12). When Jesus asks Simon which debtor loves the creditor more (7:42), he has evoked the topic of "love," which is central to Deuteronomy 6 and 7.

This topic of love is not only present in Deuteronomy 6:5 (the Shema) but continues into Deuteronomy 7, where the assertion is made that the Lord brought Israel out of Egypt, "because the Lord loved you" (7:8) and the Lord is "the faithful God who maintains covenant loyalty with those who love him" (v. 9).

> If you heed these ordinances, . . . he will love you, bless you, and multiply you. He will bless the fruit of your womb and the fruit of your ground, your grain and your wine and your oil, the increase of your cattle and the issue of your flock. You shall be the most blessed of people. . . . The LORD will turn away from you every illness. . . . (Deut 7:12-15)

When Jesus responds to Simon, he is developing a topic that his testing by the devil implicitly introduced into the discourse. He turns Simon's concerns about "sinfulness" into the topic of "love," that is, God's giving of abundant wealth. Thus, the woman's willingness to anoint Jesus' feet (Luke 7:37-38, 46) emerges as a paradigmatic instance of "love" (v. 47). The woman, Jesus asserts, knows how to enact love by multiple acts of generosity with oil, an item mentioned as one of God's "blessings" in abundance to Israel in Deuteronomy 7. Forgiveness of debts and generosity with one's possessions must have priority as one begins to discuss sinfulness and forgiveness.

When the sinful woman anoints and kisses Jesus' feet, her actions may call to mind Samuel's anointing and kissing of Saul when he made him king (1 Sam 10:1). But why does the woman anoint Jesus' feet rather than his head? The answer may lie in Luke 9:51–19:27, which presents what is often called "the Lukan travel narrative," which brings us to the Lukan version of Mark's Caesarea Philippi story.

Praying Scenes That Start Jesus' Journey to Jerusalem

Luke does not locate Jesus' discussion with his disciples about who he is either in relation to villages or the district of Caesarea Philippi. Rather, he locates the scene in an unnamed place where "Jesus was praying alone." After praying, "with only the disciples near him" (9:18), Jesus asks the disciples who the crowds say he is and then who the disciples themselves say he is, and then foretells his death and resurrection (vv. 18-22):

> [18]Once when Jesus was praying alone, with only the disciples near him, he asked them, "Who do the crowds say that I am?"
> [19]They answered, "John the Baptist; but others, Elijah; and still others, that one of the ancient prophets has arisen."
> [20]He said to them, "But who do you say that I am?"
> Peter answered, "The Messiah of God."
> [21]He sternly ordered and commanded them not to tell anyone, [22]saying, "The Son of Man must undergo great suffering, and be rejected by the elders, chief priests, and scribes, and be killed, and on the third day be raised."

As stated earlier, this abbreviated account of the scene does not include Peter rebuking Jesus or Jesus rebuking Peter. Jesus asks who the crowds say he is. The disciples' answer focuses on people's understanding of Jesus in relation to John the Baptist, Elijah, or one of the other ancient prophets. When Jesus asks them who they say he is, Peter answers, "The Messiah of God." Well and good, but what does this mean in relation to Jesus' activity as a Spirit-anointed prophetic Messiah? Jesus tells them that "the Son of Man" must suffer, be rejected, killed, and raised up. But where? The key is in Jesus' naming of "the elders, chief priests, and scribes." The only place this can happen is Jerusalem, the place where he was "presented to the Lord" by his parents when he was an infant (2:22-40), where he "sat among the teachers, listening to them and asking questions" when he was twelve years old (2:41-52), and where he refused to throw himself down from the pinnacle of the temple when the devil tested him (4:9-12).

After Jesus asserts that his messiahship requires suffering and death, he explains that this means that his followers will be required to deny themselves, take up their cross daily, and follow him (9:23-27). Then eight days later Jesus again goes to another place to pray. This time Jesus goes up "on the mountain," taking Peter, James, and John with him (v. 28). While Jesus is praying, "the appearance of his face" changes, and his clothes become "dazzling white" (v. 29). Then suddenly the three disciples see Moses and Elijah talking with Jesus, "appearing in glory" as they talk about Jesus' "departure," namely his "exodus, which he was about to accomplish at Jerusalem" (v. 31).

The emphasis in the Lukan account of the Transfiguration, then, is on Jesus' having been anointed to go to Jerusalem for his exodus to heaven. In contrast to the Markan version of the Transfiguration (Mark 9:2-14), the Lukan version has no discussion about the Son of Man rising from the dead, about the scribes' saying that Elijah must come first to restore all things, or about Elijah's already having come (Mark 9:9-13). Rather, the Lukan account emphasizes how Moses and Elijah came to Jesus "in glory" while Jesus was praying, how his clothes became dazzling white, and how his face changed as Moses' did when he spoke to YHWH on the mountain (Exod 34:29-35). In other words, instead of the Holy Spirit coming upon Jesus as it did the first time Jesus prayed in Luke (3:21-22), Jesus begins to shine in the presence of God, and Moses and Elijah come to Jesus and talk with him about his exodus to heaven from Jerusalem after he suffers and dies there (9:30-31). Since Peter, John, and James see this happen, they begin to talk with Jesus about it as Moses and Elijah start to leave (9:32-33). While Peter is suggesting to Jesus that they make dwellings for Jesus, Moses, and Elijah, the presence of God comes in a cloud and overshadows them, as YHWH came to the people of Israel in a cloud (Exod 13:21-22). After God's voice in the cloud tells the disciples, "This is my Son, my Chosen; listen to him," Jesus and the three disciples come down the mountain and Jesus resumes healing and teaching activities briefly before the narrative announces that "when the days drew near for Jesus to be taken up, he set his face to Jerusalem" (Luke 9:51, 53).

In the Gospel of Luke, therefore, two scenes where Jesus is praying introduce his long journey to Jerusalem, where he will die, rise up, and ascend into heaven. The first praying scene presents Jesus' discussion with his disciples concerning who he is. The second praying scene presents Peter, John, and James seeing Moses and Elijah come to Jesus and talk with him about his journey to Jerusalem and exodus into heaven; and then God overshadows the disciples and Jesus in a cloud and presents Jesus' identity to the three disciples as God's chosen Son, to whom they must listen. After this, Jesus sets his feet in motion "along the road" to Jerusalem (9:57), traveling through various unnamed villages and places, teaching, healing, and entering people's homes. Is it fair to suggest that the woman who anointed Jesus' feet with oil and her tears, kissing them and wiping them with her hair (7:38), prepared Jesus' feet for his long journey to Jerusalem? The Lukan Jesus never says this. But soon after the woman anoints Jesus' feet, Jesus goes "through cities and villages, proclaiming and bringing the good news of the kingdom of God" (8:1). The twelve travel with him, and women whom Jesus had cured of evil spirits and infirmities accompany them (v. 2). Luke names these women: Mary Magdalene, Joanna, the wife of Herod's steward Chuza, Suzanna, and many others (v. 3). These women travel with Jesus and his disciples to Jerusalem, and they are the ones who see Joseph of Arimathea lay Jesus' body in the tomb (23:55), who find the empty tomb on the first day of the week, and who tell the apostles about it (24:10). In other words, after the sinful woman anoints Jesus' feet with oil and her tears, Jesus' anointed feet move him decisively forward on his mission of proclaiming good news and healing until he reaches Jerusalem, where he is taken up into heaven.

Jesus as the Dining Prophetic Messiah on His Way to Jerusalem

In the midst of Jesus' journey to Jerusalem, two more invitations to dine in a Pharisee's house create dramatic encounters where Jesus' "prophetic anointment" brings forth especially strong speech from Jesus. At the second dinner, the Pharisee is concerned that Jesus did not wash his hands before he ate (another "traditional religious issue"). In response, Jesus prophetically confronts all who are present with the following topics:

1. Give for alms those things which are within (11:41).
2. Do not neglect justice and the love of God (v. 42).
3. Do not load people with burdens hard to bear (v. 46).
4. Do not kill and build tombs for prophets (who held the people of Israel responsible for social and economic expressions of love) (vv. 47-48).
5. Do not take away the key of knowledge (v. 52).

This list embellishes the central topic of "love of God" in Deuteronomy 6:5 with the topic of "justice" from Isaiah 1:17. In the final assertion by Jesus about "the key of knowledge," we recognize the topic of "knowing, remembering, and doing" from Deuteronomy 8:2-5. Jesus' list, then, builds upon and expands topics central to both Deuteronomy 6–8 and Isaiah.

At Jesus' last dinner in the house of a ruling Pharisee, his actions begin with healing (14:2-4) in a manner that reconfigures Deuteronomy 7:15: "The LORD will turn away from you every illness." In Luke 14, dropsy is a symbol of greed, which is based on the insatiable thirst and hunger of a man with this disease (Braun 1995). When Jesus heals the dropsy, he is symbolically healing the illness of greed in the presence of people of wealth. As Jesus interprets the significance of what he has done, he addresses the topic of "honor," which is a widespread Mediterranean value, with the argumentative topic: "All who exalt themselves will be humbled, and those who humble themselves will be exalted" (v. 11). As we recall, the topic of humbling oneself and being exalted is central to Deuteronomy 8:3, 14-19. Once the people of Israel receive all their wealth, they must not "exalt themselves" but "humble themselves" before God. This leads into the specific topics of Isaiah concerning "the poor, the maimed, the lame, the blind" (Luke 14:13), which is a Lukan reconfiguration of Isaiah 61 and 35. Jesus responds to a man at the dinner who says, "Blessed is he who shall eat bread in the kingdom of God!" with a parable about a man who gave a dinner that emphasizes once more the Lukan reconfiguration of Isaiah with a command to "bring in the poor and maimed and blind and lame" (14:21). Luke 14:1-24 thus presents the high point of Jesus' encounter of the Pharisees with the Deuteronomic-Isaian program of redemption. Jesus' statements at this third and final dinner in a Pharisee's house make it clear that "household" activity is "public" activity that must meet the test of justice and love, which combines emphases in Deuteronomy with emphases in Isaiah, rather than a test of friendship among the wealthy.

The Prophetic Messiah Seeks and Saves the Lost

When the Gospel's story reaches ch. 15, another topic moves into the center: seeking and saving the lost. The resource for this topic is Ezekiel 34, where God's word comes to the prophet Ezekiel after the destruction of Jerusalem and its Temple in 587-86 B.C.E. After Jerusalem and the Temple were destroyed, God's people were scattered throughout the world. In this context, one must not only heal but also seek, find, and save the lost who are scattered across the face of the earth. The words of Ezekiel 34:11-12, 16, responding to the abuse of the people by the leaders of Israel (vv. 3-10), present a challenge to Israel that moves one step beyond the program of Isaiah.

Rather than reciting some portion of Ezekiel 34 to the Pharisees and scribes who were "grumbling" at Jesus' welcoming and eating with tax collectors and sinners (Luke 15:1-2), Jesus recites a parable that enacts the central topics of Ezekiel 34. When even one sheep is lost, a shepherd will leave the flock and seek it until he finds it (Luke 15:4). When he finds it, he will rejoice, because he has found the one who was lost (v. 6). The setting for the parable (v. 2) and the closing statement by Jesus (v. 7) recall the topic of "sinfulness" from Jesus' first dinner in the house of a Pharisee (7:37, 39, 47-49). Still concerned with "sinfulness," the Pharisees and scribes grumble at Jesus' activity, this time at his acceptance of tax collectors and sinners rather than of one specific sinful woman. Occurring immediately after Luke 14, Jesus' description of the "one sinner who repents" evokes an image of a person who is "humble" rather than "exalted" (14:11).

After telling the parable of the shepherd with a hundred sheep, Jesus tells of a woman with only ten silver coins. Losing one of them, she lights a lamp, sweeps the house, and searches carefully until she finds it (15:8). Then she calls her friends and neighbors together to rejoice, since she has found the coin that was lost. Once again, then, Jesus introduces wealth, or the meagerness of wealth, as a topic. The woman exemplifies a person to whom wealth is not abundant. As Jesus tells how she rejoices with others over the coin that was lost, he moves the topic of sinfulness (v. 10) once more toward the issue of wealth, or the lack of it.

Luke 15:11-32 begins with the topic of property and the dividing of property among sons. After the younger son has sinned against heaven and his earthly father (vv. 18, 21) by wasting all his possessions (vv. 13-14), he returns to his father. The result of the repentant return is the bestowal of gifts of wealth and celebration by the father. This story reconfigures the commands to Israel in Deuteronomy 6–8 through the topic of seeking and saving the lost in Ezekiel 34. The father embodies the attributes of a shepherd who will "rescue" (Ezek 34:12) and "feed" (vv. 13-14) the lost, "bring back the strayed and bind up the injured" (v. 16) rather than simply "clothe himself" (v. 3) while failing to "bring back the strayed" (v. 4). The parable of the prodigal son, then, exhibits a father who embodies the attributes of the shepherds that God asks people to be in Ezekiel 34 rather than of the shepherds who abuse their people and fail to seek them out when they are lost.

Luke 16–18 continue to elaborate, amplify, and integrate the topics of Deuteronomy 6–8 and Isaiah as they focus on seeking and saving the lost. 16:1-8 focuses on a manager of money and follows with an elaboration that ends with the assertion that one cannot serve God and wealth (v. 13). The topic of "serving God," we recall, is central to Deuteronomy 6 (v. 13). Jesus continues with a description of the Pharisees as "lovers of money" (Luke 16:14), and when Jesus tells them that "God knows their hearts" (v. 15), the story is developing topics central to Deuteronomy 6–8 in this new context.

The parable of the rich man and Lazarus (16:19-31) ends with an appeal to "listen to Moses and the prophets" (v. 31). The parable of the widow and the unjust judge (18:1-8) features a God who will "grant justice to his chosen ones who cry out" (cf. Isa 1:17). The parable of the Pharisee and the tax collector (Luke 18:9-14) presents a model, as mentioned above, of the principle from Deuteronomy 8:2-3 about the necessity to humble oneself. The story of the rich ruler who came to Jesus, knowing the commandments (Luke 18:20; cf. Deuteronomy 6, 8) yet being unwilling to sell his possessions and give the money to the poor (Luke 18:22), sets the stage for a discussion of the relation of Jesus' followers to possessions (vv. 28-30). Throughout all this, Jesus as the prophetic Messiah anointed with both Spirit and oil explores how "those who are lost may be found" and "those who have wealth" may learn to "seek and save the lost."

Luke 19:1-10 presents the climax of the section on seeking and saving the lost (15:1–19:10). Zaccheus, who is both rich (blessed by the standards of Israel) and a chief tax collector (lost to the house of Israel), welcomes Jesus into his house and explains that he gives half of his possessions to the poor and, if he defrauds anyone, he pays it back fourfold (19:8). When Jesus sees how this person, who is "lost" in the eyes of the Pharisees, embodies the attributes of a rich man who gives generously to the poor and corrects any injustice that occurs, Jesus pronounces him "a son of Abraham."

In Jewish tradition, Abraham is the model of a wealthy man who remained generous all his life.[12] The story ends with Jesus' assertion that "the Son of man came to seek out and to save the lost" (19:10), recalling the topic he had introduced in the parable of the shepherd who, having lost one sheep, sought it until he found it (15:4). At this point in the story, the topic from Ezekiel 34 of seeking, finding, and saving the lost reaches its high point and conclusion before the transitional parable of the ten pounds, which introduces the violent dynamics of the passion narrative in 19:28–23:56.

Conclusion

Who, then, is Jesus on the basis of his anointment both with Spirit and with oil, and what are his tasks in Luke? He is a praying prophet-Messiah. He brings good news to the poor and heals people. He confronts scribes and Pharisees prophetically, challenging them to accept not only sinners but also the crippled, the blind, and the lame (14:21). In addition, he seeks and saves the lost.

It is informative that this anointed prophetic Messiah does not remain silent during the process of his crucifixion, as he does in Mark and Matthew. Rather, while hanging on the cross he prays to God to forgive those who are crucifying him, saying, "Father, forgive them; for they do not know what they are doing" (23:34). Then to the criminal who spoke out against the other criminal who was mocking Jesus' status as Messiah Jesus said, "Truly I tell you, you will be with me in Paradise" (v. 43). Then, this Spirit and oil-anointed prophetic Messiah does not cry out, "My God, my God, why have you forsaken me?" as in Mark 15:34/Matthew 27:46. Instead, he gives the Spirit with which he was anointed back to God, crying out with a loud voice, "Father, into your hand I commit my spirit" (Luke 23:46). When Jesus has given his spirit back to God like this, the stage is set for God to give his Holy Spirit to Jesus' followers, as God does in Acts 2. But before this happens, there is at least one more event we must notice. When the centurion at the foot of the cross sees Jesus die, instead of saying, "Truly this man was God's Son" (Mark 15:39/Matt 27:54), he says, "Certainly this man was *dikaios*" (Luke 23:47). The Greek word *dikaios* regularly means "righteous," and in this context it means "innocent." In Luke, there is no question about Jesus being God's Son. The reader has known

---

12. See, for instance, the Testament of Abraham.

this identity for Jesus ever since the angel Gabriel came to Mary and told her she would have a child (1:32). Rather, the question was what God's Son would do with his anointment both with Spirit and with oil. The answer the Gospel presents is an anointed life focused on food, healing, and justice for the poor supported by a life of prayer. Jesus, the specially anointed Messiah, says that justice and well-being can occur only through love and generosity nurtured through prayer and enacted by those who possess an abundance of God's blessings.

LEARNING ACTIVITIES

1. Read all places in Luke where Jesus or someone else prays: Luke 1:10; 3:21-22; 5:15-16; 6:12, 28; 9:18, 28-29; 11:1-2; 18:1, 10-11; 19:45-46; 20:47; 22:40-46.
2. Read Deuteronomy 6:1-25, which presents the Shema and interpretation of the Shema for the people of Israel who are in the wilderness on their way to the land of Canaan.
3. Read Jesus' Sermon on the Plain in Luke 6:20-49.
4. Read the three accounts in Luke of a Pharisee inviting Jesus to dinner: 7:36-50; 11:37-54; 14:1-24.
5. Read Ezekiel 34:1-31, where the word of the Lord God describes God as a shepherd who seeks the lost, brings back the strayed, binds up the injured, and strengthens the weak (v. 16).
6. Read Luke 15:1-32, where Jesus tells three parables about seeking and saving the lost.

BIBLIOGRAPHY

Braun, Willi. 1995. *Feasting and Social Rhetoric in Luke 14.* Society for New Testament Studies Monograph Series 85. Cambridge: Cambridge University Press.

Byrne, Brendan. 2000. *The Hospitality of God: A Reading of Luke's Gospel.* Collegeville: Liturgical.

Craddock, Fred B. 1990. *Luke.* Interpretation. Louisville: John Knox.

Esler, Philip F. 1987. *Community and Gospel in Luke-Acts: The Social and Political Motivations of Lukan Theology.* Society for New Testament Studies Monograph Series 57. Cambridge: Cambridge University Press.

Gospel of Luke: http://www.earlychristianwritings.com/luke.html.

Green, Joel B. 1997. *The Gospel of Luke.* Grand Rapids: Eerdmans.

Johnson, Luke T. 1991. *The Gospel of Luke.* Sacra Pagina. Collegeville: Liturgical.

Malina, Bruce J., and Richard L. Rohrbaugh. 1992. *Social-Science Commentary on the Synoptic Gospels.* Minneapolis: Fortress.

Moxnes, Halvor. 1988. *The Economy of the Kingdom: Social Conflict and Economic Relations in Luke's Gospel.* Philadelphia: Fortress.

Neyrey, Jerome H. 1991. *The Social World of Luke-Acts.* Peabody: Hendrickson.

Ringe, Sharon H. 1995. *Luke.* Westminster Bible Companion. Louisville: Westminster John Knox.

Stein, Robert H. 1992. *Luke.* New American Commentary. Nashville: Broadman.

Talbert, Charles H. 1982. *Reading Luke: A Literary and Theological Commentary on the Third Gospel.* New York: Crossroad.

Tannehill, Robert C. 1996. *Luke.* Abingdon New Testament Commentaries. Nashville: Abingdon.

Tiede, David L. 1988. *Luke.* Augsburg Commentary on the New Testament. Minneapolis: Augsburg.

6

─────────────

Sir, Give Us This Bread Always!

Like the Synoptic Gospels, the Gospel of John presents an occasion when Simon Peter confesses to Jesus who the twelve disciples think he is. Instead of being a self-contained story, however, as in the Synoptic Gospels, Jesus' discussion with his disciples in John flows out of events and topics that begin with Jesus' miraculous feeding of 5,000 people at the beginning of ch. 6. Jesus' discussion with his disciples in John follows a speech by Jesus on "food that perishes" in relation to "food that endures for eternal life" (6:27). This leads to an argument about "bread from heaven" and Jesus as "the bread of life" (v. 35). When Jesus asserts that "the bread that I will give for the life of the world is my flesh" (v. 51), this leads to dispute among the Jews that produces a statement by Jesus that "unless you eat the flesh of the Son of Man and drink his blood, you have no life in you" (v. 53). At this point, Jesus' disciples begin to complain about the "difficulty" of his teaching (v. 60), and this leads finally to a declaration by Simon Peter that those who are still going around with him consider him to be "the Holy One of God" who has "the words of life" (vv. 68-69). While this sequence still features Simon Peter as the disciple who speaks for the twelve disciples concerning who Jesus is, the overall context dramatically changes the major topics of discussion. The issue is no longer a dispute about a Messiah referred to as "the Son of Man" who must suffer, die, and rise. Rather, it is a dispute about "eating the flesh" and "drinking the blood" of "the Son of Man." To understand the overall significance of this discussion and change of topics, we must look first more carefully at all of John 6.

The Holy One of God Who Has the Eternal Words of Life

John 6 opens with Jesus' feeding of 5,000 people with five barley loaves and two fish (6:1-14), which leads people to refer to Jesus as "the prophet who is to come into the world" (v. 14). After this comes a dramatic story of Jesus walking on water, which creates a context in which Jesus announces to his disciples, "It is I; do not be afraid" (v. 20). After this opening, the middle of the chapter focuses on crowds of people, rather than in any way on Jesus' disciples (vv. 25-59). Prominent in the crowds are "the Judeans" (or "the Jews") who complain about Jesus' teaching, and they dispute with him (vv. 41-59). Jesus' argument with the Jews leads to the closing of the chapter, where Jesus' disciples complain to Jesus about his teaching, and this leads to a series of questions and answers between Jesus and his disciples about Jesus' identity (vv. 60-71). As Jesus' discussion with his disciples comes to a conclusion, Simon Peter speaks for the twelve disciples, saying that they have come to believe that Jesus has "the words of eternal life" and is "the Holy One of God" (vv. 68-69).

Like Mark, the Gospel of John features Jesus presenting a saying about "the Son of Man" to clarify an aspect of his identity. In John, however, Jesus' teaching about the Son of Man does not focus on a rejected-dying-rising Messiah. Rather, Jesus says that the only way people can have "life" in themselves is to "eat the flesh of the Son of Man and drink his blood" (6:53). As in Mark, the saying Jesus presents about the Son of Man is difficult for Jesus' disciples to understand and accept. In John, however, Jesus' statement not only produces a complaint from his disciples (vv. 60-61); it causes all of Jesus' disciples except twelve to turn away and no longer go around with him (v. 66).

This occasion, then, presents the scene in which divine selection of the twelve disciples "reveals itself" in the Johannine story. In other words, in John there is no scene like in the Synoptic Gospels where Jesus explicitly selects twelve disciples to play a special role with him in his activity, whom the narrator names for the reader.[1] Rather, in John "the twelve" are those select disciples who "have come to believe and know" that Jesus is "the Holy One of God" (6:69). Those disciples who "turn back" from Jesus and no longer travel with him object to his teaching about eating the flesh and drinking the blood of the Son of Man (v. 66). Even the "divine selection" of the twelve is a problem, however, because one of the twelve is Judas Iscariot,

---

1. Mark 3:13-19; Matt 10:1-4; Luke 6:12-16.

who will betray Jesus. As a result, the Gospel of John does not focus on Simon Peter as a problematic disciple in this scene, as Mark does by having Jesus refer to Peter as Satan when Peter rebukes Jesus for asserting that the Son of Man must be rejected and killed and rise again (Mark 8:31-33). Rather, in John the scene comes to a close with Jesus speaking about Judas son of Simon Iscariot as a devil, because he will betray Jesus (John 6:69-71).

On a first reading of Jesus' discussion with his disciples at the end of John 6, the different subject matter of Jesus' Son of Man saying might seem to create a total disconnection from anything in the Synoptic Gospels. Closer analysis, however, reveals that a special occasion of "eating" stands near the Caesarea Philippi story in the Synoptic Gospels, where Jesus discusses his identity with his disciples. In Mark, Jesus feeds 4,000 people (8:1-10) and immediately afterwards Pharisees come to him and ask him for a sign from heaven (v. 11). From the Markan perspective, then, the Pharisees either did not see or did not perceive Jesus' miraculous feeding of 4,000 people as "a sign from heaven." Then, as Jesus continues on his way with his disciples in the boat, the disciples worry about having only one loaf of bread (v. 14), which they consider to be no bread at all (vv. 16-17)! In this context, Jesus confronts them about not being able to perceive or understand the meaning of his feeding both the 5,000 people earlier in the story (6:30-44) and the 4,000 just previous to their discussion (8:1-10). The disciples' lack of understanding causes Jesus to ask them ironically, in the tradition of Isaiah 6:9-10, if they have hardened hearts that cause their eyes not to see, their ears not to hear, and their minds not to remember (Mark 8:18-21). Then, after Jesus heals a blind man through a two-step process (vv. 22-26), he discusses his identity with his disciples near Caesarea Philippi, as we have discussed in chapter 3 above.[2]

Now let us return to the beginning of John 6 and read it anew in the context of what we have learned above. In John 6, as stated above, the episodes leading up to Jesus' discussion with his disciples about his identity

---

2. In Matthew, since there is no account of Jesus' successful healing of a blind man through a two-step process, Jesus' Caesarea Philippi discussion with his disciples (16:13-28) occurs immediately after Jesus' feeding of 4,000 people (15:32-39), a request by Pharisees and Sadducees for Jesus to perform a sign from heaven (16:1-4), and Jesus' confrontation of his disciples with their lack of understanding (vv. 5-12). Since there is no account of Jesus' feeding of 4,000 people in Luke, Jesus' discussion of his identity with his disciples (Luke 9:18-27) occurs immediately after his miraculous feeding of 5,000 people (vv. 12-17). Thus, already in the Synoptic Gospels there is a noticeable relation between Jesus' feeding of a large number of people and his discussion of his identity with his disciples.

begin with Jesus' feeding of 5,000 people with five barley loaves and two fish (John 6:1-13). The Johannine narrator calls Jesus' feeding of the 5,000 a "sign" *(sēmeion)* that causes the people to say, "This is indeed the prophet who is to come into the world" (6:14). It is important to observe that the response of the people blends John the Baptist's concept of "the Coming One" *(ho erchomenos)* in the Q Gospel[3] with the response of the disciples in the Caesarea Philippi story that people say Jesus is "one of the prophets."[4] According to John, then, as a result of "the sign" the people do not simply think Jesus is "one of the prophets." Rather, they think he is that particular prophet who has been sent by God into the world. What, however, does this mean? What will this particular prophet do, and how?

From the perspective of the Johannine narrator, the immediate result of the people's perception of Jesus' identity as "the prophet who is to come into the world" is a desire to make him king (6:15). For the Synoptic Gospels, the topic of the kingship of Jesus emerges fully only in Jesus' trial before Pilate. In Mark 15:2 Pilate asks Jesus, "Are you the King of the Judeans?" After a series of events that repetitively focus on people's understanding of Jesus as king, the crucifixion of Jesus highlights an inscription on the cross that accuses Jesus of claiming to be "the king of the Judeans."[5] In early Gospel tradition, the concept of Jesus as king emerges out of Jewish belief that he is "the Messiah." This is evident from Mark 15:32, where the chief priests and scribes mock Jesus by saying, "Let the Messiah, the king of Israel, come down from the cross now, so that we may see and believe" (cf. Luke 23:2, 35-39). There is no mention of Jesus as Messiah in John 6. Rather, the discussion moves from Jesus as "*the* prophet" (6:14) directly to Jesus as king (v. 15) and then on to topics that highlight special aspects of the Johannine portrayal of the identity of Jesus.

In John 6, after Jesus withdraws to "the mountain" by himself to escape from being made king (v. 15), he walks on the sea to his disciples in the boat, identifying himself as "I am he" *(egō eimi)* when they are terrified by what they see (v. 20). Jesus responds earlier in the storyline with "I am he" when the Samaritan woman at the well says she knows the Messiah is coming. Jesus' response is "I am he *(egō eimi),* the one who is speaking to you" (4:26). Interpreters agree that this response by Jesus has a close relation to God's revelation to Moses as "I am who I am" *(egō eimi ho ōn)* in Exodus

---

3. QLuke 7:19-20//QMatt 11:3.
4. Mark 8:28; Matt 16:14; Luke 9:19.
5. Mark 15:26; cf. Matt 27:37; Luke 23:38.

3:14. Jesus' identification of himself to the Samaritan woman is the first of twenty "I am" statements in John,[6] and these statements have a close relation also to the statement in the prologue that "the Word was with God, and the Word was God" (1:1). Jesus' "I am" statements are a special way for Jesus to reveal that "whatever the Father does, the Son does likewise" (5:19). In other words, they exhibit the divine unity and purpose of the Father and the Son. After Jesus' "I am" *(egō eimi)* response to the Samaritan woman, his response to his disciples when he walks on the sea is the first of five occurrences of "I am" *(egō eimi)* in ch. 6 (vv. 20, 35, 41, 48, and 51).

Jesus as the Bread of Life

The Gospel sets the stage for the four additional *egō eimi* statements in ch. 6 by expanding the topic of bread and loaves from the feeding of the 5,000 into the biblical topos of bread/loaves/food/manna.[7] In 6:31 Jesus speaks to the crowd about "the manna in the wilderness." Then he asserts that Moses did not give them "the bread from heaven," but "my Father gave you the true bread from heaven," which is "the bread of God" which "comes down from heaven and gives life to the world" (vv. 32-33). When the crowd says, "Sir, give us this bread always" (v. 34), Jesus introduces the thesis "I am the bread of life" (v. 35: the second "I am" statement in ch. 6) and begins to build an elaborate argument based on "believing in me" and "coming to me" that is grounded in "the will of my Father."

As Jesus elaborates the argument about himself, he explains that the purpose of the bread of God is to bring eternal life to "all who see the Son and believe in him" (v. 40). At this point there is a shift in identification of the people who speak to Jesus. Up to this moment, the crowd who have seen Jesus feed the 5,000 have engaged Jesus in a series of questions and statements that invite Jesus to explain about the bread from heaven, and they ask Jesus to give them this bread always. When Jesus explains that the will of Jesus' Father is that "all who see the Son and believe in him may have eternal life; and I will raise them up on the last day" (v. 40), the people who speak are no longer simply "the crowd" but "the Judeans."

---

6. John 4:26; 6:20, 35, 41, 48, 51; 8:12, 23, 24, 28, 58; 9:5; 10:11, 30, 36, 38; 11:25; 13:19; 14:6; 15:1; 18:5, 8.

7. See 6:23, 26-27, 31-35. A topos is a "place" of reasoning that has rich cultural resources, including literary traditions, supporting its meanings and importance.

The Judeans complain that Jesus has identified himself by saying, "I am the bread that came down from heaven" (6:41: the third "I am" statement in ch. 6). Then they add that he is simply "Jesus, the son of Joseph" and that they know his father and mother. How, then, can Jesus say he has come down from heaven (v. 42)? After Jesus tells the Judeans not to complain, he elaborates his argument further, supporting it this time with what "is written in the prophets" (v. 45). In this context Jesus presents the fourth "I am" statement in John 6 by repeating the saying with which he began in v. 35: "I am the bread of life" (v. 48). This time, however, Jesus adds new dimensions, explaining that "*Whoever eats of this bread* will live forever; and *the bread that I will give* for the life of the world *is my flesh*" (v. 51).

Jesus' reference to his flesh as "the living bread" that people "will eat" produces a scene in which the Judeans "dispute among themselves" saying, "How can this man give us his flesh to eat?" (6:52). As Jesus responds, he asserts that it is necessary that they "eat the flesh of the Son of Man and drink his blood," or they will have no life in them (v. 53). When Jesus elaborates this argument, he asserts, "my flesh is true food and my blood is true drink" (v. 55), and "whoever eats me will live because of me" (v. 57). As Jesus completes his argument, he reiterates that "this is the bread that came down from heaven, not like that which your ancestors ate, and they died" (v. 58). The one who eats this bread will live forever.

Here we have one of the most distinctive, and indeed startling, aspects of the identity of Jesus in the Gospel of John. According to Jesus' assertions in John 6, the Son is "living bread" that people eat. Indeed, people must not only eat the flesh of the Son of Man, but they must drink his blood to have eternal life (v. 54). This sounds like cannibalism, and these statements caused early Christians considerable difficulty in the broader context of the Roman world. In the history of Christianity, of course, these verses have created considerable controversy over the nature of divine presence in celebrations of the Last Supper. It is impossible for us to turn to a discussion of these issues here. Rather, we will continue to explore the relation of this language on the lips of Jesus to other aspects of John in comparison with the other Gospels.

In John 6, the conversations between Jesus and "the crowd," and then between Jesus and "the Judeans," set the stage for Jesus to have a conversation with his disciples about his identity. Like the Caesarea Philippi story, the disciples begin with what they have heard. In this scene, the disciples have heard what Jesus said to the Judeans about eating his flesh and drinking his blood, and they do not like it! Therefore, in contrast to the Caesarea

Philippi story, where Jesus initiates the conversation, in John the disciples initiate it by saying, "This teaching is difficult; who can accept it?" (6:60). Then the disciples "complain" (v. 61) much like the Judeans (v. 41). Their complaint concerns eating the flesh and drinking the blood of the Son of Man, which is an expansion of simply "giving his flesh to eat," about which the Judeans complained (v. 52). Asking his disciples, "Does this offend you?" (v. 61), Jesus explains that "It is the spirit that gives life; the flesh is useless. The words that I have spoken to you are spirit and life" (v. 63). Then Jesus says, "But among you there are some who do not believe" (v. 64). In response to the disciples, then, Jesus "spiritualizes" the eating and drinking in terms of "digesting," if you will, the words of Jesus. Here there are at least two things we should notice. First, from the opening chapter of John the reader has learned that Jesus is "the Word." Here, it would seem, Jesus as "the Word" does his work by speaking "words" that lead a person to belief, which in turn fills a person with eternal life. The words Jesus speaks, then, are spirit and life which people are to "digest," that is, "consume into themselves." At the end of Jesus' discussion, then, Jesus "draws back" from what one might call a cannibalistic understanding of what he has said by presenting a "spirit/life/word" understanding of his presence in the world and of the nature of people's "eating and drinking" of the Son of Man. Second, in the Gospel of Thomas, which we will discuss in a later chapter, Jesus speaks of drinking from his mouth, saying, "Whoever drinks from my mouth will become like me; I myself shall become that person, and the hidden things will be revealed to him" (Gospel of Thomas 108). As the Gospel tradition develops, then, it becomes possible to think of drinking the words from Jesus' mouth as water that flows as eternal life into a person.

It is noticeable that even after Jesus has presented a "spirit/life/word" interpretation of eating the flesh and drinking the blood of the Son of Man, many of Jesus' disciples turn back and no longer go around with Jesus (6:66). Perhaps in John, then, the reader is to understand that "the twelve" who remain are those who can understand the "spirit/life/word" meaning of eating the flesh and drinking the blood of the Son of Man. The rest of the disciples turn away because they are not able to "believe and know" what this means. At the end of John 6 Jesus has an abbreviated interchange with his inner circle of twelve disciples that presents a Johannine version of the Caesarea Philippi story in the Synoptic Gospels. Jesus asks the twelve, "Do you also wish to go away?" (v. 67). To this Simon Peter responds, "Lord, to whom can we go? You have the words of eternal life. We have come to believe and know that you are the Holy One of God" (vv. 68-69). At this point

Jesus answers, "Did I not choose you, the twelve? Yet one of you is a devil" (v. 70). Then the narrator comments that Jesus was speaking about Judas son of Simon Iscariot, one of the twelve, who would betray him (v. 71).

The Last Supper

One may wonder what the relation of this discussion about consuming the words of the Son of Man as spirit and life might be to the rest of the Johannine Gospel. There are many ways we could explore this. We will explore it in relation to Jesus' Last Supper in John and to Jesus' Farewell Discourse, which occurs immediately after the meal (chs. 13–17).

One of the most significant differences between John and the Synoptic Gospels is their presentation of the disciples' Last Supper with Jesus. In the Synoptic Gospels, as many will know, the Last Supper occurs on Thursday evening and is a Passover Meal. Jesus sends two of his disciples ahead into Jerusalem to prepare the meal,[8] and during the meal Jesus takes two of the regular items at a Passover Meal, bread and wine, and changes their focus from a meaning in relation to Israel's exodus from Egypt to Jesus' death on the cross. What is important to know at this point is that Passover could (and still can!) begin at sundown on any day of the week, because it is based on a calendar guided by sighting the full moon.[9]

In John, Jesus' Last Supper on Thursday evening is not a Passover Meal. The reason is, according to John, that the year Jesus was crucified Passover began on Friday evening after Jesus was crucified. The advantage of this chronology is that Jesus' death on the cross occurs while the Passover lambs are being slaughtered in Jerusalem on Friday afternoon in preparation for the Passover Meal in the evening. In John's Gospel, then, Jesus dies "like a Passover lamb" (cf. John 1:36). This chronology has invited into the

8. Mark 14:12-16 and the parallels.

9. Since a lunar calendar is based on months established by sighting the full moon, the beginning of Passover on the fourteenth day of Nisan can occur on different days of the week in different years. This is different from the Christian practice of always having Palm Sunday begin Passion Week, which leads to resurrection day on Easter Sunday. It is possible that the Synoptic Gospel chronology for Passover on the year when Jesus was crucified is based on the Jewish lunar calendar regularly followed by the priests associated with the Jerusalem Temple and that the Gospel of John timing is based on a Jewish solar calendar followed by the people at Qumran, who considered themselves "Sons of Light" (cf. John 12:36: "While you have the light, believe in the light, so that you may become sons of light").

Johannine account of the crucifixion the scene of the breaking the legs of those being crucified, which does not occur in any of the Synoptic Gospels. The Judeans "asked Pilate to have the legs of the crucified men broken and the bodies removed" (19:31). When they got to Jesus, he was already dead, so they did not break his legs (v. 33). Then the narrator says, "These things occurred so that the scripture might be fulfilled, 'None of his bones shall be broken'" (v. 36). These words from Exodus 12:46 refer to the lambs that are killed for Passover each year. The disadvantage of the Johannine chronology, of course, is that wine, which is abundant at Passover meals but not at regular meals, is not present at Jesus' Last Supper (13:1-30).

So what occurs at the Last Supper in John, and how might it be related to the events and discussions in John 6?

In the Gospel of John, instead of Jesus sending two disciples into Jerusalem to prepare the Passover Meal, Jesus "knew that his hour had come to depart from this world and go to the Father" (13:1). Then the narrator introduces the principle that Jesus enacts during the meal: "Having loved his own who were in the world, he loved them to the end" (v. 1). The drama of the Last Supper in John, then, is Jesus' enactment of "loving his own in the world." But how could Jesus better demonstrate this than by interpreting the bread they are eating as "his body broken for you" and the wine they are drinking as "the new covenant in my blood"?

Again as many will know, the major event of the Last Supper in John is Jesus' washing of the disciples' feet. During the supper Jesus, "knowing that the Father had given all things into his hands, and that he had come from God and was going to God, got up from the table, took off his outer robe, and tied a towel around himself" (13:3-4). At this point, Jesus pours water into a basin and begins to wash the disciples' feet and wipe them with the towel (v. 5). When Simon Peter objects, Jesus tells him, "Unless I wash you, you have no share in me" (v. 8). In response to this, Simon Peter says, "Lord, not my feet only but also my hands and my head" (v. 9). Then Jesus says that one who has bathed does not need to wash, except for his feet. But then he adds, "And you are clean; though not all of you" (v. 10), referring, of course, to Judas, who was to betray him. As one can see, then, Jesus' washing of the disciples' feet is the central action of Jesus during the Last Supper in John, rather than his blessing, breaking, and distributing a loaf of bread and giving thanks and passing a cup of wine to all of them.

But Jesus' washing of the disciples' feet is only the first of a series of scenes in which Jesus acts and speaks in ways that elaborate his "loving his own to the end." After he washes their feet he returns to the table and asks the twelve what he has done to them (13:12). But he does not wait for an answer. Rather, he speaks to them about their calling him Teacher and Lord and tells them that, if their Teacher and Lord has washed their feet, they "also ought to wash one another's feet" (v. 14). Next he explains to them that he has given them "an example" of how they should act toward one another (v. 15). Jesus thus transforms his actions into words, which are teachings about the entire range of actions he embodies while he is on earth. Another way to say this is that during the Last Supper in John Jesus becomes "embodied Word" of the entire system of God's bringing of eternal life to those who believe in the Son of Man. As Simon Peter said at the end of John 6: "Lord, to whom can we go? You have the words of eternal life" (6:68). Regularly throughout the Gospel of John, but in special ways during and immediately after the Last Supper, Jesus presents words to his disciples designed to bring eternal life into them through belief.

It is remarkable how similar Jesus' teaching of his disciples during the Last Supper sounds like Jesus' teaching about the implications of the rejection, death, and resurrection of the Son of Man in the Synoptic Gospels. At the end of Jesus' teaching his disciples about the rejected-dying-rising Son of Man in Mark, he also teaches them that the implications of this kind of Messiah is that "whoever wishes to become great" among them must become a servant, and "whoever wishes to be first" must be "slave of all" (Mark 10:43-44). Then he asserts: "For the Son of Man came not to be served but to serve, and to give his life as a ransom for many" (v. 45). In John 13, Jesus does not speak about the Son of Man until v. 31, and even then, as we will see, there is no mention of the Son of Man's rejection, suffering, death, and resurrection. There is, however, an uncanny relation between many of the things Jesus teaches about the rejected-dying-rising Son of Man in the Synoptic Gospels and the things Jesus enacts and teaches at the Last Supper in John 13. As Jesus says in John 13:16-17: "Very truly, I tell you, servants are not greater than their master, nor are messengers greater than the one who sent them. If you know these things, you are blessed if you do them."

In relation to the Synoptic Gospels, it is amazing to realize that in all the discussion at the Last Supper in John there is no reference to Jesus' body or blood. In addition, at the meal there is no reference to a cup or to wine Jesus gives as "the blood of the Son of Man" or as the new covenant in Jesus' blood. There are, however, five references to bread. None of these references speak of Jesus "breaking" the bread, because in John the bread does not signify Jesus' body broken on the cross. In fact, as we have seen above, the concept of Jesus' body "broken" on the cross would conflict with the Johannine portrayal of Jesus' crucifixion. Jesus' body is pierced with a spear while he is on the cross, which fulfills the Scripture "They have looked on the one whom they have pierced" (John 19:37; Zech 12:10). But if Jesus' body were "broken" (19:32), the Scripture signifying Jesus as the Passover lamb would not be fulfilled: "None of his bones shall be broken" (John 19:36; Exod 12:46). In fact, even in the feeding of the 5,000, Jesus simply gives thanks and distributes the bread without breaking it (6:11). This differs noticeably from Jesus' action in the Synoptic Gospels of "breaking the loaves" before distributing them in the feeding of the 5,000 (Mark 6:41), the feeding of the 4,000 (Mark 8:6), the Last Supper (Mark 14:22), and Jesus' meal with disciples after his resurrection in Luke 24:30.[10] In fact, it even differs from Paul's wording about the bread in the meal on the night when Jesus was betrayed (1 Cor 11:24).

So none of the five references to bread during the Last Supper story in John's Gospel signify Jesus' "broken" body. So what do they signify? The bread at the Last Supper functions as "betrayal" bread. In the opening statements about the meal the narrator states that "[t]he devil had already put it into the heart of Judas son of Simon Iscariot to betray him" (13:2). Then, when Jesus is interpreting the meaning of his washing of their feet, which is the major event during the Last Supper, he says, "I am not speaking of all of you; I know whom I have chosen. But it is to fulfill the scripture, 'The one who ate my bread has lifted his heel against me'" (v. 18; Ps 41:9). After Jesus has interpreted the meaning of the washing, Jesus turns to the topic of "one of you will betray me" (13:21). When the disciples wonder which of them it is, Jesus answers, "It is the one to whom I give this piece of bread when I have dipped it in the dish." Then after he dips the piece of bread into the dish, he gives it to Judas son of Simon Iscariot. Then the narrator says, "After he received the piece of bread, Satan entered into him" (vv. 26-27). The final comment of the narrator for the scene is: "So, after receiving the piece of bread, he immediately went out. And it was night" (v. 30).

The Farewell Discourse

If there is no reference to wine or the cup as the new covenant in Jesus' blood and no reference to bread as Jesus' body broken for believers, what is

---

10. Cf. Matt 14:19; 15:36; 26:26; Luke 9:16; 22:19.

the overall effect of Jesus' Last Supper with his disciples in John? The answer surely lies in the statement Jesus makes to his disciples at the beginning of his Farewell Discourse immediately after the Last Supper: "I give you a new commandment, that you love one another. Just as I have loved you, you also should love one another. By this everyone will know that you are my disciples, if you have love for one another" (13:34-35). In this statement, I would argue, Jesus transforms his actions throughout all of John into "word." Jesus' "new commandment" is "the word of spirit and life" that most clearly reveals the inner meaning of Jesus' coming into the world to bring eternal life to those who believe in him.

In relation to the other Gospels, it may seem ironic that the inner revelation of the meaning of Jesus in the Gospel of John should exist in a commandment. As we have seen in chapter 4, Matthew in particular stands out for its emphasis on enacting "righteousness that exceeds that of the scribes and Pharisees" (Matt 5:20). In Matthew, Jesus argues that it is necessary to fulfill "the least" of the commandments (v. 19) and to do what the scribes and Pharisees teach, "because they sit on Moses' seat" (23:2). The key to this, of course, is that fulfillment of the commandments is to become so internalized and automatic within the follower that when the Son of Man comes the righteous will say, "Lord, when was it that we saw you hungry and gave you food, or thirsty and gave you something to drink? And when was it that we saw you a stranger and welcomed you, or naked and gave you clothing? And when was it that we saw you sick or in prison and visited you?" (25:37-39). John, it would seem, is so oriented toward seeing, believing, and receiving eternal life that the idea of fulfilling commandments is virtually foreign to it.

There are, however, ten instances in John where Jesus speaks explicitly about one or more commandments. As we will see, these commandments not only concern people who become believers. Rather, they concern the way in which the Word came into the world as flesh and acted and spoke in the flesh. The first time Jesus refers to a commandment in the Johannine story, he explains to the Judeans how love between the Father and the Son is embedded in a commandment God the Father gave to the Son and the Son's fulfillment of that commandment: "For this reason the Father loves me, because I lay down my life in order to take it up again. No one takes it from me, but I lay it down of my own accord. I have power to lay it down, and I have power to take it up again. I have received this command from my Father" (10:17-18).

The second time Jesus refers to a commandment occurs just before the

Last Supper in a context where "many, even of the authorities, believed in him, but because of the Pharisees they did not confess it, for fear that they would be put out of the synagogue" (12:42). In this context, Jesus explains how his role in the world is not to judge (in contrast to his role in the Synoptic Gospels, which includes his activity as the Son of Man who comes in the future and judges between the righteous and the wicked). The reason is that in John judgment has already occurred with Jesus' coming into the world. The Father has given all judgment to the Son (5:22), and the judgment occurred when the light came into the world and exposed people's deeds (3:19-21). It is not necessary, therefore, for Jesus to judge people's deeds individually, because "those who believe in him are not condemned, but those who do not believe are condemned already" (3:18). This means that "the Son of Man" can focus entirely on saving the world rather than judging it. As Jesus explains:

> [47]I do not judge anyone who hears my words and does not keep them, for I came not to judge the world, but to save the world. [48]The one who rejects me and does not receive my word has a judge; on the last day the word that I have spoken will serve as judge, [49]for I have not spoken on my own, but the Father who sent me has himself given me a commandment about what to say and what to speak. [50]And I know that his commandment is eternal life. What I speak, therefore, I speak just as the Father has told me. (12:47-50)

In Jesus' second reference to the commandment the Father has given him, then, one notices how "the word itself" functions as judge. The word itself is so much an internal part of the will and nature of God the Father that it serves on its own as judge before God the Father. There need not be any other judge than the word itself! Jesus explains that his words function this way because his life on earth is an enactment of "a commandment about what to say and what to speak" that God the Father gave to him when he sent him into the world. Then Jesus adds, "And I know that his commandment is eternal life" (12:50). In other words, the inner nature of God's will and being is eternal life, eternal living being. According to John, in Jesus as "the Word" God the Father was able to formulate a commandment that revealed to the world the innermost nature of God as eternal being that manifests itself in love both for the Son and for the world. There is no special interest, therefore, in having the Son function as judge while he is on earth, or even in the future. Rather, the interest of God the Father is to have the Son come into the world and enact in deed and word the inner "commandment" that guides the storyline of the Word becoming flesh and living on earth until the Son returns to the Father. This "commandment," as Jesus says, "is eternal life" (12:50), because it enacts on earth the inner nature of God the Father as eternal loving being. That enactment on earth is God's speech that creates the reality of eternal life within those who believe.

Another dimension of this commandment, as Jesus says clearly in 10:17-18, is the necessity that the Son be willing to fulfill the commandment of the Father to lay down his life and take it up again. This "commandment" drives the story to the Last Supper, the betrayal, the crucifixion, the death, the burial, and the resurrection. The inner nature of this commandment is so complex, however, that the Gospel shows Jesus explaining it and embodying it in an extended sequence of questions, answers, and statements more than four chapters long, regularly called Jesus' Farewell Discourse (13:31–17:26). For our purposes here, we will interpret only Jesus' statements about commandments in the Farewell Discourse.

Immediately after Judas leaves the Last Supper, Jesus goes out and begins his Farewell Discourse to the eleven disciples. In contrast to the Synoptic Gospels, Jesus does not continue to talk about "the betrayal of the Son of Man." Rather, in the Johannine Farewell Discourse Jesus asserts: "Now the Son of Man has been glorified" (13:31). In John, the betrayal, crucifixion, and death of Jesus is a demonstration of the love of God the Father and the Son. It is not a story of suffering, therefore, but of revealing the true nature of the Father and the Son, who together bring eternal life into the world. In this context, Jesus gives to the eleven "a new commandment," which is: "Love one another. Just as I have loved you, you also should love one another" (v. 34). Jesus explains that everyone will know that they are his disciples if his disciples have love for one another. Later he says, "If you love me, you will keep my commandments" (14:15). Then he explains: "They who have my commandments and keep them are those who love me; and those who love me will be loved by my Father, and I will love them and reveal myself to them" (v. 21). When one of the eleven named Judas (not Iscariot) says to Jesus, "Lord, how is it that you will reveal yourself to us, and not to the world?" Jesus answers, "Those who love me will keep my word, and my Father will love them, and we will come to them and make our home with them. Whoever does not love me does not keep my words; and the word that you hear is not mine, but is from the Father who sent me" (vv. 22-24). Jesus ends this particular discussion with, "I will no longer talk much with you, for the ruler of this world is coming. He has no power over me; but I do as the Father has commanded me, so that the world may know that I love the Father. Rise, let us be on our way" (vv. 30-31). In John, therefore, Jesus does not go out to Gethsemane and pray to God, "Abba, Father, for you all things are possible; remove this cup from me; yet, not my will but yours be done" (Mark 14:36). Rather, he explains to his disciples how the Father gave him a commandment to lay down his life, that he is fulfilling that commandment, that this commandment shows God's love for both the Son and the world, and that Jesus' disciples must show love to one another to enact their belief in this storyline.

As Jesus continues his explanation to the disciples, he moves beyond a discussion of his own glorification to glorification of God the Father:

> [8]My Father is glorified by this, that you bear much fruit and become my disciples. [9]As the Father has loved me, so I have loved you; abide in my love. [10]If you keep my commandments, you will abide in my love, just as I have kept my Father's commandments and abide in his love. [11]I have said these things to you so that my joy may be in you, and that your joy may be complete. [12]This is my commandment, that you love one another as I have loved you. [13]No one has greater love than this, to lay down one's life for one's friends. [14]You are my friends if you do what I command you. (15:8-14)

After Jesus has spoken for a lengthy time in the Farewell Discourse answering the disciples' questions and elaborating his own statements, they finally say, "Now we know that you know all things and do not need to have anyone question you; by this we believe that you came from God" (16:29-30). In contrast to the Synoptic Gospels, then, in the Gospel of John the eleven disciples come to a clear understanding of who Jesus is and how his fulfillment of the commandment God gave to him brings eternal life to the world. In addition, they understand their responsibility to fulfill the commandment to love one another to show both God's love and Jesus' love for them.

In the final chapter of the Farewell Discourse, then, when Jesus prays to God the Father, he does not focus on his own suffering, as he does in the Synoptic Gospels. Instead, Jesus prays to the Father, "Glorify your Son so that the Son may glorify you" (17:1). Then Jesus prays for those who have received the words God gave to him and he in turn has given to them (v. 8). Finally, Jesus prays not only for those who already believe but for those "who will believe" through the word of those who believe (v. 20). Jesus concludes his prayer to God with: "I made your name known to them, and I will make it known, so that the love with which you have loved me may be in them, and I in them" (v. 26). In John, then, the identity of Jesus is especially embedded in the commandment God gave to him to be willing to lay down his life and to take it up again, which makes known the love of the Father both for the Son and for the world. The implications of this are present in the new commandment Jesus gives to his followers, "Love one another. Just as I have loved you, you also should love one another" (13:34).

Conclusion

In summary, we have learned that John's Gospel also contains a scene in which Simon Peter speaks for the twelve disciples, identifying Jesus in a context of disagreement and dispute. When Peter speaks, he asserts that Jesus is "the Holy One of God" who has "the words of eternal life" (6:68-69). But, unlike the Synoptic Gospels, the topic of dispute is not the Son of Man's suffering, death, and resurrection but "eating the flesh and drinking the blood of the Son of Man" (vv. 51-58).

As we have explored Jesus' identity in John, we have observed the absence in Jesus' Last Supper with his disciples (ch. 13) of any "institution of a ritual" concerning eating bread and drinking wine in relation to Jesus' body and blood. Rather, the supper features a foot-washing ritual and a "new commandment" that Jesus' disciples "love one another." This means that in John Jesus' identity is "embedded" in a "foot-washing" action of love and service, and in a commandment to "love one another," rather than in a "ritual of remembrance" that focuses on eating bread and drinking wine.

As we explored the relation between John 6 and Jesus' Last Supper in John 13, we have observed that Jesus' "final statement" in John 6 about eating and drinking is that "It is the spirit that gives life; the flesh is useless. The words that I have spoken to you are spirit and life" (6:62-63). These "final statements" in John 6 raise a serious question concerning proper ritual activity in emerging Christianity in relation to Jesus as "the bread from heaven" who "has the words of eternal life." What kinds of "regular ritual activities" will enact "proper remembrance" of Jesus and lead believers in Jesus into proper actions and beliefs? We will discover in the chapters to follow that John's Gospel introduced topics and issues concerning Jesus as light and life that later writers would explore in elaborate ways and, in some instances, portray in remarkable ways. In the centuries to come, John's presentation of Jesus' identity was so full of meaning, significance, and divinity that a selection of Johannine topics and issues was present in one way or another in virtually every new presentation of Jesus thereafter.

LEARNING ACTIVITIES

1. Read the story of the manna in the wilderness in Exodus 16:1-36; Numbers 11:7-9; and Psalms 78:24-25; 105:40.

2. Read all the "I am" sayings and note the different titles that Jesus uses for himself in John (4:26; 6:20, 35, 41, 48, 51; 8:12, 23, 24, 28, 58; 9:5; 10:11, 30, 36, 38; 11:25; 13:19; 14:6; 15:1; 18:5, 8).

3. In relation to the "I am" sayings, read Exodus 3:1-15.

4. Read John 6:66-71 alongside 9:35-41, attentive to how Jesus' concluding discussions build upon and elaborate the events that happen just before.

5. Reread John 6:60-71 and determine how the twelve disciples are selected according to John's Gospel.

6. Read Mark's Last Supper account (14:12-25) and contrast it with John 13:1-30. Note how the Last Supper in John focuses on the "love commandment," which reveals important aspects of Jesus' identity (see 13:34-35).

7. Read Mark 14:22 (cf. 6:41; 8:6) and 1 Corinthians 11:24 to observe how John's Last Supper account (13:1-30) treats bread in a distinctive way. Then read John 6 to see how the Gospel presents bread in relation to Jesus.

8. Read Exodus 12:43-51 (particularly v. 46) in relation to John 19:31-37 to see the theological significance of the Passover lamb in the Johannine crucifixion account.

BIBLIOGRAPHY

Barrett, C. K. 1978. *The Gospel According to St. John.* 2nd ed. Philadelphia: Westminster.

Beasley-Murray, George R. 1991. *The Gospel of Life: Theology in the Fourth Gospel.* Peabody: Hendrickson.

———. 1999. *John.* 2nd ed. Word Biblical Commentary. Nashville: Thomas Nelson.

Brown, Raymond. 1966, 1970. *The Gospel According to John.* 2 volumes. Anchor Bible. New Haven: Yale University Press.

Bruner, Frederick Dale. 2012. *The Gospel of John: A Commentary.* Grand Rapids: Eerdmans.

Dunn, James D. G. 1996. "John and the Synoptics as a Theological Question." Pages 301-33 in *Exploring the Gospel of John: In Honor of D. Moody Smith.* Ed. R. Alan Culpepper and C. Clifton Black. Louisville: Westminster John Knox.

Gospel of John: http://www.earlychristianwritings.com/john.html.

Käsemann, Ernst. 1978. *The Testament of Jesus: A Study of the Gospel of John in the Light of Chapter 17.* Trans. Gerhard Krodel. Philadelphia: Fortress.

Keener, Craig. 2003. *The Gospel of John: A Commentary.* Grand Rapids: Baker.

Lincoln, Andrew T. 2005. *The Gospel According to Saint John.* Black's New Testament Commentaries. Grand Rapids: Baker.

Martyn, J. Louis. 2003. *History and Theology in the Fourth Gospel.* New Testament Library. Louisville: Westminster John Knox.

Michaels, J. Ramsey. 2010. *The Gospel of John.* New International Commentary on the New Testament. Grand Rapids: Eerdmans.

Moloney, Francis J. 1998. *The Gospel of John.* Sacra Pagina. Collegeville: Liturgical.

O'Day, Gail R. 1995. "The Gospel of John: Introduction, Commentary, and Reflections." Pp. 491-865 in *The New Interpreter's Bible,* vol. 9. Nashville: Abingdon.

Smith, D. Moody. 1995. *The Theology of the Gospel of John.* Cambridge: Cambridge University Press.

———. 1999. *John.* Abingdon New Testament Commentaries. Nashville: Abingdon.

Thompson, Marianne Meye. 1993. *The Incarnate Word: Perspectives on Jesus in the Fourth Gospel.* Peabody: Hendrickson.

7

My Mouth Is Utterly Unable to Say
What You Are Like!

T his chapter moves beyond Gospels in the New Testament to a Gospel
outside the biblical canon. The Gospel of Thomas is one of those Gospels regularly called "extracanonical," which means "outside the canon," or
"apocryphal," which means "hidden away" but more commonly means "of
questionable authorship." The extracanonical Gospels show us how participants in emerging Christianity expanded early Gospel traditions as they
explored and tested their understanding and beliefs about the relation of
Jesus to God, the nature of God's created world, and the innermost nature
of human beings. These Gospels are especially interesting when they are
read in relation to Gospels in the New Testament. Therefore, the approach
in this book is for each chapter to approach an extracanonical Gospel in a
manner that helps readers both expand their knowledge of Christian tradition and deepen their understanding of one or more Gospels inside the
New Testament.

This chapter interprets Thomas especially in relation to John, although
it also continues the focus on special scenes in which Jesus and his disciples raise questions about Jesus' identity in all the New Testament Gospels.
As the chapter unfolds, the reader will notice that the Gospel of Thomas
contains many beliefs and ideas difficult to understand. This shows us how
certain groups of Christians during the century after the writing of the canonical Gospels tried to describe the divine, the nature of eternity, and the
innermost nature of being human — all of which a person cannot see —
through scenes in which Jesus and his disciples ask questions and give answers on a wide range of topics. Thomas presents Jesus in dialogue with
his disciples in a manner in some ways reminiscent of Socrates' famous

discussions with people in Plato's dialogues. Through the literary form of dialogue, namely question and answer, Thomas shows us how some early Christians were trying to push their thinking and believing both inwardly and outwardly into regions beyond both time and space. They were in their own way creating speculative or imaginative Christian philosophy. In other words, they were focusing beyond moral and ethical beliefs and actions into issues concerning the innermost nature of being itself in relation to God and the world.

In this chapter we explore the Gospel of Thomas especially through the scene in logion 13 where Jesus asks his disciples to compare him to something. Three of his disciples answer, and Thomas, after whom the Gospel is named, gives the best answer. Basically Thomas's answer is that it is impossible to compare Jesus to anyone else. To understand why this is a good answer in the Gospel of Thomas, we must understand, first, the relation of this Gospel to the Old Testament/Hebrew Bible.

Old Testament/Hebrew Bible

One thing in common among Q, Mark, Matthew, Luke, and John is that if a person is having difficulty understanding who Jesus is, some verses in the OT/HB will be of help. In other words, for the New Testament Gospels Jesus is a person who is somehow like but greater than Moses, David, Solomon, Elijah, Elisha, Jonah, Isaiah, Daniel, or others. The view in the Gospel of Thomas, in contrast, is that the OT/HB provides no help with understanding who Jesus is. The reason is that Jesus is of a different nature than prophets, kings, messiahs, and the like. One needs to know things like what Jesus says in logion 77: "I am the light that is over all things. I am all: from me all came forth, and to me all attained." In the Gospel of Thomas, Jesus as the light over all things becomes known through the sayings he speaks. Thus, in logion 38 Jesus says, "Often you have desired to hear these sayings that I am speaking to you, and you have no one else from whom to hear them. There will be days when you will seek me and you will not find me." It is not possible to see the light and understand it from anyone other than Jesus, because only Jesus is "the light from whom all came forth."

The issue about the importance of the OT/HB comes to a head in logion 52:

His disciples said to him: "Twenty-four prophets have spoken in Israel, and they all spoke of you."

He said to them: "You have disregarded the Living One who is in
your presence, and have spoken of the dead."

In the Gospel of Thomas, all the OT/HB prophets are dead, so they do not
have a living voice full of eternal light with which to speak about "the light
from whom all came forth." In contrast to the dead prophets, Jesus is "the
Living One," namely the post-resurrection Jesus full of eternal life and
light. When Jesus speaks, life and light come forth in the form of "sayings"
that give humans access to eternal life. As Jesus says at the beginning in
logion 1: "Whoever discovers the interpretation of these sayings will never
die (not taste death)." Jesus, then, does not redeem people through his actions, that is, by dying on the cross or performing miracles of healing.
Rather, he saves people through the sayings he speaks.

Sayings of Jesus

The problem, of course, is that the sayings Jesus speaks in Thomas are difficult to understand. The Gospel does not pretend otherwise. It openly admits that the most important sayings of Jesus, those sayings that can lead a
person into eternal life, have meanings that the ordinary person regularly
cannot comprehend. Jesus communicates this difficulty in the opening of
the Gospel when he presents a version of "seek and you will find" that varies from its form in the Synoptic Gospels. In logion 2 it says:

Jesus said, "Those who seek should not stop seeking until they find.
When they find, they will be disturbed. When they are disturbed,
they will marvel, and will reign over all."

A Greek fragment of this logion adds: "And after they have reigned they will
rest." Logion 60:6 adds: "Seek for yourselves a place for rest, lest you become a carcass and be eaten." As this chapter proceeds, we will come to see
how becoming "a carcass" and being "eaten" means "to be consumed by the
world." The alternative is "fasting" from the world, which allows a person to
"find the kingdom" (logion 27). In Thomas the focus is not simply on persistently asking, seeking, and knocking, as in Matthew 7:7//Luke 11:9.
Rather, a person can enter into eternal rest, the Gospel of Thomas version

of salvation, only through a long, persistent practice of seeking meaning in the sayings attributed to Jesus. After a long period of seeking, a person can begin to find the important things that have the potential to lead a person into eternal rest. But the process is not easy. A major hurdle is that the things a person finds in Jesus' sayings may seem absurd, ridiculous, outlandish, impractical, unpopular, simplistic, or many other things. As Jesus says in logion 2, when a person finds what the sayings mean, the person becomes disturbed. If a person persists in the midst of the disturbance, however, within time the person will begin to marvel. What the person finds is so great that it has a miraculous quality: through what amounts to a miracle of understanding the person becomes a superior being on earth. Indeed, the superiority comes in such great magnitude that the best analogy is that the person becomes like "a king over all understanding within all humans."

King of Knowledge

Royalty in the Gospel of Thomas, then, is not some kind of messianic royalty in the line of David, or some kind of super-prophetic or priestly royalty. One can properly call it wisdom royalty. The concept of royalty moves beyond any kind of traditional concept of a political Messiah in the line of David, a prophetic Messiah in the line of Moses, Elijah, or Elisha, or priestly royalty with lineage from Moses, Aaron, Levi, Zadok, or the order of Melchizedek. Royalty is being "a king of knowledge." It is knowledge that leads a person to eternal life in the form of eternal rest. "Finding" in sayings of Jesus, then, is acquiring the ability to know and understand things that allow the person to overcome death. Knowing is the status of ruling over all things, including death.

A Righteous Angel?

So when Jesus asks the disciples to compare him to something, the question is, Who answers and to what do they compare Jesus? The opening of the scene in logion 13:1-2 is as follows:

> Jesus said to his disciples, "Compare me to something and tell me what I am like."
>
> Simon Peter said to him, "You are like a righteous heavenly messenger."

Naturally, Simon Peter is the first disciple to answer, continuing the tradition of Peter's response to Jesus in the Caesarea Philippi scene in the Synoptic Gospels and in John 6:68-69. In the Gospel of Thomas Peter does not respond out of a prophetic-apocalyptic blend of thinking about prophets, kings, and messiahs. Rather, he responds out of what we might call "fully developed" pre-creation–apocalyptic thinking.

This kind of thinking could begin with the presentation of the heavenly Son of Man in Matthew who "comes in his glory, and all the angels with him" (25:31). This Son of Man is a righteous, descending heavenly messenger who "will separate people one from another as a shepherd separates the sheep from the goats." The unrighteous "will go away into eternal punishment, but the righteous into eternal life" (vv. 32, 46).

Peter is smart enough to expand this thinking with understanding like we find in 1 Enoch, which speaks of "the Son of Man" as the heavenly "prototype of the Before-Time [God]" "to whom belongs righteousness, and with whom righteousness dwells" (46:2-3). This heavenly Son of Man is the Chosen One who was "concealed in the presence of the Lord of the Spirits [God] prior to the creation of the world and "has revealed the wisdom of the Lord of the Spirits to the righteous and holy ones" (48:6-7).

This would seem to be a pretty good answer concerning Jesus' identity in the Gospel of Thomas! In other words, Peter does not say that Jesus is a powerful earthly Messiah (Mark 8:29), the Messiah the Son of the living God (Matt 16:16), or the Messiah of God (Luke 9:20). Indeed, the term Messiah or its Greek translation "Christ" never occurs in the Gospel of Thomas. Peter is smart enough not to suggest that Jesus is a prophetic, political, or miracle-working Messiah, or any other kind of Messiah. Rather, Jesus is a righteous "revealing" messenger. Therefore, Peter's mind moves to some kind of heavenly personage, and he suggests that Jesus is a righteous "revealing" personage. Why is this not good enough to explain who Jesus is?

The problem seems to be that Peter's thinking is still limited by pre-creation–apocalyptic thinking like we find in 1 Enoch. This thinking, from the perspective of the Gospel of Thomas, is limited by "temporal" conceptuality, namely it understands Jesus as a personage who functions within "time." For Peter, Jesus has come to earth as a righteous heavenly messenger related to a kingdom that is "coming" in the future. This is not correct. Every time the disciples ask about a "coming kingdom," Jesus corrects them. For the Gospel of Thomas, the kingdom is already here, both on earth and inside every person. As it says in logion 113:

His disciples said to him, "When will the kingdom come?"

"It will not come by watching for it. It will not be said, 'Look, here!' or 'Look, there!' Rather, the Father's kingdom is spread out upon the earth, and people do not see it."

The kingdom is not something that comes in the future. The kingdom is already in the world and inside everyone living in it. Therefore, there will be no time in the future when the Son of Man comes to bring in the kingdom. Rather, "the Living One" is "in your presence," "before your face" in the form of the sayings of Jesus, and these sayings can lead a person to see and understand the kingdom that is both inside every person and everywhere in the world.

Heavens and Earth Will Roll Up

While the kingdom will not "come in the future" according to the Gospel of Thomas, it is difficult to understand the kingdom clearly. One of the reasons is that there is much "end time" imagery in the Gospel, and it is natural to think of the imagery in the "ordinary" ways we usually think about it. In Thomas, Jesus works hard to change his disciples' ordinary ways of thinking about end-time things. For example, it is true, Jesus says in logion 111, that sometime in the future the heavens and the earth will "roll up like a scroll." But this is not the coming of the kingdom. As it says in logia 110-12:

> 110 Jesus said, "Let one who has found the world, and has become wealthy, renounce the world."
>
> 111 Jesus said, "The heavens and the earth will roll up in your presence, and whoever is living from the Living One will not see death."
>
> Does not Jesus say, "Those who have found themselves, of them the world is not worthy"?
>
> 112 Jesus said, "Damn the flesh that depends on the soul. Damn the soul that depends on the flesh."

According to Jesus in the Gospel of Thomas, the rolling up of the heavens and earth will simply be something that happens to the world and has nothing to do with the kingdom. The world is simply a place where people live, and people need to find out how to separate themselves from the world, because the world is nothing of any real importance or substance, and in no way can it offer any kind of hope for redemption. The world simply "is," a person lives in it, and a person needs to learn how not to be a part of it. Jesus teaches what is regularly called asceticism, an approach where people renounce or reject material possessions and daily benefits as a way of moving spiritually toward redeemed, eternal life. As it says in logion 1, "Whoever finds the meaning of these words will not die." Finding the meaning results in "knowing oneself" and "knowing who is in your presence," namely the Living One. Both of these aspects of "knowing" are the key. Issues about the "coming" of the kingdom are simply misleading. The disciples need to know how to examine the present, not the future. They need to know that the Living One is standing before them, speaking to them through his sayings. As it says concerning the kingdom in logion 3:1-5:

> [1]Jesus said, "If your leaders say to you, 'Look! the kingdom is in the heaven,' then the birds of the heaven will arrive first before you. [2]If they say to you, 'It is under the earth,' then the fish of the sea will enter it, arriving first before you. [3]But the kingdom of Heaven is inside you and outside. [4]Whoever knows himself will find it. [5]And when you know yourselves, you will understand that you are the children of the Living Father. But if you will not know yourselves, you are impoverished and you are poverty."

The sayings about the kingdom being in the heaven or under the earth seem to mean that when the heavens and earth roll up, if the kingdom is in the heaven, the living things in that realm will enter the kingdom first, but if the kingdom is under the earth, the living things in that realm will enter the kingdom first. If humans in the realm of the world have not "found" the kingdom in themselves, then they will be part of the world that rolls up rather than among "the living" who enter the kingdom. Whoever knows himself or herself, then, will find the kingdom and become part of the living, because the kingdom is inside oneself. Knowing the kingdom is knowing that a person is a child of the living Father, and a child of the living Father is a living being in the world. The only way to know that a person is a child of the living Father is to know "what is in front of you," namely the Living One who speaks the words of eternal life. When a person understands the meaning of the words of eternal life spoken by the Living One, then one can find the kingdom and become a Living One in the world. As Jesus says in logion 5:

¹"Understand what is in front of you, and what is hidden from you will be revealed to you. ²For there is nothing hidden that will not be manifested."

Peter's response that Jesus is like a righteous heavenly messenger is good in the sense that it is not focused on Jesus as some kind of earthly prophet, Messiah, or miracle worker. Peter has turned his mind upward, but this has limited him to apocalyptic thinking about the heavens: personages who descend from heaven and ascend back up to heaven, a time in the future when heavenly messengers will assist God in bringing the kingdom to fulfillment, and a time in the future when all people will be judged on the basis of righteousness. For the conceptual world of the Gospel of Thomas, this is not good enough. Jesus is not some kind of apocalyptic personage, some kind of heavenly messenger. A primary reason is that he is not limited to "heaven." He is someone beyond the space of heaven, as well as beyond the way heaven engages with "time" to bring "this age" to an end and to bring "the coming age" into being. Jesus is someone beyond a heavenly personage, because he is a non-time personage who himself is the source of all time, since "when light came forth" time actually began. Before that "time," there was no such thing as time. We will need to explore this much more below to get closer to an understanding. Matthew's answer to Jesus' question can help us to take one step closer toward understanding this idea.

A Wise Philosopher?

As soon as we begin to probe into "pre-time," the time before time, we enter the realm of "speculative philosophy," namely philosophical thinking that moves beyond understanding "nature," namely the world in which things "exist" in a "natural" state. We move beyond "natural philosophy" to an attempt to understand what things were like before there was any "world." This leads us to Matthew's answer to Jesus in logion 13:3:

> Matthew said to him, "You are like a wise philosopher."

This would seem to be quite a good answer to Jesus' question, perhaps in some ways better than Peter's. Instead of attempting to understand the "heavenly" nature of Jesus, Matthew accepts the intellectual challenge of understanding the meaning of Jesus' sayings. Jesus says so much about "knowing" and "understanding" that he seems to be a philosopher-sage, a person filled with a special kind of wisdom that surpasses that of any other sage. Surely Jesus is "like a philosopher," for example, when he speaks directly about having "the keys of knowledge" and criticizes the Pharisees and the scholars in logion 39 for how they use those keys:

> Jesus said, "The Pharisees and the scholars have taken the keys of knowledge and have hidden them. They have not entered nor have they allowed those who want to enter to do so."

Jesus' critical statement about the Pharisees and the scholars would seem to suggest that "someone greater than the Pharisees and the scholars is here," namely one who is like a wise philosopher who has the keys of knowledge and gives these keys to others. Thus, Jesus enters and allows others to enter also. Even logion 67 would seem to suggest that Jesus is like a wise philosopher:

> Jesus said, "Those who know all, but are lacking in themselves, are utterly lacking."

It would seem from this saying that Jesus has a special ability, like a very special wise philosopher, to help people not only to know all but to overcome "lack in themselves." In other words, Jesus helps people to "know themselves" as Socrates in particular did when he functioned as a "midwife of knowledge" in Athens, helping people to bring understanding to birth within themselves.

Truth

Even beyond these assertions about knowledge, there are other sayings in the Gospel of Thomas that appear to support Matthew's answer. In logion 6, when the disciples question Jesus he emphasizes that everything must be faced with "truth":

> [1]His disciples questioned him and said, "How should we fast? How should we pray? How should we give alms? What diet should we observe?"
> [2]Jesus said, "Do not tell lies, [3]and what you hate, do not do. [4]For

everything, when faced with truth, is brought to light. [5]For there is nothing hidden that will not be manifested."

Jesus' answer is startling, but the emphasis on truth suggests that Jesus is approaching fasting, praying, giving alms, and dieting in a philosophical way that focuses on what is really true in contrast to those things that only appear to be true. Socrates certainly comes to mind again here. Indeed, bringing things to "light" seems to suggest that Jesus has special enlightenment and has a goal of leading others into this enlightenment. As it says in logion 11:

> [1]Jesus said, "This heaven will pass away, and the one above it will pass away. [2]The dead are not alive, and the living will not die. [3]In the days when you ate what is dead, you made it something living. When you are in the light, what will you become? On the day when you were one, you became two. When you are two, what will you become?"

This saying is even more difficult, but if a person understands the philosophical system it begins to become clear. When heaven and earth pass away, as we have seen above, the dead will not be alive, but the living will not die. In other words, the dead will simply be dead and remain dead in the earth that passes away. The living, in contrast, will enter "eternal rest," which can be described as the kingdom or the place of light. When people are in the light, they will become one, because they will return to their original pre-Adam state when males were not separated from females. So the question is: What will you become when you are two (male and female), as you are now? Will you become dead or will you become living? If you become living, when heaven and earth pass away, you will return to the place of living, where humans lived prior to their earthly form when they became divided into male and female.

The Beginning and the End

Continuing in this philosophical mode, a person can begin to understand the nature of the beginning and the end. As it says in logion 18:

> [1]The disciples said to Jesus, "Tell us, how will our end come about?"
> [2]Jesus said, "Have you discovered the beginning that you seek the

end? Because where the beginning is, the end will be also. ³Whoever will stand in the beginning is blessed. This person will not die."

When the disciples ask about the end of their lives, it is obvious to Jesus they are not yet thinking beyond time. Thus, Jesus responds to them about the "time" when all time began, namely the beginning. If they understand how all time "began," namely if they understand "the beginning," they will understand that the end is only the end of time or the end of the world. These "ends" are nothing of real substance, since what really "is" lies beyond time. What really "is" always was and always will be. So the beginning of things and the end of things are simply ways of "worldly" thinking. Indeed, the problem is that humans become totally preoccupied with thinking in terms of earthly or worldly "time." To understand Jesus, it is necessary to think beyond time. So, Jesus says, "Whoever will stand in the beginning is blessed. This person will not die." But how can this be? How can a person "stand in the beginning"?

The Gospel of John and the Gospel of Thomas

Perhaps it will help if we go back to the Gospel of John in the New Testament for a moment and compare how "the beginning" is talked about there with how it is talked about in the Gospel of Thomas. In John, there is no attempt to get a person to think "entirely beyond time." Rather, the goal is to help a person live within time, namely to live within "now," in a way that is related to the beginning, to the end, and to non-time. Therefore, John's Gospel starts with a storyline about the beginning:

> In the beginning was the Word, and the Word was with God, and the Word was God. He was in the beginning with God. All things came into being through him, and without him not one thing came into being. What has come into being in him was life, and the life was the light of all people. The light shines in the darkness and the darkness did not overcome it. . . . And the Word became flesh and lived among us, and we have seen his glory, the glory as of a father's only son, full of grace and truth. (John 1:1-5, 14)

The Gospel of John presents "a beginning storyline." In other words, it wants a person to think about time in relation to the beginning. In fact, it wants a person to think not only about the beginning, but about the relation of the beginning to the end and to "now." In "the beginning" God and the Word were united and all things "came into being" through the Word. The nature of all things that came into being through the Word was "life." This "life" was not visible, just as God is not visible (no one has ever seen God: John 1:18). When "the world" came into being, "life" became visible as "light" in the world. The reasoning is that the world without "life" is darkness. The primary nature of "life" in the world, therefore, is "light." The primary nature of the Word, in contrast, is "life," which may be invisible or visible. In a place where all is "life," light is not visible, because there is no darkness there. When life comes into a place where there is no life and all is darkness, on the other hand, "life" is visibly present as "light." Thus Jesus, who is "life," is visibly present as "the light" in the world, where all is darkness. The important things for John, therefore, are to believe in the light so that one may become a child of light (12:36) and to follow the light so that one may have the light of life (8:12).

In the Gospel of Thomas the procedure concerning "the light of life" is more complicated. On the one hand, "belief" and "following" are not avenues for eternal life. There are no occurrences of "follow" in the Gospel and only one occurrence of "believe." Jesus immediately rejects the concept of "belief" as a proper response, as it says in logion 91:

> They said to him, "Tell us who you are so that we may believe in you."
> He said to them, "You examine the face of heaven and earth, but you have not come to know the one who is in your presence, and you do not know how to examine the present moment."

The essential action, according to this Gospel, is "coming to know who is in your presence," not "believing" or "following."

The "Word Storyline" in the Gospel of John

Perhaps it can help to return to the Gospel of John yet one more time before continuing with Thomas. In John the primary nature of the Word is "life." In the world, where all is darkness, the nature of the Word of life is "light." This creates a storyline in which the Word "comes into" the world as light, then at a certain time the light/Word of life departs from the world and sends an Advocate after him to be with his disciples after he has returned to "the Father." John, then, contains a storyline of the Word as the Son of the Father. The Word, who was with God, brought all things into being through his function as "life," after which the Word "came" into the world as "light." When the light came into the world, it "became flesh," and the light dwelled in flesh among humans as the Son of the Father.

As the storyline continues in John beyond "the beginning," Jesus explains to people the relation of the beginning and the end to "now," in which they are living. In other words, in John Jesus makes people keenly aware that they live in time. During the story, there comes "a time" when Jesus "leaves" the world. Jesus explains to his disciples that after he leaves the world there will be a time in which he will send the Advocate (the Paraclete) to his followers to remind them of the past, help them understand it, and guide them as they live in the present in relation to both the past and the future. These things happen in John through presentation of "a time" after the Son leaves the world when the Son will ask the Father to send the Advocate to be with those who believe in him, "a time" when the Father will send the Advocate, the Holy Spirit, to be with them, and "a time" when the Advocate will teach them everything and remind them of everything Jesus has said to them (14:16, 26).

The "Time Storyline" in the Gospel of Thomas

In the Gospel of Thomas, in contrast to John's Gospel, there is no sequence of events that include Jesus' coming into the world and becoming flesh, his staying in the world for a period of time, his leaving the world, his asking the Father to send an Advocate, anticipation of the coming of an Advocate, or explanation of the activity of an Advocate within "time" after Jesus has departed. In addition, there is never any "time of conversation" between the Son and the Father in Thomas. Here it is important to contrast with the Gospel of Thomas Jesus' long conversation with the Father in John 17, as well as various other times of conversation between the Son and the Father in John.[1]

The reason there are no conversations between the Son and the Father in the Gospel of Thomas seems to be that there is no relation "in time" between Jesus and God the living Father. The relation between Jesus and the Father is "beyond time." God the Father "is," and Jesus' relation to the Fa-

---

1. See John 11:41-42; 12:27-28; 17:1-26.

ther is a relation of "being" the light over all things (logion 77). There are no "time events" that occur between Jesus and God the living Father, because there is no "time" in God the Father and actually no "time" in Jesus either. The only things in God the Father, according to logion 50, are "motion" (cf. Gen 1:2) and "rest" (cf. Gen 2:2), and neither of these is understood as "time." Accordingly, Jesus is "the light over all things," which contains the innermost attributes of motion and rest in the Father.

In contrast to Genesis 1:2, where "the Spirit of God moved across the face of the waters," in the Gospel of Thomas Jesus is the light above God's Spirit who is the source of movement in all creation. Also in contrast to Genesis 2:2, which says that God rested, in the Gospel of Thomas Jesus is the light that "rests" above all that moves or rests in the created world. Jesus is, then, the light above all movement and rest in the created order. The movement and rest in Jesus as the light over all are a manifestation of God the Father, in whom there are both movement and rest. The emergence of movement and rest from God is not the beginning of time, as it is in Genesis. Rather, Jesus as the light above all contains the innermost attributes of God's movement and rest and is the source of all movement and rest in the created world. This means that in the Gospel of Thomas Jesus himself is not the beginning of time, namely the beginning of a storyline within time. Jesus, as the light above all who emanated from movement and rest in God the Father, is not only beyond time: he is "the light" who is the source of "time" in the created world.

In this Gospel, then, time does not begin when the Word, who is with God and is God, brings all things into being through life. Rather "the beginning" is "a place of light" (logion 50). What came into being was "the place of light," which is the kingdom, rather than "all things" (John 1:3). How did it come into being? The answer seems to be that Jesus self-generated from the living Father as light, and light established itself as Light over All in "the place of light," which is the kingdom. Understanding "place" can help us, and an important verse for this is Ezekiel 3:12: "Behind me I heard a great roaring sound, 'Blessed is the Presence (Glory) of the Lord, in His place.'" The Presence (Glory) of the Lord moves from its "place" to other places and then returns (cf. Ezek 10:4, 18-19). In the Gospel of Thomas, Jesus is the self-generated light (the Presence/Glory of the Lord) from the Living Father who established its "place" as the Light over All. This "place" is the kingdom, which is both the "beginning" and the "end." "Time" is related to the place of light, because, as "the kingdom," the place of light is the beginning and the end. The basic storyline of the place of light as the kingdom is that all the chosen come from the kingdom and return to the kingdom. Thus, "time" is the "going and coming" of the chosen from the kingdom, which is the place of light.

In the Gospel of Thomas, then, the beginning place is "the kingdom" (logion 49). But it is also the place of "the end." Time "begins" in the relation between Jesus and the world, not in any relation between the Son and the Father. Jesus is the source of the world and all things (including people) in the world. This "source" activity produces "time"; that is, it produces "the beginning." This Gospel is careful not to present any "activities" between the Father and the Son "at any time," which could lead to a perception that God the Father somehow functions within "time." Rather, time begins entirely in Jesus' nature as "source" of the world and all that is in it, including people.

Now that we see how Jesus is the "source" of the world in the Gospel of Thomas, we can revisit Jesus' answer to the disciples' question about their end in logion 18:2-3, where Jesus says:

> ²Have you discovered the beginning that you seek the end? Because where the beginning is, the end will be also. ³Whoever will stand in the beginning is blessed. This person will not die.

What can it mean for a person to "stand in the beginning" in relation to "the end"? This is a highly interesting statement by Jesus in relation to Ephesians 1:3-4, which says:

> ³Blessed be the God and Father of our Lord Jesus Christ, who has blessed us in Christ with every spiritual blessing in the heavenly places, ⁴just as he chose us in Christ before the foundation of the world to be holy and blameless before him in love.

The letter to the Ephesians tells "the saints who are in Ephesus and are faithful in Christ Jesus" (1:1) that God the Father chose them "in Christ before the foundation of the world," that is, before "the beginning," with a goal in the future "to be holy and blameless before him in love," that is, to be with God "in the end." The understanding of the beginning and the end in Ephesians and the Gospel of Thomas seems very close in these two statements, except that there is no concept of being "in Christ" in Thomas.

Rather, Jesus says some "will stand" in the beginning. Here the concept of standing appears to come from how both Jews and Christians thought of angels worshiping before the seated and enthroned God.[2] The Gospel of Thomas does not have the apocalyptic imagery of angels or God the Father sitting on a throne, because the place of God the Father is an invisible realm beyond space, time, and image. The goal for those who seek is to "stand in the beginning," namely to stand at the place where non-space, non-time, and non-image became space, time, and image. But how can the chosen arrive there? In logia 49-50 Jesus says the chosen "came from" there and will "return" there:

> 49[1]Jesus said, "Congratulations to (blessed are) those who are alone and chosen, for you will find the kingdom. [2]For you have come from it, and you will return there again."
>
> 50[1]Jesus said, "If they say to you, 'Where have you come from?' say to them, 'We have come from the light, from the place where the light came into being by itself, established [itself], and appeared in their image.'
>
> [2]If they say to you, 'Is it you?' say, 'We are its children, and we are the chosen of the living Father.'
>
> [3]If they ask you, 'What is the evidence of your Father in you?' say to them, 'It is motion and rest.'"

In the Gospel of Thomas, then, there is a clear storyline whereby the chosen "came from" the light and will "return to" the light. This storyline goes back to "the beginning of all things." Instead of being "chosen in Christ" before the foundation of the world (Eph 1:4), "the chosen" are "from the light," from that place "in the beginning" where the light came into being by itself, established itself, and appeared in human image. It also is helpful for us to see that Thomas calls this beginning place "the kingdom" (logion 49). The kingdom is both the beginning and the end, because it is the place of light outside time where light came into being by itself, established itself, and appeared in human image. But there is so much in logia 49-50 it will help if we look at one thing at a time.

---

2. DeConick 2007: 98-99: 1 Enoch 39:12-13; 40:1; 47:3; 68:2; 2 Enoch 21:1; Testament of Abraham 7-8.

Light and Kingdom

First, let us notice that in the Gospel of Thomas God does not "create" light, as Genesis 1:3 presents it. Light did not come into being through "an event in time" when God said, "Let there be light." Light is beyond time. There was not "a time" when God created light, because God does not function "in time." This means that God is not a creator. Rather, God is the living Father, the one in whom all eternal life is present in the form of motion and rest. Light simply "self-generated" from the living Father. In other words, light self-generated out of "life" in the living Father. After Light came into being by itself, it did not disappear but "established itself." Perhaps it can be debated whether the process whereby light came into being and established itself was the beginning of time, but it seems most likely that this happened outside time. Light was and is simply "a manifestation" of the Father's living being that had no beginning and will have no end. This means that "time" began when the world and all things in it "came into being" through light. Within "time" there "will be" an end when the heavens and the earth roll up. In other words, since the world exists and functions within "time," the world will end. But this does not mean that light or the place of light will end.

Second, let us remind ourselves once again that in the Gospel of Thomas Jesus calls "the place of light" outside of time "the kingdom." The place "from which" those who are alone and chosen came and "to which" they will return is "the kingdom." In other words, the kingdom is not a place that begins and ends: it has no beginning or end. It is also not something that "comes." Thus, it does not come to earth. The kingdom is an eternal place of light outside time. Therefore, it is at both the beginning and the end, that is, in the place outside time from which things came into being at the beginning and to which things return when the end comes.

Third, let us notice that those who "find the kingdom" are "the chosen of the Living Father." "The chosen" are mentioned in the Gospel of Thomas only in logia 49 and 50. First Jesus presents a beatitude about the chosen in logion 49: "Congratulations to (blessed are) those who are alone and chosen, for you will find the kingdom. For you have come from it and you will return there again." Then in logion 50 Jesus says: "If they say to you 'Is it you?' say, 'We are its children, and we are the chosen of the living Father.'" So the children of the living Father are the chosen of the living Father. Because they are the chosen ones, when they are in the world they will be able to find the kingdom and return to it.

Fourth, let us notice that the children of the living Father are not only chosen but are also "alone." This reference to their "solitariness" may have started with a concept that each person "by himself/herself alone" has to find the kingdom "through his or her own individual seeking." But during the 2nd and 3rd centuries c.e. it came to mean that each person needed to be celibate, and finally that each needed to be "a monk" (the word in Coptic is *monachos,* "alone" or "only"). As Christianity emerged, then, the emphasis on the necessity for each individual to seek the meaning of the sayings of Jesus encouraged asceticism, "fasting from the world." This, then, grew into celibacy, that is a single, unmarried person who perhaps lives in the desert. And finally it came to mean a person who dedicated himself or herself to the life of "a monk" or "nun" in a monastic community.

Fifth, let us notice that the evidence for being children of the Father is "in" those who are chosen. In logion 50:3 this evidence is "motion" and "rest," and the question that immediately arises is how anyone can "see" this evidence. Logion 83 seems to speak to this through the topic of "images":

Jesus said, "Images are visible to people, but the light within them is hidden in the image of the Father's light. He will be disclosed, but his image is hidden by his light."

People can see images, Jesus explains, but they are not able to see "the light within themselves," because it is hidden "in the image of the Father's light." What, then, is the image of the Father's light? The "evidence" in the children of the Father's light is motion and rest, but what is the "image" of this motion and rest? A clue may lie in the relation of logion 84 to a statement in logion 50:1. In logion 84 it says:

Jesus said, "When you see your likeness, you are happy. But when you see your images that came into being before you and that neither die nor become visible, how much you will have to bear!"

This seems to mean that the disciples enjoy seeing their likeness when they are in the world. In the future, however, they will see "their images that came into being before them." These images were never visible to them when they were in the world, because they never become visible in the world. The reason seems to be that these images, which never die, are "hidden in the image of the Father's light" (logion 83). While they are not able to see this image that never dies while they are in the world, perhaps this leads us back to the importance of Jesus in the world.

Jesus "Appears" in the World

To get a clear picture of "who" Jesus might be in the Gospel of Thomas, let us recall once again for a moment that in John's Gospel the Word "became flesh" and dwelled among us (1:14). In Thomas, however, Jesus "appeared" in flesh but did not "become" flesh. We see this when Jesus tells his story in logion 28:

> Jesus said, "I took my stand in the midst of the world, and in flesh I appeared to them. I found them all drunk, and I did not find any of them thirsty. My soul ached for the children of humanity, because they are blind in their hearts and do not see, for they came into the world empty, and they also seek to depart from the world empty. But meanwhile they are drunk. When they shake off their wine, then they will change their ways."

Jesus does not "come into" the world and "leave" the world in the Gospel of Thomas as he does in John's Gospel. Rather, Jesus "takes his stand" in the world, that is, manifests himself in the world like the place of light as it manifested itself as the kingdom. Jesus manifests himself in the world by being "present" in it, "before the face" of the disciples. Since flesh is something of "the world," Jesus does not "enter into flesh." In scholarly terms, then, Jesus is a "docetic" Jesus in the Gospel of Thomas. Jesus only "seems" (Greek: *dokeō*) to be fleshly, but he really is not. He "appears" to be a fleshly person, but he cannot actually be flesh or he would be "impregnated" by the nature of the world and thereby "imprisoned" in it. Jesus is "totally pessimistic" about the world and shows no characteristics whatsoever of being "of" it. This Gospel, then, presents a "docetic" Jesus, a Jesus who only might seem to be a human flesh and blood Jesus, but is really a being of another sort.

If we think we are having some success understanding Jesus' sayings because we have "learned" his philosophical system, we begin to realize something more is at stake when we confront sayings of Jesus like what we find in logion 24:

> His disciples said, "Show us the place where you are, for we must seek it."
>
> He said to them, "Anyone here with two ears had better listen! There is light within a person of light, and it shines on the whole world. If it does not shine, it is dark."

Where is the place Jesus is? Is Jesus saying that he himself is light within a person of light? If this is what he is saying, then Jesus is certainly something different from a wise philosopher who "brings light" into other people. This sounds as if Jesus himself is the light within a person of light, this light shines on the whole world, and, if it ("he") does not shine, the world is dark. Here we do well to remember logion 77, discussed above, where Jesus says that he is the light that is over all things, that he is all, that from him all came forth, and that to him all attained. Indeed, he goes on to say, "Split a piece of wood; I am there. Lift up the stone, and you will find me there." If Jesus is the light over all things and all attains to him, then he could very well be the light in a person of light. But this would mean that Jesus is, in the final analysis, something very different from a wise philosopher. Indeed, he is something or someone very different from any kind of person anyone on earth knows, and for this reason his "wisdom" is something that lies beyond any "philosophical" system. Indeed, Jesus says something very close to this in logion 43:

> His disciples said to him, "Who are you to say these things to us?"
> "You do not understand who I am from what I say to you. Rather, you have become like the Judeans, for they love the tree but hate its fruit, or they love the fruit but hate the tree."

In this saying Jesus explicitly states that his disciples do not understand who he is on the basis of what he says to them. What they get is "conflicting understanding." Either they love the goal but do not understand the daily practice that will lead to the goal, or they love a certain kind of daily practice and love this "worldly" activity so much that they completely lose sight of the goal, which must be "fasting from the world." As Jesus says in logion 27: "If you do not fast from the world, you will not find the kingdom."

Impossible to Say Who Jesus Is

This leads us finally, then, to Thomas' discussion with Jesus and the disciples in 13:4-8 after Jesus has asked the disciples to compare him to something and tell him whom he is like:

> [4]Thomas said to Him, "Teacher, my mouth is wholly incapable of saying whom You are like."

⁵Jesus said, "I am not your teacher. Because you have drunk, you have become intoxicated by the bubbling spring which I have measured out."

⁶And He took him and withdrew and told him three words.

⁷When Thomas returned to his companions, they asked him, "What did Jesus say to you?"

⁸Thomas said to them, "If I tell you one of the words which he told me, you will pick up stones and throw them at me; a fire will come out of the stones and burn you up."

Thomas, unlike Peter and Matthew, knows that it is absolutely impossible to compare Jesus to anyone or anything, because Jesus is different from anyone else or anything else. But, unwittingly, Thomas' mouth calls Jesus "Teacher," which is an assertion that compares Jesus to a person who instructs students. Overall Thomas has said the right thing. But his address to Jesus as "Teacher" reveals that he still has not been able to get his mind completely right about who Jesus is. Ironically Thomas has become *too focused* on words of life that flow from Jesus' mouth! One wonders how this could be possible. Again, however, we have to remind ourselves we are not in John's Gospel, where Jesus says in 4:14: "Those who drink of the water that I will give them will never be thirsty. The water that I will give them will become in them a spring of water gushing up to eternal life." In the Gospel of Thomas, what flows from Jesus' mouth should not be compared to water that gushes up to eternal life. Rather, as it says in logion 108:

> Jesus says: "Whoever drinks from my mouth will become like me; I myself shall become that person, and the hidden things will be revealed to him."

As discerning as Thomas has been, then, he still has fallen into the trap of "the children of humanity," who are drunk. Thomas is not just a child of humanity, but he still has a ways to go to "find the kingdom," even though he is "a child of the Father's light." Therefore Jesus tells him, "Because you have become drunk, you have become intoxicated by the bubbling spring I have measured out."

When Jesus takes Thomas away from the other disciples and tells him three words, we are not told the three words Jesus told him! One wonders what they might have been. Because he talks about fire coming out of the stones and burning the disciples up, did Jesus tell Thomas something like logion 82?

> Jesus said, "Whoever is near me is near the fire, and whoever is far from me is far from the kingdom."

Richard Valantasis thinks the reference to fire is related to logion 10, where Jesus says that he has cast fire upon the world and is guarding it until it blazes: "These disciples who insist upon being a part of the world will find themselves calling forth the destructive fire by their own insecurity" (Valantasis 77). April DeConick thinks the three words "must be a reference to the unutterable and unpronounceable Name of God, the *Shem hammephorash.*" Perhaps, then, the words were *"AHYH ASHR AHYH"* as found in Exodus 3:14: "I AM WHO I AM." DeConick suggests that the mention of fire may indicate that "Thomas, by drinking from Jesus' bubbling fount, has been transformed into Jesus' equal, has drawn near to the fire and survived (cf. [logia] 108 and 82). Why will the disciples be burned by fire from the rocks? As C. Murray-Johns has intimated in his article, the gravest of dangers awaits the unprepared person who attempts to encounter God — death by fiery annihilation rather than transformation into a being of light or fire" (DeConick 2007: 85).

Conclusion

In the Gospel of Thomas, then, Jesus is a manifestation of God who transcends angelic forms, all forms of wisdom tradition, and even a Word-flesh personage. He is a self-generated manifestation of the one whose name is unutterable. His presence is known through a human-like image with a voice that speaks words that can help the chosen ones in the world to return to the place of light.

Jesus is not "the Word who was with God," as in the Gospel of John. Also, Jesus is not "life" through whom all things were created. Rather, Jesus is the Living One who is "the light over all things" who emanated from God the living Father, in whom are motion and rest. When Jesus emanated from the Father as the light over all things, this light established itself as the place of light, which is the kingdom. This place of light contains both the beginning and end of time, namely it is both the beginning and the end. It also contains the motion and rest of God the Father.

In the Gospel of Thomas, all the elect have come from the place of light and will return to the place of light when they seek and find the kingdom through the Living One, namely Jesus, who is in their presence. Jesus' sayings are the means by which they can come to this knowledge and become "kings of wisdom" who rule over all others in the created world, take off their earthly clothing, and return to the place of light, which is the kingdom, where they will dwell in the motion and rest of God the Father.

When Jesus asks the disciples to compare him to something, then, the challenge before the disciples is amazingly difficult. Simon Peter gives quite a good answer when he suggests that Jesus is a righteous heavenly messenger. But his answer is not good enough, because angels assist God within "time" to bring in God's kingdom on earth. Jesus, in contrast to angels, functions outside time as "the light over all." While Matthew's answer that Jesus is a wise philosopher might seem to be more appropriate, since Jesus' mode of thinking is so complex, in many ways the answer is less perceptive than Peter's answer. In the Gospel of Thomas, Jesus is a personage far beyond any human being like a philosopher.

Thomas's answer, in contrast to both Peter's and Matthew's, is right on target. The mouth of no human is able to properly express who Jesus is! Humans must speak, of course. But none of their words are able to explain what an incredible personage Jesus is. The only remedy is to have sayings from Jesus, the Living One. When people seek until they find within Jesus' sayings, they will be disturbed when they find. When they are disturbed, however, they will begin to marvel! When they marvel, then they will begin to know the Living One who is in their presence. And when they know the Living One, they will know that they themselves have come from the place of light, they will take off their earthly clothes and return to the place of light, and in the place of light they will dwell in the motion and rest of the Living Father.

LEARNING ACTIVITIES

1. To see how the Gospel of Thomas stresses the enigmatic nature of Jesus' sayings, read logion 2 in conjunction with Matthew 7:7//Luke 11:9.

2. Read Matthew 25:31-46 and 1 Enoch 46 and 48 in comparison with Simon Peter's likening of Jesus to a "heavenly messenger" in Gospel of Thomas 13:1-2.

3. Read John 1:1-5, 14 and note how this storyline concerning the Word's existence and activity in relation to time differs from what one finds in the Gospel of Thomas (e.g., logion 50).

4. Read John 11:41-42; 12:27-28; 17:1-26 to appreciate the sort of conversations between Jesus and God the Father that are lacking in the Gospel of Thomas.

5. Read Genesis 1:2; 2:2 to appreciate Jesus' claim in Gospel of Thomas 50 that the only things existing in God the Father are "motion" and "rest."

6. Read Ezekiel 3:12; 10:4, 18-19 to see how one might begin to understand Jesus' statement in Gospel of Thomas 50 that the beginning is "a place of light."

7. Read Ephesians 1:3-4 to see one formulation of what it means to stand "in the beginning" in relation to "the end."

8. Read 1 Enoch 39:12-13; 40:1; 47:3; 68:2; 2 Enoch 21:1; and Testament of Abraham 7–8 — concerning angels worshiping before God — to see what it might mean in Gospel of Thomas 18:3 for some to "stand in the beginning."

9. When you find the time, read all of the Gospel of Thomas. Then consider how each disciple's response in logion 13 coheres with the Gospel's conceptual world.

BIBLIOGRAPHY

DeConick, April D. 2007. *The Original Gospel of Thomas in Translation: With a Commentary and New English Translation of the Complete Gospel.* New York: T & T Clark.

————. 1996. *Seek to See Him: Ascent and Vision Mysticism in the Gospel of Thomas.* New York: E. J. Brill.

Ehrman, Bart D., and Zlatko Pleše. 2011. *The Apocryphal Gospels: Texts and Translations.* Oxford: Oxford University Press, pp. 303-49.

Foster, Paul. 2009. *The Apocryphal Gospels: A Very Short Introduction.* New York: Oxford University Press, pp. 31-41.

Foster, Paul (ed.). 2008. *The Non-Canonical Gospels.* New York: T & T Clark, pp. 13-29.

Gospel of Thomas: http://www.earlychristianwritings.com/thomas.html.

Klauck, Hans-Josef. 2003. *Apocryphal Gospels: An Introduction.* New York: T & T Clark, pp. 107-22.

Kloppenborg, John S., Marvin W. Meyer, Stephen J. Patterson, and Michael G. Steinhauser. 1990. *Q Thomas Reader.* Sonoma: Polebridge.

Miller, Robert J. 2010. *The Complete Gospels: Annotated Scholars Version.* 4th ed. revised and expanded. Santa Rosa: Polebridge, pp. 279-303.

Murray-Jones, C. 1992. "Transformational Mysticism in the Apocalyptic-Merkavah Tradition," *Journal of Jewish Studies* 48:1-31.

Pagels, Elaine. 2003. *Beyond Belief: The Secret Gospel of Thomas.* New York: Vintage.

Patterson, Stephen J. 1993. *The Gospel of Thomas and Jesus.* Sonoma: Polebridge.

Perkins, Pheme. 2007. *Introduction to the Synoptic Gospels.* Grand Rapids: Eerdmans, pp. 68-72.

Perrin, Nicholas. 2007. *Thomas, the Other Gospel.* Louisville: Westminster John Knox.

Plisch, Uwe-Karsten. 2008. *The Gospel of Thomas: Original Text with Commentary.* Stuttgart: Deutsche Bibelgesellschaft.

Valantasis, Richard. 1997. *The Gospel of Thomas.* London: Routledge.

8

Can Anyone Teach Jesus to Read?

In Qur'an 19:33 when Jesus is born as the Word he speaks from the cradle, saying: "Peace be upon me the day of my birth, the day of my death, and the day of my being raised up alive." Naturally, the sounds the Word made as a baby were not the inarticulate sounds of crying. Rather, the Word pronounced a blessing on his mission as God's servant in the world. What would the Word do if he were a five-year-old boy? A member of the Christian community toward the end of the 2nd century decided to explore this possibility. The Word as a five-year-old would clearly have an upper edge on everyone else, but would he thoroughly understand how to use his power? The writer of the Infancy Gospel of Thomas shows us a way to think about this.

When the writer of Infancy Thomas wanted to start with the Word on earth as a five-year-old, the Gospel of Luke provided him with a way to conclude the story. At twelve years of age, seven years after the beginning of the story, Jesus shows off his special wisdom before the leaders of the Jerusalem Temple. This provides a "canonical" conclusion for the story about Jesus' boyhood. Whatever the Word was at five, he will become the Lukan "twelve-year-old 'adult' boy" by the end of the story.

So how should the story begin? Well, of course, Jesus should be playing creation at the beginning of the story. Why? Because the first thing the Word does at the beginning of the Gospel of John (1:3) is to create the world. But what would be the "special dynamic" of the story? Well of course the story would have to contain the dynamic that "the world received him not." But why would the world not receive him? Because, of course, he could do powerful "signs." So the story must begin with one or more powerful signs to get the story going.

Then how should the middle of the story proceed? If every word the five-year-old "Word Jesus" spoke "instantly happened," this boy would create havoc. Like the Gerasene demoniac, he would have to be "tamed." So how should people try to tame him? Why not try to teach him his letters, which is the underlying principle of "Greek civilization" that created the educational system of *paideia* that was the foundation of Roman civilization?

In the last chapter we saw how the Gospel of Thomas reoriented topics in the Gospel of John. In this chapter we see how the Infancy Gospel of Thomas (InfThomas) blends the Gospels of Luke and John in its presentation of the boyhood of Jesus from five to twelve years of age. We also will see some instances of relationships to some aspects of the Gospels of Mark and Matthew.

InfThomas ends with a version of the Lukan story of twelve-year-old Jesus in the Temple. Thus, it is clear that the author knew Luke and used it as a source for the overall story. But what about the stories that come earlier in this story of the life of Jesus from age five to twelve? Can we see any relation between any of the other stories and Luke? In this chapter we will show that some of the statements by the boy Jesus and many statements by people about Jesus sound like statements related to John's Gospel. In the midst of the "Johannine" way of thinking about Jesus, however, there is one point in particular where InfThomas has a fascinating relation to Luke's Gospel, namely in the attempt to teach Jesus to read. Other information suggests that the author of InfThomas also had access to traditions in Mark and Matthew.

Five-Year-Old Jesus Plays Creation

The opening scene in InfThomas presents Jesus as a five-year-old boy playing with rushing water in a stream. As the scene unfolds, Jesus' gathering of the water into ponds so that water and earth are separated from one another points to God's creation of the world in Genesis 1. When Jesus separates water and earth "with command only," it becomes obvious that he is making a game out of being "the Word" who creates things in the world. As we start to interpret InfThomas, therefore, it will help if we remind ourselves of the manner in which the opening verses of John's Gospel reformulate the creation of the world in Genesis 1.

While Genesis 1:1 starts with "In the beginning God created the heavens and the earth," John starts with "In the beginning was the Word, and the Word was with God, and the Word was God." It thus replaces an emphasis on "God" in Genesis 1 with a focus on "the Word" who is with God in the beginning. As the Gospel of John continues, the Word, rather than God, is the subject of the statements that follow. Indeed, John 1:1 may say that the Word "was" God: it at least says that he was "divine" *(theos)*. In any case, v. 2 reasserts that the Word was in the beginning "with" God. As v. 3 begins, the narrator tells about things that "came into being" *(egeneto)* "through" the Word. In other words, the hearer becomes aware that "the Word" was the primary actor and agent of creation.

If we look back at Genesis 1, we notice there that God created things by speaking "words." This helps to make clear that John's Gospel has "personified" the words God spoke in Genesis 1, making the words into a "personage" called "the Word" who created all things in the world. John 1:3 says that the Word created "all things"; indeed, nothing came into being that "the Word" did not create. V. 4 continues with the assertion that the Word created "life." In Genesis 1, God does not create living things until 1:20: "And God said, 'Let the waters bring forth swarms of living creatures, and let birds fly above the earth across the dome of the sky.'" It is important for us to notice that the first living thing God creates in Genesis 1 is birds that fly, because this will help us understand the beginning of InfThomas. So let us return to the opening of InfThomas.

As the story opens in InfThomas, five-year-old Jesus is playing on the Sabbath. When we become aware that Jesus is playing "creation," we remember that John presents "the Word" as though he were an "adult" personage producing creation as the story opens. The Sabbath, of course, should be a day of rest. InfThomas presents Jesus playing a "game" of creation, as little boys play games. But those who see Jesus see what he is playing as work. Jesus does two things while playing with water: he gathers it into ponds and makes the water pure "with command only." To understand what Jesus is doing it will help to go back to Genesis and carefully read 1:9-10: "And God said, 'Let the waters under the sky be gathered together into one place and let the dry land appear.'" God thus performed two actions that separated water from land only by giving commands. In other words, God causes these things to happen without "forming" a special place for the water to gather, which could, for instance, imply action by God's right hand in the process of creation. Imitating this "commanding" action by God, in InfThomas five-year-old Jesus makes the rushing water "gather together" and "purifies" the water with command only (2:2). But what exactly are the two actions? The first is clear: Jesus has separated water from earth by gathering the water together. The second is more challenging to understand: Jesus made whatever dirt was still in the water separate itself out from the water, making the water "pure" from any "earth" whatsoever. With command only, then, the boy Jesus has imitated God's actions in Genesis 1:9.

The next thing Jesus does in InfThomas is to make soft clay and form it into twelve sparrows (2:3). This takes us to God's creation of living things in Genesis 2:19: "out of the ground the Lord God formed every animal of the field and every bird of the air." The boy Jesus thus imitates God's action.[1] When a Jewish man sees Jesus make the clay and form birds out of it on the Sabbath, he detects a problem, since Jesus' "play" is actually producing "created things" as God did for six days before resting on the seventh (Gen 2:2-3). When the man complains to Jesus' father Joseph, Joseph comes and scolds Jesus for playing in such a manner that he is actually "working." In response to Joseph's complaint, Jesus produces even more incredible "work" on the Sabbath: he shouts to the sparrows, "Be off, fly away, and remember me, you who are now alive!" and the sparrows fly noisily away. At this point, of course, the boy Jesus has produced what we would call a "miracle" on the Sabbath, something the Pharisees regularly complain about concerning the adult Jesus in the New Testament Gospels.[2] In addition, however, we need to see that InfThomas is reformulating the speech of God in Genesis 1:20, where God says, "Let birds fly above the earth across the dome of the sky." Even beyond this, though, we also need to see that InfThomas, with "you are now alive," is reformulating John 1:3-4, which emphasizes that what "came into being" in the Word was "life."[3]

In Jesus' actions, then, of making ponds of water, purifying the water, then making soft clay, forming twelve birds out the clay, and shouting them to life, Jesus is separating water from earth and creating the first living creatures in relation both to Genesis 1-2 and to John 1. A comparison of the texts looks as follows:

---

1. The Greek words in InfThomas 2:3 are *poiēsas* ("made") and *eplasen* ("formed"). The Septuagint (the Greek Old Testament) uses forms of *poiein* ("make") in Gen 1:1, 7, 16, 21, 25-27, 31; 2:2-4, 18 and *eplasen* ("formed") in Gen 2:19.

2. Jesus' miracles on the Sabbath in the New Testament Gospels: Mark 3:1-6//Matt 12:9-14//Luke 6:6-11; Luke 13:10-17; 14:1-6; John 5:1-18; 7:21-24; 9-10; cf. Mark 1:21-34//Luke 4:31-41; Mark 2:23-28//Matt 12:1-8//Luke 6:1-5.

3. The Greek word in InfThomas 2:6 is *zōntes*, and in John 1:3 it is *zōē*.

Jesus Plays Creation

Genesis	Infancy Gospel of Thomas
1⁹And **God said**, "Let the **WATERS** under the sky be **GATHERED** together into one place, and let the dry land appear." And it was so.	2¹When this boy, Jesus, was five years old, he was playing at the ford of a rushing stream. ²He was **GATHERING** the flowing **WATER** into ponds and made the **WATER** instantly pure. He did this **with a single command**.
2¹⁸. . . the Lord God said, "I will **make** . . . ." ¹⁹So **out of the ground** the LORD God **SHAPED** *(eplasen)* every animal of the field and **every bird of the air**.	2³He then **made soft clay** and **SHAPED** *(eplasen)* it into **twelve sparrows**. He did this on the sabbath day, and many other boys were playing with him. . . .
1²⁰**And God said**, "Let the waters bring forth swarms of **LIVING** creatures, and **let birds** FLY above the earth across the dome of the sky." ²¹So God created . . . every **LIVING** creature that moves, of every kind . . . and every winged **bird** of every kind. And God saw that it was good.	2⁶**Jesus** simply clapped his hands and **shouted** to the sparrows: "Be off, **FLY** away, and remember me, you who are now **ALIVE!**" And **the sparrows** took off and **flew** away noisily.
John 1³What has come into being ⁴in him was **LIFE**.	

Once we have seen how InfThomas opens, it will be no surprise for the reader that as InfThomas continues people say things about Jesus like what they might say about God after reading Genesis 1.

The next important event in the life of the boy Jesus occurs when another boy takes a willow branch and makes the water drain out of the pond where Jesus had gathered the water together. When the boy does this, Jesus becomes angry and curses him, telling him he will "dry up like a tree" and "never produce leaves or root or bear fruit" (3:2). Immediately the boy withers and dies as the fig tree withers and dies when cursed by the adult Jesus in Mark 11:12-14, 20-21 (cf. InfThomas 3:1-4). In InfThomas, some people respond with: "Where has this boy come from? Everything he says happens instantly!" (4:3). This is how Psalm 33:9 refers to the power of God's voice when God created the world: "For he spoke, and it came to be; he commanded, and it stood firm." But it is also related to the statement of the blind man after Jesus healed him in John's Gospel: "You do not know where he comes from, and yet he opened my eyes" (9:30). After the parents of the dead boy complain to Joseph in InfThomas and Jesus talks firmly back to Joseph when he scolds him, the people who see it become afraid and say, "Every word he says, whether good or bad, has become a deed — a marvel even!" (5:3). This response of people builds in the story until near the end, when Jesus raises a child from the dead, the crowd of onlookers marvel and say, "Truly this child was a god or a heavenly messenger of God — whatever he says instantly happens" (17:4). Throughout InfThomas, then, people respond to the actions of the boy Jesus with language that sounds both like a natural response to the creative power of God's voice at the time of the creation of the world and like the way people speak about Jesus in the Gospel of John.

Three Teachers Attempt to Teach Jesus His "Letters"

As the story in InfThomas continues further, three different teachers attempt to teach Jesus his "letters," namely to teach him the Greek alphabet. The goal of these teachers is to change the boy Jesus from an unruly child, a person who acts like an "unlettered" barbarian,[4] to a "lettered" person who will act according to "civilized" rules and laws of behavior. When a teacher named Zaccheus offers to help Joseph bring the boy Jesus under his control by teaching him his letters, Joseph tells him, "No one is able to rule this child except God alone. Don't consider him to be a small cross, brother" (6:3).[5] At this point Jesus begins to teach Zaccheus the teacher, telling Zaccheus that he himself, Jesus, is "the Lord of these people," "is present" with all of them, "has been born" among them, and "is with" them (6:5). As Jesus speaks to Zaccheus, words from the Gospels of Matthew and Luke echo in the background: "they shall name him Emmanuel, which means 'God with us'" (Matt 1:23), "to you is born this day in the city of David a Savior, who is the Messiah, the Lord" (Luke 2:11), and "where two or three are gathered in my name, I am there among them"

---

4. *Barbaroi* meant people who did not speak Greek (Herodotus 1.58); in other words they spoke *bar bar*. This lack of "civilization" also made them "unruly," barbarous. Xenophon, *Anabasis* 5.4.34 describes the Mossynoecians as the most barbarous *(barbarōtatoi)* people of all the countries over which they traveled, "the furthest removed from Greek customs. For they habitually did in public the things other people would do only in private, and when they were alone they would behave just as if they were in the company of others, talking to themselves, laughing at themselves, and dancing in whatever spot they chanced to be, as though they were giving an exhibition to others."

5. Jesus interprets this "cross" to the teacher a bit later, saying: "When you see the cross that my Father mentioned, then you'll believe that everything I've told you is true" (6:8).

(Matt 18:20). But then the boy moves into a mode of speaking that sounds like the adult Jesus in the Gospel of John: "I existed when you were born . . . I will teach you a wisdom that no one knows except for me and the one who sent me to you."[6] Then Jesus continues: "when the world was created, I existed along with the one who sent me to you."[7] After this, the teacher Zaccheus tells Joseph,

> [4]This child is no ordinary mortal; he can even tame fire! Perhaps he was born before the creation of the world. [5]What sort of womb bore him, what sort of mother nourished him? — I don't know. . . . [11]What great thing he is — god or angel or whatever else I might call him — I don't know. (7:4-5, 11)

The emphasis on Jesus being "born before the creation of the world" points in particular to the adult Jesus in John's Gospel. In other words, the emphasis in InfThomas is that Jesus is a "pre-creation" Jesus, rather than a "prophetic" Jesus who confronts people like Isaiah or Jeremiah, or an "apocalyptic" Jesus who will come in the future on a cloud as "the Son of Man" accompanied by angels.

After Zaccheus tells Joseph that the boy Jesus is a god or angel or something else, Jesus becomes happy, blesses all who are infertile so they may bear fruit, heals the blind, and cures those who are deaf in the understanding of their heart so they might hear (8:1). Then he says, "I've come from above so that I might save those who are below and summon them to higher things, just as the one who sent me to you commanded me."[8] At this point in the story, InfThomas begins to refer to Jesus' positive acts of healing and raising from the dead as "signs," the language the Gospel of John uses for Jesus' wondrous acts.[9] When Jesus raises a dead child who has fallen off a roof, the child's parents "praised God for the sign that had happened and worshiped Jesus" (9:6). When Jesus spreads out his cloak and carries water in it after the water jar fell and broke, his mother "saw the sign that had occurred, kissed him; but she kept to herself the mysteries that she had seen him do" (11:4). Then when Jesus sows only one measure of grain that yields one hundred measures the narrator notes that Jesus was

---

6. InfThomas 6:6; cf. John 7:16; 12:49; 14:24.

7. InfThomas 6:10; cf. John 1:1; 3:34; 6:38; 7:29; 8:16.

8. InfThomas 8:2; cf. John 10:18; 12:49.

9. John 2:11, 18, 23; 3:2; 4:48, 54; 6:2, 14, 26, 30; 7:31; 9:16; 10:41; 11:47; 12:18, 37; 20:30.

eight years old when he did this sign (12:4). Instead of referring to Jesus' wondrous works as "powers" *(dynameis)* as do Mark, Matthew, and Luke, InfThomas repeatedly uses the Johannine word "signs" *(sēmeia)* for the wonders Jesus performs. In the midst of this, however, that his mother Mary "kept to herself the mysteries that she had seen him do" (cf. Luke 2:19, 51) reminds us that Luke's Gospel is still very much present in the background of the story.

At this point in the story Joseph takes Jesus to another teacher with the resolve that Jesus should not remain illiterate. When the teacher becomes exasperated and hits Jesus on the head, Jesus curses him and the teacher loses consciousness and falls "facedown on the ground" (14:4). But then a teacher who is a close friend of Joseph offers to use flattery to teach Jesus, and Jesus happily goes with him (15:1-2). This creates a scene that reformulates the scene in Luke 4:16-23, where Jesus stands up to read on the Sabbath in his hometown synagogue at Nazareth:

Luke 4	Infancy Gospel of Thomas 15
[16]When he came to Nazareth, where he had been brought up, **HE WENT INTO THE SYNAGOGUE.**	[3]**JESUS WENT BOLDLY INTO THE SCHOOLROOM**
	and found **A SCROLL** lying on the desk. He took the **SCROLL** but
HE STOOD UP TO READ, [17]and the **SCROLL** of the prophet Isaiah was given to him. **HE UNROLLED THE SCROLL** and	**DID NOT READ THE LETTERS** *(ta grammata)* in it.
FOUND THE PLACE WHERE IT WAS WRITTEN *(gegrammenon)*:	Rather, he opened **HIS MOUTH** and
[18]"The **SPIRIT OF THE LORD** is upon me. . . ." [21]"Today this Scripture has been fulfilled in your hearing."	**SPOKE BY THE HOLY SPIRIT** and taught the law to those standing there.
[22]All testified of him and **MARVELED** at the **GRACIOUS WORDS** that **CAME FROM HIS MOUTH.**	[4]A large crowd gathered and stood listening to him, and they **MARVELED** at the maturity of his teaching and **HIS READINESS OF HIS WORDS** — a mere child able to say such things.
They said, "Is not this **JOSEPH'S SON?**"	[6]But the teacher said to **JOSEPH**, ". . . already he is full of much **GRACE** and **WISDOM**. So I'm asking you, brother, to take him back home."

²³He said to them, "Doubtless you will recite to me this proverb, 'Doctor, **HEAL** yourself!' And you will say, 'Do here also in your **HOME** town the things that we have heard you did at Capernaum.'"

⁷When the child heard this, he immediately smiled at him and said, "Because you have spoken and testified rightly, that other teacher who was struck down will be **HEALED**." And right away he was healed. Joseph took his child and went **HOME**.

Instead of a synagogue, Jesus goes into a schoolroom. Instead of having a scroll given to him, he "finds" a scroll lying on the desk. And instead of "opening" the scroll, in InfThomas Jesus "does not read the letters in it." With this act, the boy Jesus is refusing to perform as a "lettered" person, namely one who can read aloud the letters in a written scroll. Rather, simply opening "his mouth," he speaks "by the Holy Spirit" and teaches "the law" to those standing there.

The story has a connection to what Jesus does when the devil tests him in Luke: he responds with Torah he knew from memory (Luke 4:1-12). In InfThomas Jesus at eight years of age is able to "recite" Torah "by the Holy Spirit," rather than reading it. Normally, a Jewish boy becomes an adult member of the community through his Bar Mitzvah, where he displays that he is able to read publicly from the Torah. In InfThomas, Jesus "becomes an adult" already by age eight! But more than this, he does not even have to read the letters to be able to recite the Torah with maturity and eloquence. The people "marveled at the maturity of his teaching and the readiness of his words," and the teacher tells Joseph he is amazed that already Jesus "is filled with much grace and wisdom" (InfThomas 15:4, 6).

When we compare Jesus' schoolroom performance with his performance as a young adult in his hometown synagogue in the Gospel of Luke, we notice a number of things in common. First, in Luke Jesus finds a portion of Isaiah that says, "the Spirit of the Lord is upon me," and he asserts, "Today this scripture has been fulfilled in your hearing" (4:18, 21). In InfThomas, the narrator says that Jesus "opened his mouth and spoke by the Holy Spirit" (15:3). Second, after Jesus speaks, the people marvel at the "eloquence" (grace) of the words that came out of his mouth. Regularly this is the major test of a person's ability to read or recite publicly: the gracefulness, namely the beauty and eloquence of the performance of the words. Third, we notice that the people refer to Jesus as "Joseph's son" in the Lukan scene, and Joseph is the prominent parent in the scene in InfThomas. Fourth, we notice that in the Lukan scene Jesus begins to speak immediately about his curing of people, and in InfThomas he immediately responds by saying, "that other teacher who was struck down will be healed" (15:7). In other words, part of the maturity of Jesus' knowledge is Jesus' control of "whatever he says" so that every miraculous thing he causes with his speech brings benefit to humans rather than death.

Indeed, from this point on in InfThomas, Jesus never becomes angry with anyone and never curses anyone. For this reason, all his speech only "creates" beneficial circumstances. When a viper bites his brother James' hand, Jesus blows on the bite and immediately the pain stops, the viper bursts apart, and James gets "better on the spot" (16:1-2). Then when an infant in the neighborhood dies, Jesus touches the child's chest and says, "I say to you, infant, don't die but live, and be with your mother" (17:3). Immediately the infant looks up and laughs, and Jesus tells the mother to give the infant her breast to feed on. A year later when a man falls off a building that is being constructed, Jesus takes the dead man's hand and says, "I say to you, sir, get up and go back to work" (18:2). At this point, the man gets up and worships Jesus, and the crowd marvels and says, "This child is from heaven — he must be, because he has saved many souls from death, and he can go on saving all his life" (18:3). The episode after this is the final story in InfThomas: Jesus displays his wisdom in the Jerusalem Temple at twelve years of age. Once he speaks "by the Holy Spirit" at eight years of age, then, he has become a disciplined, benevolent adult who only brings life and healing into the world.

So what has happened in InfThomas, and how is this different from what Jesus does in the Gospel of Luke? In InfThomas Jesus has refused to learn "how to read" from human teachers. As a person who was "born before the creation of the world" (7:5), he participated in the creation of the world along with his "Father" and heard the Torah as it was spoken to Moses. There is no need, therefore, for him to learn Greek to become a civilized person. Rather, the challenge he faces, once he is born into "flesh" as a young boy, is to bring "whatever he says" into a mode that only brings benefit to people, because whatever he says happens. Instead of learning this "discipline" through "external" teaching, Jesus learns it "internally" through his own trial and error, which gradually brings "the Holy Spirit" into his thinking and action. When Jesus was five years old, his "play" was based simply on imitating the activities of his "Father," from whom all things came into being. During his eighth year, however, he "masters" his emotions and speech by bringing the presence of the Holy Spirit into his eyes, heart, mind, and mouth. From this time on, he has the ability to use his breath, his touch, and his mouth to restore people to health, life, and the ability to return to their daily work.

But this raises a very interesting question about Jesus in Luke's Gospel that it has not been natural for interpreters to see. Jesus "stood up to read" (4:16) after he entered the synagogue, but did he actually read? What the text says is that he was given a scroll of the prophet Isaiah and he unrolled the scroll and found the place where it was written: "The Spirit of the Lord is upon me . . ." (v. 17). But it never says that he read this text aloud to the people. Rather, the narrator says Jesus "found the place" where the words appear, then the narrator presents the words that were written there, and then the narrator says Jesus "rolled up the scroll, gave it back to the attendant, and sat down" (v. 20). Did Jesus read from the scroll, or did he speak the words to the people without looking at the words? The narrator does not say. Rather, the narrator says Jesus began to say to them, "Today this scripture has been fulfilled in your hearing" (v. 21). Could it be that having found this Scripture in Isaiah Jesus recited it "by heart" to them rather than reading it? Scholars observe, actually, that we have no written copy of Isaiah that presents the words exactly as they are presented in Luke. In contrast, the version in Luke blends verses from Isaiah 58:6 into 61:1-2, as oral recitation of biblical verses often do, especially when they are longer than one verse or clause. Is the Spirit of the Lord, rather than "written" Scripture, guiding the mouth of Jesus in Luke? Scholars regularly refer to this blending of verses as "editing."[10] But this may not do justice to the strong influence of "oral speech" on writing during the 1st and 2nd centuries C.E. Interpreters also notice that the words of Isaiah in Luke 4:18-19 "relate closely to the Lukan portrait of Jesus and provide an interpretation of his ministry."[11] Should we consider the possibility that the author is more interested in showing the reader "what the Holy Spirit spoke" than what might be present in any "written text" of Isaiah?

Whatever we may think of the author of the Gospel of Luke and his view of the influence of the "Holy Spirit" on the words of Scripture, it may be helpful for us to observe that there is no occasion in InfThomas where the narrator presents actual words that Jesus or anyone else "recites" from Scripture. Rather in one place, and one place only, there are words in InfThomas that exist somewhere else in a written text available to us. These words are present in the last scene in InfThomas, which we have al-

10. E.g., Tannehill 1996: 92.
11. Tannehill 1996: 91.

ready observed exists in Luke 2:41-52. Interestingly enough, InfThomas does not contain "exactly the same words" we find in Luke. As we compare the two, we will discover that the InfThomas version expands the final part of the opening, the middle, and the closing of the scene. Let us start by comparing Luke 2:42-47 and InfThomas 19:1-5, which present the opening of the story about Jesus in the Jerusalem Temple at twelve years of age:

Luke 2	Infancy Gospel of Thomas 19
	1
⁴¹Now every year **his parents went to Jerusalem for the festival of the Passover.** ⁴²And when he was **twelve years old,** they went up **as usual** for the festival.	¹When he was **twelve years old his parents went to Jerusalem, as usual, for the Passover festival,** along with their fellow travelers.
	2
⁴³When the festival was ended and **they started to return, the boy Jesus** stayed behind in **Jerusalem,** but **his parents** did not know it. ⁴⁴**Assuming that he was in the group of travelers,** they went a **day's journey.** Then **they started to look for him among their relatives** and friends.	²After Passover **they started to return** home. But while on their way, **the boy Jesus** went back up to **Jerusalem. His parents,** of course, **assumed that he was in the group of travelers.** ³After they had traveled one **day's journey, they started to look for him among their relatives.**
⁴⁵**When they did not find** him, **they returned to Jerusalem to search for him.**	**When they did not find** him, **they** were worried and **returned** again **to** the city **to search for him.**
	3
⁴⁶**After three days they found him in the temple, sitting among the teachers, listening to** them **and asking them questions.** ⁴⁷**And everyone** who heard him was amazed at his understanding and his answers.	⁴**After three days they found him in the temple** area, **sitting among the teachers, listening to** the law **and asking them questions.** ⁵All eyes were on him, **and everyone** was astounded that he, a mere child, **could interrogate the elders and teachers of the people and explain the main points of THE LAW and THE PARABLES OF THE PROPHETS.**

There are only small variations in the wording of the first and second parts of the opening of the story. As the story begins, Luke emphasizes that Jesus' parents went up to Jerusalem for the Passover "every year"; InfThomas considers the phrase "as usual" sufficient to describe the faithful yearly participation of Jesus' parents in the Passover festival in Jerusalem. InfThomas emphasizes the presence of "fellow travelers" with them. In the second part of the opening, Luke says Jesus "stayed behind" in Jerusalem and his parents "did not know it"; InfThomas says Jesus "went back up to Jerusalem." Luke mentions that Jesus' parents look for Jesus even among "friends"; InfThomas mentions only relatives but adds that Jesus' parents "were worried." These are very small variations, seemingly without significant consequence, simply the kind of variations customary for writers who are "composing" rather than trying to be "scribes" who copy a manuscript verbatim.

The InfThomas version, however, presents major expansion in the final part of the opening. First, it asserts that Jesus was listening to "the law" as he sat among the teachers. Second, it emphasizes that "all eyes were on him." Third, instead of a generalized statement that everyone who heard Jesus was amazed at his understanding and answers, InfThomas asserts that everyone was astounded that Jesus, "a mere child, could interrogate the elders and teachers of the people and explain the main points of the law and the parables of the prophets." In other words, in InfThomas the emphasis is on the law and the prophets.

Concerning the law (Torah), the word translated "main points" refers to "head points" *(kephalaia),* which can mean "chief points" but also comes to refer to "headings" or "divisions" in the Torah. In Palestine the Torah came to be divided into 154 sections to be read aloud in public worship over a three-year period, while in Babylonia it was divided into 53 or 54 sections to be read through in a year. Hearers of the story in InfThomas could think either that Jesus was teaching "major topics" in the Torah or that he was teaching them how to navigate through the divisions of the Torah. Concerning the prophets, Jesus' teaching of "the parables of the prophets" has a fascinating relation to Sirach 38:34–39:3:

> [34]How different the one who devotes himself to the study of the law of the Most High! 39[1]He seeks out the wisdom of all the ancients, and is concerned with prophecies; [2]he preserves the sayings of the famous and penetrates the subtleties of parables; [3]he seeks out the hidden meanings of proverbs and is at home with the obscurities of parables.

In InfThomas, the twelve-year-old Jesus is praised as the exemplary Jewish "wise man" who devotes himself to the study of the law of the Most High. This mere child teaches "the elders and teachers of the people" and leads them into understanding of aspects of the law and the prophets which they themselves might not otherwise be able to understand! InfThomas emphasizes that Jesus uses a question and answer approach to teaching similar to Socrates' dialogical method of interrogating people with established reputations in Athens. Jesus, then, as "a mere child" who refused to be taught Greek letters is using what is regularly called a Greek philosophical "Socratic method" of teaching to lead the learned teachers in Jerusalem into greater understanding.

When we turn to the middle of the story, again we find expansion in the final part:

Luke 2	Infancy Gospel of Thomas 19
	1
[48]When his parents saw him they were astonished; and **his mother said to him, "Child, why have you** treated us like **this? Look,** your father and I **have been searching for you in great anxiety."**	[6]**His mother MARY** came up and **said to him, "Child, why have you** done this **to us? Look, we have been searching for you in great anxiety."**
	2
[49]He **said to them, "Why were you searching for me? Did you not know that I must be in MY FATHER'S HOUSE?"**	[7]Jesus **said to them, "Why were you searching for me? Did you not know that I must be in MY FATHER'S HOUSE?"**
	3
[50]But they did not understand what he said to them.	[8]Then the scholars and Pharisees said, "Are you **THE MOTHER OF THIS CHILD?"** [9]She said, "**I AM.**" [10]And they said to her, "You more than any woman are to be congratulated, for **GOD HAS BLESSED THE FRUIT OF YOUR WOMB!** For we've never seen nor heard such glory and such virtue and wisdom."

Instead of mentioning Jesus' "parents" in the first part, InfThomas focuses entirely on Jesus' mother, giving her name as "Mary" and emphasizing how she "came up" to Jesus and confronted him concerning his actions. When Jesus responds to his mother with the same words as in the Lukan account, his statement about his "Father's house" is more dramatic because the hearer presupposes that Jesus' "mother Mary" actually knows who Jesus' "real" Father is.

This leads to the expansion in the third part of the middle of the scene. Instead of simply saying that "they," namely Jesus' parents, "did not understand what he said to them," InfThomas presents the scholars and Pharisees in the Temple as eager to know if Mary is the mother of this brilliant child. When they ask her, Mary answers with those special words Jesus uses throughout the Gospel of John, "I am."[12] This is Mary the bearer of God, *theotokos,* who is responding to the scholars and Pharisees, identifying herself on the basis of the manifestation of God through her. At this point the scholars and Pharisees respond with words that are on the lips of Elizabeth and Mary herself in Luke: "You, more than any other woman, are to be congratulated, for God has blessed the fruit of your womb!" (cf. Luke 1:42, 48).

When the scholars and Pharisees move beyond praise of Jesus' virtue and wisdom to praise of his "glory," they have moved into language characteristic once again of John's Gospel. In fact, InfThomas has given this scene a relation to the wedding at Cana in John 2:1-11. In that scene, Jesus' mother creates a context in which Jesus "revealed his glory; and his disciples believed in him" (2:11). In InfThomas, Mary's direct confrontation of her son creates a context in which the scribes and Pharisees are able to witness to the "glory" of Mary's son Jesus which, in their words, is greater than anything they have seen or heard before.

This leads to the closing of the scene, which again in the third part expands Luke's words so they move into testimony about Jesus like what one hears in John:

Luke 2	Infancy Gospel of Thomas 19
	1
[51]Then he went down with them and came to Nazareth, **and was obedient** to them.	[11]Jesus got up and **WENT TO HIS MOTHER, and was obedient** to his parents.
	2
HIS MOTHER treasured all these things in her heart.	**HIS MOTHER treasured all** that had happened.
	3
[52]**And Jesus continued to grow in wisdom and in years, and** in divine and human favor.	[12]**And Jesus continued to grow in wisdom and in years, and** he was **GLORIFIED BY HIS [DIVINE] FATHER.** (added later) [13]She **[MARY] GLORIFIED HIM** [Jesus] with the Father and the Holy Spirit both now and always and forever and ever. Amen.

12. Also cf. YHWH's manifestation as divine in Septuagint Exod 3:14; Isa 41:4; 43:10-11; 46:4.

The wording in the closing of the episode in InfThomas creates a sequence in which Jesus "went to his mother" in the first part, his mother treasures everything that has happened in the second part, and Jesus is "glorified" by his divine father in the final part. With the addition of "his mother" in the first part and "glorified by his Father" in the last part, InfThomas has moved the verses once again beyond a "Lukan" view of Jesus into a "Johannine" view of Jesus. When InfThomas says that Jesus was "glorified by his Father," words from John 17 reverberate in the background, where Jesus looks up to heaven and says, "Father . . . glorify your Son" (17:1). Later scribes built on this reverberation by adding InfThomas 19:13: "She [Mary] glorified him [Jesus] with the Father and the Holy Spirit both now and always and forever and ever. Amen."

Conclusion

In this chapter we have seen how some Christians during the 2nd and 3rd centuries could blend aspects of the Gospel of Luke with John's Gospel to present Jesus as "the Word" even as a boy. This blending of the two Gospels gave writers an opportunity to explore the nature of God's powerful "creating" word, which immediately brings what it says into being, with a "human" Jesus who was born as a little child and only gradually grew up into adulthood.

One of the remarkable things about this Gospel is its presentation of Jesus in a context of the Greek educational system of *paideia,* in which learning the Greek alphabet was the beginning process for becoming a "civilized" person. How would Jesus as "boy Word" respond to a Greek teacher who was accustomed to striking his students with a stick as part of his "taming" of unruly children? Also, would the "boy Word" ever submit to the process of changing from destructive action to benevolent action by means of learning "Greek letters"? What, then, was to be the relation of the Greek educational *paideia* system to teaching about the Bible and about Jesus? These issues remained very important throughout the third, fourth, and fifth centuries C.E. Indeed, Augustine addressed the issue of the relation of Christian thinking, belief, and practice to classical education and oratory in many of his writings until his death in the 5th century (d. 430 C.E.). Even in the 21st century, the question of the relation of Christian belief and understanding to public school education has not gone away. Indeed, it is as present as ever.

LEARNING ACTIVITIES

1. Read more about Jesus in the Qur'an in Bruce 1974: 167-77.
2. Read further description of the ideal Jewish wise man in Sirach 39 in the Old Testament Apocrypha.
3. Read all of Infancy Thomas in one of the editions listed below or on-line.
4. Read John 1:1-5 to see how the Evangelist refashions aspects of the creation account in Genesis 1–2.
5. Read Mark 11:12-14, 20-21 where the adult Jesus curses a fig tree, and note how the fate of the fig tree compares with that of the boy in the Infancy Gospel of Thomas 3:1-4.
6. To see the Johannine view of Jesus' miracles as signs, read John 2:11, 18, 23; 3:2; 4:48, 54; 6:2, 14, 26, 30; 7:31; 9:16; 10:41; 11:47; 12:18, 37; 20:30.
7. Read Luke's account of Jesus' testing in the wilderness in 4:1-12 to see the importance of memorizing Torah for Jewish adults.
8. Read Isaiah 58:6 and 61:1-2 and observe how Jesus blends these verses in Luke 4:18-19.
9. Read Luke 1:42, 48 in relation to the blessing of Mary's womb in Infancy Gospel of Thomas 19:10.
10. Read John 2:1-11 and note how Mary's actions set the stage for Jesus to reveal his glory.

BIBLIOGRAPHY

Aasgaard, Reidar. 2011. *The Childhood of Jesus: Decoding the Apocryphal Infancy Gospel of Thomas.* Cambridge: James Clark.

Bruce, F. F. 1974. *Jesus and Christian Origins outside the New Testament.* Grand Rapids: Eerdmans.

Ehrman, Bart D., and Zlatko Pleše. 2011. *The Apocryphal Gospels: Texts and Translations.* Oxford: Oxford University Press, pp. 3-29.

Foster, Paul. 2009. *The Apocryphal Gospels: A Very Short Introduction.* Oxford: Oxford University Press, pp. 63-72.

Foster, Paul (ed.). 2008. *The Non-Canonical Gospels.* New York: T & T Clark, pp. 126-38.

Hock, Ronald F. 1995. *The Infancy Gospels of James and Thomas.* Santa Rosa: Polebridge.

Infancy Gospel of Thomas: http://www.earlychristianwritings.com/infancythomas .html.

Klauck, Hans-Josef. 2003. *Apocryphal Gospels: An Introduction.* New York: T & T Clark, pp. 73-78.

Miller, Robert J. 2010. *The Complete Gospels: Annotated Scholars Version.* 4th ed. revised and expanded. Santa Rosa: Polebridge, pp. 379-89.

Perkins, Pheme. 2007. *Introduction to the Synoptic Gospels.* Grand Rapids: Eerdmans, pp. 247-49.

Tannehill, Robert C. 1996. *Luke.* Abingdon New Testament Commentaries. Nashville: Abingdon.

Xenophon. 1992. *Anabasis.* Trans. Carleton L. Brownson. Loeb Classical Library. Cambridge: Harvard University Press.

9

I've Seen a New Miracle!

In the last chapter we saw how InfThomas blends a Johannine view of Jesus as the Word who created the world with a Lukan view of Jesus as a
person who can recite Scripture with graceful beauty and wisdom. The
special creativity of the 2nd-century Christian writer who composed the
story began as Jesus got into trouble while playing creation on the Sabbath
at age five. The trouble increased when Jesus refused to learn from three
teachers who tried to teach him his Greek letters to tame his unruliness.
Gradually, however, Jesus learned on his own how to recite the Torah
beautifully by heart in a schoolroom by age eight, how to control the immediate effects of his speech so he only brought benefit and healing to humans, and how to teach both the Torah and the prophets with astonishing
skill to scholars and Pharisees in the Jerusalem Temple at age twelve. A
special result of the story is the gradual movement of Jesus' father Joseph
into the background while his mother Mary moves into the foreground as
the most fortunate and blessed mother in the world for giving birth to a
child of such glory, virtue, and wisdom.

The Birth of Jesus in the Infancy Gospel of James

In this chapter we look at the Infancy Gospel of James (InfJames), which
presents twenty-five short chapters in which one of the dramatic
highpoints is the birth of Jesus. The priestly holiness first of Mary's parents, Joachim and Anna, and secondly of Mary herself stands in the foreground as the story begins. When Mary gives birth to Jesus, however, the

story blends a Johannine emphasis on Jesus as the light of the world with a Synoptic emphasis on the healing body of Jesus. The story ends with Herod's decision to kill all infants two years of age and under, and this leads to an unusual story of the killing of Zechariah, the father of John the Baptist. Since our focus is on people's views of Jesus rather than other people like John the Baptist and his father, we will not present any detailed analysis and interpretation of the events in InfJames 21–25, which tell about the events after Herod becomes angry that the astrologers have tricked him by not telling him where Jesus was born and decides to kill all infants two years and younger. Rather, the emphasis will be on the sequence of events that leads to the birth of Jesus as the light who comes into the world and becomes flesh as a suckling child.

The first special focus of this chapter will be on how InfJames extends the Lukan story backwards beyond the births of John the Baptist and Jesus to the birth of Mary to Joachim and Anna. In this context, a second focus will be on a significant number of events in InfJames that are a reworking of the birth of the priest-prophet Samuel to his parents Elkanah and Hannah in 1 Samuel 1–2. Samuel is an important person, because he anointed the first two kings of Israel, Saul and David. This means he is an important priest-prophet in the storyline from the first kings of Israel to Jesus, the Messiah of Israel. The third focus of this chapter will be on the way in which InfJames interweaves a Lukan approach that focuses on the women with a Matthean approach that focuses on Joseph. The fourth focus will be on the surprising way in which Johannine topics and perspectives come into Mary's conception of Jesus "by the word *(logos)* of God" in her womb and gives birth to Jesus in a manner by which she remains a virgin. The fifth and final focus, then, will be on the surprising way in which Jesus' birth as the light of the world who comes into the darkness and becomes flesh, a Johannine emphasis, answers the question of "who Jesus is" in InfJames when he is born in a totally unusual way to Mary.

The Birth of Mary

InfJames begins with Joachim, who will become the father of Mary, experiencing rejection of his double offerings at the Jerusalem Temple because he and his wife Anna have not borne a child for the people of Israel. This opening scene (1:1–11) is reminiscent both of the opening of 1 Samuel, where Elkanah, who will become the father of Samuel, gives annual sacrifices to the Lord at Shiloh, and of the opening of Luke's Gospel, where Zechariah, who will become the father of John the Baptist, experiences a special visitation of the angel of God while he is offering the incense offering in the Temple.

As the story continues, there is a shift to Joachim's wife Anna that is like the focus on Hannah with the birth of Samuel in 1 Samuel 1–2 and on Elizabeth and Mary with the births of John the Baptist and Jesus in Luke. Anna's severe lamentation and frustration finally lead her to take off her mourning clothes, wash her face, put on her wedding dress, and go out to her garden in the middle of the afternoon to walk (2:7-8). When she sits down under a laurel tree and prays to the Lord about Sarah and her son Isaac, she looks up and sees a nest of sparrows (2:9–3:1). This sends her into even deeper lamentation, which produces six woes from her lips that begin with "Poor me!" The first is "Poor Me! Who gave birth to me? What sort of womb bore me? . . . I was born under a curse. . . . I have been reviled and mocked and banished from the temple of the Lord my God" (3:2-3). The next five begin with "Poor me! What am I like?" As these statements unfold, Anna laments that she is not like the birds of the sky, domestic animals, wild animals, the waters, or the earth, all of which are productive in the presence of God (3:4-8). This long sequence of woes is, of course, the opposite of Hannah's song of exaltation in 1 Sam 2:1-10, of Mary and Elizabeth's pronouncement of beatitudes on one another, and of Mary's Magnificat of gratitude to God for how blessed she is in Luke 1:39-55.

Continuing with a storyline related to that of Luke, suddenly an angel of the Lord appears to Anna. The scene is like the angel Gabriel's appearance to Mary in Luke 1:26-38. The angel tells Anna that the Lord has heard her prayer and that she will give birth to a child who will be talked about all over the world (4:1). When Anna says that she will offer the child to the Lord her God whether it is a boy or a girl (v. 2), the story is suddenly reminiscent of Hannah's willingness to dedicate Samuel to the temple in 1 Samuel 1:11, 22.

At this moment two angels report to Anna that her husband is coming with his flocks, because an angel of the Lord had come to him and told him that the Lord God had heard her prayer and that she is pregnant (4:3). This now makes the story like the storyline in Matthew, where Joseph is the one to whom the angel continually comes to give instructions surrounding the birth of Jesus. Joachim summons his shepherds and instructs them to bring ten lambs without spot or blemish for the Lord God, twelve calves for the priests and council of elders, and one hundred goats for all the people (vv. 5-7). When Joachim comes to Anna, she throws her arms around his neck and tells him how blessed she is to be pregnant with child, which now makes the story like the time when Elizabeth is five months pregnant in Luke 1:24 and expresses her gratitude for what the Lord has done for her. As the story continues, it temporarily keeps its focus on Joachim offering priestly gifts, which again is like the focus on Zechariah at the beginning of Luke's Gospel. When Joachim is able to make his offerings at the altar of the Lord, rather than be prevented because he and his wife have not borne a child for Israel, he expresses satisfaction that the Lord God has been merciful to him and forgiven all his sins (5:1-4).

Again there is a shift back to a storyline like that of Luke. When Anna gives birth in the ninth month of her pregnancy, she says her soul is magnified on the day, which of course is like the opening line of Mary's Magnificat in Luke 1:46. When the prescribed days are completed, Anna cleanses herself of the flow of blood, offers her breast to the infant, and gives her the name Mary (5:8-10). When Mary is six months old, Anna puts her on the ground and she walks seven steps into her mother's arms. When Anna picks her up, she tells her child that she will never walk on the ground again until she takes her into the Temple of the Lord (6:1-3). She turns Mary's bedroom into a sanctuary, does not permit anything profane or unclean to go into the child's mouth, and sends for the undefiled daughters of the Hebrews to come and keep her amused (6:4-5).

On Mary's first birthday, Joachim gives a great banquet, inviting the high priests, priests, scholars, the council of elders, and all the people of Israel. Then he presents Mary to the priests and they bless her in the name of "the God of our fathers" and give her "a name that will be on the lips of future generations forever," which is reminiscent of a line in Mary's Magnificat in Luke 1:48 (InfJames 6:6-7). At this point everyone says, "So be it. Amen," and Joachim presents Mary to the high priests and they bless her in the name of "the Most High God," which is like Simeon's blessing of Jesus in the Jerusalem temple in Luke 2:27-32. When Anna takes the child Mary up to her sanctuary bedroom, she gives Mary her breast and sings a song to her that blends statements of Elizabeth to Mary when she visited her and of Mary's Magnificat beyond the first line, when Mary thanks God for visiting her, taking away her disgrace, and giving her the fruit of God's righteousness (cf. Luke 1:42, 47-49). Then Anna makes Mary rest in her sanctuary bedroom while she herself goes out and serves her guests. When the banquet is over, the guests leave in good spirits praising the God of Israel (InfJames 6:8-15).

Dedication of Mary in the Temple

When Mary reaches two years of age, Joachim suggests that they take Mary up to the Temple of the Lord so that the Lord will not be angry with them and consider their gift unacceptable. But Anna proposes that they wait until Mary is three so that she will not miss her father or mother, and Joachim agrees (7:1-3). This exchange between Joachim and Anna appears to have a relationship to Hannah's offering of Samuel to the temple of Shiloh a year after Elkanah and all the household go there to offer sacrifice and vow of thanksgiving after Samuel is born (1 Sam 1:21-28). When Mary turns three, Joachim suggests that they have undefiled Hebrew daughters go along with them to the Temple, each with a lighted lamp, so that the child will not turn back. When they do this, the priest welcomes Mary, kisses her, and blesses her, saying: "The Lord God has exalted your name among all generations. In you the Lord will disclose his redemption to the people of Israel during the last days" (InfJames 7:5). The priest's statement is like statements in Luke in which Mary herself thanks God for making her name known to all generations and Zechariah prophesies that his son John will reveal God's redemption to the people of Israel during the last days (Luke 1:68, 77). When the priest sets Mary down on the third step of the altar, the Lord showers favor on her, she dances, and the whole house of Israel loves her (InfJames 7:9-10).

Once Mary is in the Temple, she is fed there "like a dove" with the hand of an angel (8:2). This is like the angels feeding Jesus (Mark 1:13; Matt 4:11) and Elijah (1 Kgs 19:5-8) when they are in the wilderness for forty days. When Mary turns twelve, the priests meet to decide what to do with Mary, since her menstrual flow will pollute the sanctuary of the Lord God (8:3-4). They decide to put the high priest in charge of the procedure by which Mary will be removed from the Temple. The high priest is Zechariah, the priest who becomes the father of John the Baptist in Lukan tradition. When he goes into the Holy of Holies to seek instructions from God concerning what to do with Mary, a scene emerges that is like the opening scene in Luke 1:11, where an angel appears to Zechariah telling him that his wife Elizabeth will have a child named John.

In InfJames 8:7-8, an angel appears to Zechariah and tells him to assemble all the widowers of the people, and each is to bring a staff. When Zechariah gathers all of them and prays, a dove comes out of the staff of the widower named Joseph and perches on Joseph's head (9:3-6). When Zechariah announces to Joseph that the lot has chosen him to take "the virgin of the Lord" into his care and protection, Joseph protests that he already has sons and is an old man, while she is only a young woman; therefore, people will make fun of him. Zechariah warns Joseph that he must not resist God's will or his fate could be like that of Dathan, Abiram, and Korah, who were swallowed up by the earth splitting open when they resisted God's will during the time of Moses (Num 16:31-32). So Joseph takes Mary home, but he then leaves to fulfill a contract to build houses for many months (InfJames 9:7-12).

While Joseph is away, the high priest has assistants bring all "the true virgins from the tribe of David" to the Temple and cast lots to decide who will spin the threads for a special veil that is to be made for the Temple. The lot falls to Mary to spin "the true purple and scarlet threads" (the threads of royalty), while the lot falls on others to spin the other colored threads. Then the narrator says, "It was at this time that Zechariah became mute, and Samuel took his place until Zechariah regained his speech" (InfJames 10:1-10). This is, of course, a reference to the event in Luke's Gospel where the angel makes Zechariah mute until John the Baptist is circumcised because Zechariah did not believe the words of the angel that he and his wife would have a son even though both of them were very old (Luke 1:20-23, 62-64).

Mary, Blessed among Women

While Joseph is away, the storyline again becomes like that of Luke's Gospel. One day when Mary goes out to fetch water a voice speaks to her saying: "Greetings, favored one! The Lord is with you. Blessed are you among women" (cf. Luke 1:28, 42). When she becomes terrified, runs home, and immediately takes up where she left off spinning the purple thread, an angel suddenly stands before her, saying, "Don't be afraid, Mary. You see, you've found favor in the sight of the Lord of all. You will conceive by means of his word *(en logou autou)*" (11:5; cf. Luke 1:30-33). When Mary hears that she will conceive in this unusual way, she asks the angel, "If I actually conceive by the Lord, the living God, will I also give birth the way women usually do?" The angel says "No" and continues with words that combine statements made to Mary in Luke 1:35 and to Joseph in Matt 1:21: ". . . the power of God will overshadow you. Therefore, the child to be born will be called holy, son of the Most High. And you will name him Jesus — the name means 'he will save his people from their sins.'" Mary replies,

"Here I am, the Lord's slave before him. I pray that all you've told me comes true" (InfJames 11:7-9).

After Mary finishes her spinning and takes the purple and scarlet thread to the high priest, he praises her, saying: "Mary, the Lord God has extolled your name and so you will be blessed by all the generations of the earth" (InfJames 12:2; cf. Luke 1:46, 48). Mary rejoices and goes to visit her relative Elizabeth. When she knocks on Elizabeth's door, Elizabeth leaves her spinning of scarlet thread, runs to the door and greets Mary. Then Elizabeth blesses her, saying, "Who am I that the mother of my Lord should visit me? You see, the baby inside me has jumped for joy and blessed you" (InfJames 12:3-5; cf. Luke 1:43-44). Temporarily forgetting the mysteries told her by the angel Gabriel, Mary looks up to the sky and says, "Who am I, Lord, that every generation on earth will congratulate me?" (InfJames 12:6; cf. Luke 1:26, 48). Then, after spending three months with Elizabeth, during which her pregnancy starts to show, Mary, who is twelve, fourteen, fifteen, sixteen, or seventeen years of age depending on which manuscript one follows, becomes frightened, returns home, and hides from the people of Israel (InfJames 12:7-9; cf. Luke 1:56). Most editors consider the strongest textual reading to be sixteen, even though it conflicts with other evidence in the text. If a person follows the statement in 8:3 about Mary's age being twelve, it would appear that Mary's age at the time of her pregnancy would logically still be twelve.

The Reaction of Joseph

When Mary is six months pregnant, Joseph returns home from his building projects and finds Mary pregnant. This shifts the storyline back to a mode like the Gospel of Matthew. Joseph is certain that an evil deed has been performed and is at a loss to know how to correct the situation. He compares the situation to the story of Adam, when the serpent came and deceived and corrupted Eve (13:1-5; cf. Gen 3:1-20). When Joseph confronts Mary, asking her how she could have done this (cf. Gen 3:13), she says she is innocent and has never had sex with any man (cf. Luke 1:34). When Joseph asks her where the child came from, she says she does not know. This has an interesting relation to the question posed to the healed blind man, "where Jesus has come from," in John 9:29-30 and to Jesus' statement to people in John 6:38: "I have come down from heaven." We will see below how aspects of John's Gospel hover near in various places in InfJames.

At this point in the story Joseph becomes very fearful and decides he will "divorce her quietly," as in Matthew 1:19. In addition, however, as Joseph thinks about the terrible results if he discloses Mary's pregnancy to the people of Israel, he fears he will "hand innocent blood over to a death sentence," which reverberates with the statement of the people in Matthew 27:25, where Pilate says he himself is "innocent" of "Jesus' blood" and the people say, "His blood be on us and on our children!" Then the story continues as it does in Matthew with an angel of the Lord suddenly appearing to Joseph in a dream and telling him, "Don't be afraid of this girl, because the child in her is the Holy Spirit's doing. She will have a son and you will name him Jesus — the name means 'he will save his people from their sins'" (InfJames 14:5-6; cf. Matt 1:20-21). At this point Joseph gets up, praises the God of Israel, and begins thereafter to protect Mary, according to the charge made to him when she was given to him from the Temple.

Vindicated before the High Priest

The next set of events adds entirely new scenes to a storyline related to that of Matthew's Gospel. When Annas the scholar comes to the home of Joseph to ask why he has not attended the assembly since returning home, he sees that Mary is pregnant. When Annas tells the high priest that Joseph has violated the virgin he received from the Temple of the Lord, the high priest sends Temple assistants to verify her pregnancy. When the assistants find her pregnant, they bring her and Joseph to the court in the Temple. When the high priest asks Mary why she has humiliated herself, she says, "As the Lord God lives, I stand innocent before him. Believe me, I've not had sex with any man." This, of course, repeats what she told the angel when the angel said she would become pregnant through special divine means (InfJames 15:13; cf. 13:8; Luke 1:34). When Joseph also pleads innocence of any wrongdoing, the high priest tells him not to perjure himself and accuses him of having intercourse with her, not disclosing his act to the people of Israel, and not humbling himself before God's mighty hand so that his offspring might be blessed. After this Joseph remains silent (InfJames 15:1-18). The high priest commands Joseph to return the virgin to the Temple, causing him to burst into tears. Then the high priest gives "the Lord's drink test" to both Joseph and Mary and sends them into the wilderness. But when they return unharmed, he decides not to condemn them and dismisses them (16:1-7). Joseph and Mary return home "celebrating and praising the God of Israel" (v. 8).

On the Way to Bethlehem

After this, the story presents a version of the information surrounding the birth of Jesus in the Gospel of Luke. Emperor Augustus makes a decree that everyone in Bethlehem of Judea must be enrolled in the census. Clear about enrolling his sons but unclear whether to enroll Mary as his daughter or his wife, he saddles his donkey, has Mary get on it, and starts out. As they travel along, one moment Joseph sees Mary sulking as though in discomfort, and another moment he sees her laughing. This causes Joseph to imagine two peoples in front of him, one weeping and mourning and the other celebrating and jumping for joy. This surely is related to the statement of Simeon in Luke 2:34 that Jesus will cause the fall and rising of many in Israel. Halfway through the trip, Mary asks Joseph to help her down from the donkey, because the child inside her is about to be born (InfJames 17:1-10).

Joseph takes Mary inside a cave he finds nearby, stations his sons to guard her, and goes to find a Hebrew midwife in the country around Bethlehem. From this point on, Joseph tells the story in first person singular, "I." He says that as he was "walking along and yet not going anywhere" he saw the vault of the sky standing still and then the clouds "pausing in amazement" and the birds of the sky "suspended in midair." Then on the earth he saw a bowl with workers reclining around it with their hands in the bowl. Some were "chewing and yet did not chew," some were "picking up something to eat and yet they did not pick it up," some were "putting food in their mouths and yet did not do so," and all were looking upward. Next he saw sheep being "driven along and yet the sheep stood still," and he saw the shepherd "lifting his hand to strike them, and yet his hand remained raised." Then he saw the current of the river and saw goats "with their mouths in the water and yet they were not drinking." Then suddenly everything and everybody went on with what they had been doing (18:1-11). Throughout all this, then, it is clear that "the world stood still, and yet it did not" while Joseph was looking for a midwife to attend Mary while she gave birth to Jesus.

The Birth of Jesus

Then Joseph sees a woman coming down from the hill country, whom he questions and finds out is a Hebrew midwife. By asking Joseph questions, the midwife receives the information that Joseph is an Israelite and that his fiancée Mary, who was raised in the Temple of the Lord and whom he obtained through lot as his wife, is pregnant by the Holy Spirit. When the midwife questions the information she has received, Joseph invites her to come and see, which she does.

The next event is the birth of Jesus. But how will the birth occur? What special events will occur around it? What will be the special emphases in the story? We have already seen how the whole world "stood still, and yet did not stand still" while Joseph was looking for a midwife. But now that he has found one, what special things will happen when the midwife comes to Mary? Joseph and Mary are not in a place where there is a manger, like in Luke 2:7. So there can be no talk at this point of a child in swaddling cloths lying in a manger. But what if the story would blend some other aspects of the Gospel of Luke with the Gospel of John?

The attentive reader will have already noticed above that in InfJames 11:5 "the *word*" the angel brought to Mary was the *logos* of God, and talk of the *logos* in relation to God is Johannine talk. In addition, a scholar trained in study of the New Testament will know there are two major Greek words for "word" in the New Testament writings. The term *rhēma* occurs sixty-eight times in the New Testament, referring to the word of God, a word of Scripture, or simply a word. Then there is the well-known, theologically charged, term *logos,* which appears more than three hundred times in the New Testament and is in the foreground at the beginning of John: "In the beginning was the *word,* and the *word* was with God, and the *word* was God" (1:1). In Luke, when Mary tells the angel Gabriel, "Let it be with me according to your *word,*" the word is *rhēma* rather than *logos.* When in InfJames 11:5 the angel tells Mary, "You will conceive by means of his *word,*" the Greek term is *logos,* the special Johannine term for "word." One could think this change is not important, since *logos* is such a common word in the New Testament. But could it be a clue that the narrator of InfJames is thinking in relation to John's Gospel? What if the *word* the angel brings to Mary is the Johannine *Word* and this *Word* is present in the womb of Mary? What if the *Word* in Mary's womb is "life" that is not yet actually flesh? How could "life" grow so it causes Mary's womb noticeably to swell, but this "life" would not "actually" be flesh? And how could this "life" be born in an unusual way? What if this "*word*-life" were born as "the light" that "shines in the darkness," and then "becomes flesh" and "dwells" among humans, as in John 1:5, 9, 14?

An initial question is how it would be possible to get darkness to be present in the story. Here is how it happens in InfJames. As Joseph and the midwife stand in front of the cave, a dark cloud overshadows it. This is the dark cloud that brings God's presence, as it brought the God of Israel to the tabernacle in the wilderness in Exodus 40:34-35.[1] When the dark cloud "overshadows" the cave in InfJames 19:14, the midwife declares, "My soul is magnified today, because my eyes have seen a paradoxical wonder that salvation has come to Israel." These are words closely related to assertions by Simeon when he saw the baby Jesus in the temple in Luke 2:30, 32. But why would the midwife say this? As a Hebrew midwife who knows about God's presence in the history of Israel, she recognizes God's presence in the dark cloud that "overshadows" the cave. This is why she says she "has seen" salvation come to Israel.

People familiar with the Gospel of Luke will know that the angel Gabriel told Mary she would become pregnant when the Holy Spirit "comes upon her" and the power of the Most High "overshadows" her (1:35). When we read the story in InfJames 11, it seemed that the narrator was simply repeating the Lukan story with a few minor variations when the angel was talking to Mary. The story was slightly changed, but now we must go back and see how the story actually dramatically changes what the angel says in Luke. In contrast to the story in Luke, in InfJames 11:5 the angel does not tell Mary she will "conceive" when the Holy Spirit comes upon her and the power of the Most High overshadows her (cf. Luke 1:35). Rather, the angel tells Mary, "You will conceive by means of his *word (logos)*" (InfJames 11:5). In other words, as "the Word" caused all things to come into being when the world began in John 1:3-4, so in InfJames "the Word" causes Jesus to "begin to come into being" in the womb of Mary. Since this claim by the angel in InfJames suggests that Mary will conceive in a highly unusual way, Mary asks the angel if she will "give birth the way women usually do" (11:6). At this point, the angel says, "No," and explains to Mary "how the birth will occur." The birth will take place, the angel says, by "the power of God overshadowing you" (v. 7).

We must notice that there is at this point no mention in InfJames of "the Holy Spirit" coming to Mary, either in the angel's statements to Mary

---

1. Cf. Exod 16:6, 10; 29:42-46; 1 Kgs 8:10-11.

or in the story of Jesus' birth. At another point in the story in InfJames the angel of the Lord tells Joseph, "Don't be afraid of this girl, because the child in her is the Holy Spirit's doing" (14:5; cf. 19:9). But in the statements of the angel to Mary, "the Word" makes Mary pregnant. In other words, in InfJames the child Jesus comes into being "in Mary" through the Word (11:5; cf. John 1:3). This is not yet, however, the "overshadowing" of Mary by "the power of the Most High" (cf. Luke 1:35). In InfJames, the child Jesus comes into being "in the world" when the "power of God" overshadows Mary at the birth of Jesus in the cave (11:7; 19:13). This overshadowing is the presence of God coming into the world as "the true light" (cf. John 1:9). Therefore, when the darkness withdraws from the cave, it leaves "a great light," which is "the true light . . . coming into the world" (cf. John 1:9). Gradually the light "becomes flesh" (cf. John 1:14) in the form of a baby that suckles at Mary's breast. When the "overshadowing" occurs, the midwife exclaims that her soul is magnified, because today her eyes have seen a paradoxical mystery that salvation has come to Israel. In InfJames, therefore, the story of the conception and birth of Jesus blends Lukan and Matthean features of Jesus' birth with Johannine features. In InfJames, Jesus comes into being "in Mary's womb" by being conceived by the *logos*/ Word (11:5; cf. John 1:3) and then is begotten as the light that comes "into the world" and becomes flesh through the overshadowing of Mary in the cave (19:13-16; cf. John 1:9, 14).

Now let us build on this insight a bit more by going back to the scene where Joseph returned home from his building projects and asked Mary where the child in her womb came from (InfJames 13:9-10). It has been normal for translators to present Joseph's question as: "Then where did the child you're carrying come from?" And Mary replied, "As the Lord my God lives, I don't know where it came from" (Hock 57). But the word "child" is not present in the Greek text of Joseph's question. Rather, the question is: "From where then is this in your womb?" And Mary's answer is "As my Lord lives, I don't know from where it is in me." This careful translation is important, because it can be a real question exactly what is in Mary's womb. From the perspective of InfJames, it appears that what Mary carries in her womb is something like "the Word through whom life comes into being" (John 1:4). In other words, what is in Mary's womb is not actually a fleshly fetus that will be born in the usual physical way. Rather, it is "God's Word," which comes into the world as the light of the world and then becomes flesh and dwells among humans on earth. In the midst of a Lukan-Matthean account of the birth, infancy, and young adulthood of

Mary, then, Jesus is born as the Johannine Word, who comes into the world as the light of the world and then becomes flesh in the name of Jesus, who "will save his people from their sins" (InfJames 11:8//Matt 1:21).

As the story continues, there is still another point of contact with John's Gospel. The midwife exclaims that she has seen a new spectacle *(kainon theama)* and then leaves. Immediately she meets another midwife named Salome. This is excellent. The story has already provided two witnesses to the extraordinary birth of Jesus, namely Joseph and the Hebrew midwife. But now we have a "doubting Thomas midwife" who will bring another Johannine dimension to the story. When the Hebrew midwife meets Salome, she tells her she has seen a virgin give birth, which they both know is impossible. Salome says, "As the Lord my God lives, unless I insert my finger and examine her, I will never believe that a virgin has given birth" (19:19: cf. John 20:25). When Salome inserts her finger into Mary, her hand begins to disappear, consumed by flames. Therefore Salome falls on her knees in the presence of the Lord and prays to God to remember her, since she is a descendant of Abraham, Isaac, and Jacob, and she reminds God that she has been "healing people in your name" and receiving payment for her service from God. In the context of this intense petitioning worship of God, an angel appears and tells Salome to hold out her hand to the child and pick him up, and she will have joy and salvation.

The healing that occurs with the infant Jesus is like the healing that happens when the woman with the flow of blood in Matthew, Mark, and Luke touches Jesus and the flow stops. The immediate reaction of the woman in Luke 8:47 is to fall down before Jesus and declare "in the presence of all the people why she had touched him, and how she had been immediately healed." In InfThomas, Salome speaks, saying: "I will worship him because he has been born to be the king of Israel," and she is instantly healed and leaves the cave vindicated. Just before she leaves, however, a voice tells her, "Salome, Salome, do not report the marvels you have seen until the child goes to Jerusalem" (20:12). This command is like Jesus' commands especially in Mark's Gospel to healed people not to tell what has happened to them! Luke and Matthew also contain commands like this, but scholars regularly think of Mark as the Gospel that established this tradition of "secrecy" and presented it most persistently through his story about Jesus. So in this story of Jesus' birth it is as if the writer has incorporated aspects of all four New Testament Gospels into his telling of the story.

Fleeing Herod

When Joseph is ready to depart for Judea, the narration shifts once again to a storyline related to that of Matthew's Gospel. A tumult arises over astrologers who are inquiring about "the newborn king of the Judeans" (21:2). After Herod interrogates them, he tells them to continue their search and report back to him when they find him, so he himself can go and pay homage to the newborn king. In InfJames 21:10 the astrologers follow the star to the cave and it stops directly over the head of the child. InfJames 21:11 specifically notes that not only seeing the child but also "his mother Mary," they "took gifts out of their pouches — gold, pure incense, and myrrh." Then, since they were advised by an angel not to go into Judea, they returned to their country by another route.

As the story continues, Herod's anger that he has been tricked by the astrologers leads to his decision to send out executioners to kill all the infants two years old and younger (cf. Matt 2:16). This leads to a fascinating relocation of Mary's wrapping of Jesus in strips of cloth and laying him in a manger (Luke 2:12). In InfJames 22:1-4, Mary wraps Jesus in strips and cloth and puts him in a manger used by cattle to hide him from Herod's executioners! The remainder of the story in InfJames tells about God's miraculous prevention of the death of the infant John the Baptist when a mountain opens up and allows Elizabeth to take the child inside for protection. Then the story ends with the executioners killing the high priest Zechariah, John's father, at the altar. The account of Zechariah's death contains statements and events that recall the accounts of the crucifixion of Jesus and the finding of the empty tomb in the New Testament Gospels. We will not discuss these in detail here, since our focus is on who Jesus is in the Gospels inside and outside the New Testament.

Who Do People Say Jesus Is?

Who, then, do people say Jesus is in InfJames? The angel Gabriel tells Mary, "The child to be born will be called holy, son of the Most High. And you will name him Jesus — the name means 'he will save his people from their sins'" (11:7-8). Elizabeth refers to Jesus as "my Lord" when Mary comes to visit her (12:5). An angel of the Lord tells Joseph, "You will name him Jesus — the name means 'he will save his people from their sins'" (14:6). The Hebrew midwife says, "My soul is magnified, because today my eyes have seen a miracle in that salvation has come to Israel" (19:14; cf. 17-18). The midwife Salome says, "He has been born to be the king of Israel" and so worships him (20:10). Astrologers refer to Jesus as "the newborn king of the Judeans" (21:2), and Herod asks the high priests what has been written about "the Anointed" and the astrologers about "the one who has been born king" (21:4, 7).

All the things people say about Jesus sound like what people say in the Gospels of Luke and Matthew. But there are special moments in InfJames where an additional story is being told. God's word *(logos)* comes into Mary's womb and makes her pregnant (11:5). When Joseph wonders, "From where did this in your womb come?" and Mary does not know (13:9-10), the answer really is Jesus' answer in John 6:38: "I have come down from heaven." When Jesus is born, he comes as the light who comes into the darkness and becomes flesh (InfJames 19:12-16; John 1:9, 14). As a result, heaven alone does not respond to Jesus' birth through a multitude of angels praising God and saying, "Glory to God in the highest heaven, and on earth peace among those whom he favors" (Luke 2:14). Rather, all the earth "stood still, yet it did not." Joseph was walking and yet going nowhere. All the clouds paused, and the birds "were suspended in midair." Workers reclined to eat and "chewing, yet did not chew," "picking things up to eat, yet did not pick things up," and "putting food in their mouths, yet did not put food." "Instead, they were all looking up." Sheep were being driven and yet stood still; the shepherd lifted his hand to strike them, yet his hand remained raised. Goats were drinking water from the current of the river, yet were not drinking. "Then all of a sudden everything and everybody went on with what they had been doing" (18:3-11). In other words, everything stood still, and yet it did not, when Jesus was born. Everything was for a moment "beyond time" and "beyond movement through space," and yet it was still within time and within movement in space at the same time. When Jesus was born, everything moved beyond time and space, yet it did not move in time or in space. The Word was coming as the light into the world and becoming flesh, and this was the moment when everything was no longer in time and space, and yet it still was in time and space.

So words that seem to come from Luke and Matthew about Jesus being the newborn king of Israel who will take away the sins of the world are actually Johannine words pointing to the Word coming as light into the darkness, becoming flesh, and dwelling among humans on earth. Is it any wonder, then, that in InfJames the star the astrologers follow does not simply stop over the house where Mary and Joseph take Jesus (as in Matt

2:10)? Instead, in InfJames the star leads the astrologers to the cave and stops "directly above the head of the child" (InfJames 21:10). So where does the aura of glory come from that we associate with Jesus in paintings throughout the centuries? For InfJames, the first aura of glory above Jesus' head would have been the star that traveled from the east until it stopped directly over the light that came into the world and became flesh as a little suckling child in a cave.

Conclusion

As we conclude this chapter, it may help the reader to know that around 180 C.E. a Christian named Tatian created a "four-Gospels-in-one." Scholars call this Gospel the Diatessaron, which means "through four" in Greek. Tatian created this "one Gospel" by interweaving virtually all the verses in Matthew, Mark, Luke, and John together. His four-in-one Gospel begins, naturally, with "In the beginning was the Word," and after the Johannine prologue it presents the Lukan story of the birth of John the Baptist. After this, it interweaves the Lukan and Matthean stories of Jesus' birth and continues to interweave Luke, Matthew, Mark, and John together story by story until the end.

The reason for mentioning this is that, in some ways, InfJames is a "four-gospel-in-one" story about the birth of Jesus. In this instance, the story begins with an extension of the Lukan story of the births of John the Baptist and Jesus backwards to the birth of Mary, reworking aspects of the birth of Samuel in 1 Samuel 1–2 in the process. As the story proceeds, however, the writer subtly interweaves topics and meanings from John, and at one point even Mark. So who do people say Jesus is in InfJames? He seems to be a Lukan, Matthean, Markan, and Johannine Jesus who makes the world stand still, and yet it does not.

LEARNING ACTIVITIES

1. Read the entire story of the earth swallowing up Dathan, Abiram, and Korah during the time of Moses in Numbers 16:1-35.
2. Read the story about the birth of Samuel and his parents' taking him to the temple in 1 Samuel 1–3.
3. Read about Gabriel's appearance to Mary in Luke 1:26-38 alongside Infancy Gospel of James 4:1-2.

4. Read the story of Simeon's blessing of Jesus in Luke 2:27-32 alongside Infancy Gospel of James 6:7-9.
5. Read the stories of angels feeding Elijah in 1 Kings 19:5-8 and Jesus in Mark 1:13//Matthew 4:11.
6. Read the story of Zechariah in Luke 1:20-23, 62-64 in comparison with Infancy Gospel of James 10:1-10.
7. Read how the serpent deceives and corrupts Eve in Genesis 3:1-20.
8. Read how the Word as "light" "shines in the darkness," "becomes flesh," and "dwells" among humans in John 1:5, 9, 14.
9. Read how the cloud brings God's presence to the tabernacle in Exodus 40:34-38.
10. Read about the "great light" in Matthew 4:16 (cf. Isa 9:2) in conjunction with Infancy Gospel of James 19:15.
11. Read the story of "doubting Thomas" in John 20:24-29 alongside that of the second midwife Salome in Infancy Gospel of James 19:18–20:12.
12. Read about Herod's infanticide and the flight of Joseph, Mary, and the infant Jesus to Egypt in Matthew 2:13-18.

BIBLIOGRAPHY

Ehrman, Bart D., and Zlatko Pleše. 2011. *The Apocryphal Gospels: Texts and Translations.* Oxford: Oxford University Press, pp. 31-71.

Elliott, J. K. 2006. *A Synopsis of the Apocryphal Nativity and Infancy Narratives.* Leiden: Brill.

Foster, Paul. 2009. *The Apocryphal Gospels: A Very Short Introduction.* New York: Oxford University Press, pp. 72-85.

Foster, Paul (ed.). 2008. *The Non-Canonical Gospels.* New York: T & T Clark, pp. 110-25.

Hock, Ronald F. 1996. *The Infancy Gospels of James and Thomas.* Santa Rosa: Polebridge, pp. 2-83.

Infancy Gospel of James: http://www.earlychristianwritings.com/infancyjames.html.

Klauck, Hans-Josef. 2003. *Apocryphal Gospels: An Introduction.* New York: T & T Clark, pp. 65-72.

Miller, Robert J. 2010. *The Complete Gospels: Annotated Scholars Version.* 4th ed. revised and expanded. Santa Rosa: Polebridge, pp. 361-78.

Perkins, Pheme. *Introduction to the Synoptic Gospels.* 2007. Grand Rapids: Eerdmans, pp. 244-47.

Terian, Abraham. 2008. *The Armenian Gospel of the Infancy.* Oxford: Oxford University Press.

10

Has the Savior Spoken Secretly to a Woman?

What would a Gospel look like if a person decided to feature Mary Magdalene as the only follower of Jesus who really understood who Jesus was and how he was trying to redeem humans? A major question would be what scene or scenes in the New Testament Gospels should be featured or developed in this "Gospel of Mary." When we were discussing the Gospel of Thomas in a previous chapter, we saw how the famous Caesarea Philippi story in the New Testament Gospels, where Jesus asks the disciples who people think he is and then who they themselves think he is, is reconfigured so Thomas rather than Peter gives the best answer. Likewise, when we looked at InfThomas we saw how the writer rewrote the Lukan story about Jesus as a twelve-year-old boy in the Jerusalem Temple to serve as a dramatic conclusion to a Gospel that started with Jesus playing creation as a five-year-old boy. In addition, in the chapter above on InfJames we saw how the writer reconfigured scenes around the births of Samuel in 1-2 Samuel in the Old Testament, of John the Baptist and Jesus in Luke, and of Jesus in Matthew to present a story from the birth of Mary to Mary's giving birth to Jesus in a miraculous way that maintains her virginity.

So how did the writer of the Gospel of Mary create a story that features Mary Magdalene as the follower of Jesus who understood Jesus so well that she could become the leader who helped the male disciples overcome their fear, distress, and confusion and successfully go out in mission to the world?

Rewriting Mary Magdalene's Encounter
with the Resurrected Jesus in John 20

For the writer of the Gospel of Mary, the key for presenting Mary Magdalene as the follower of Jesus who becomes the special teacher of the disciples lies in the events surrounding the empty tomb in John 20. In John,
Mary Magdalene is the only person who goes to Jesus' tomb on the first
day of the week, and she finds the stone removed (20:1). Mary's immediate
response is to run and tell Simon Peter and the disciple whom Jesus loved
what she has found, which results in their running to the tomb and also
seeing it empty, but then they return to their homes (vv. 2-10). When Mary
looks into the tomb one more time while she is weeping after the two disciples have left, she sees two angels, who ask her why she is weeping. She tells
them someone has taken away her Lord, and she does not know where
they have laid him (vv. 11-13). When she turns around, however, Jesus asks
her why she is weeping and whom she is looking for, but she thinks the
person speaking to her is the gardener. When she requests that the man tell
her where he has laid the body, if he has carried it away, Jesus speaks her
name, "Mary!" Mary turns and speaks to Jesus in Hebrew calling him
"rabbouni," which means "teacher." Then Jesus tells Mary two basic things:
(a) "Do not hold me, because I have not yet ascended to the Father" and
(b) "Go to my brothers and say to them, 'I am ascending to my Father and
your Father, to my God and your God'" (vv. 14-17). Mary Magdalene goes
to the disciples and announces to them, "I have seen the Lord." Then v. 18
says: "And she told them that he had said these things to her."

So what exactly were "these things" that Mary Magdalene told the disciples after she went to them and said, "I have seen the Lord"? Of course
she told them all that we read in John 20:11-18. But are we getting "the full
picture" in John of "all the things" Jesus said to Mary and "all the things"
Mary said to the disciples? The writer of the Gospel of Mary thinks that
there is much more to tell. According to this Gospel, Mary was involved in
conversations on the evening of that day (John 20:19) and a week later
(v. 26) when Jesus said "Peace be with you" a number of times in preparation for his final departure from them (vv. 19, 21, 26).

Also, there is the issue of the nature of Jesus' body after his crucifixion,
burial, and resurrection. When Jesus talked to Mary in the garden he said,
"Do not hold on to me, because I have not yet ascended to my Father"
(20:17). Why should she not hold on to him? Is there something about his
body, crucified and dead but now alive, that we should know about?

Would it be all right for her to hold on to him if he had already ascended to the Father and has now descended? Later Thomas says, "Unless I see the mark of the nails in his hands, and put my finger in the mark of the nails and my hand in his side, I will not believe" (v. 25). A week later Jesus tells Thomas, "Put your finger here and see my hands. Reach out your hand and put it in my side. Do not doubt but believe" (v. 27). So what is the nature of Jesus' resurrected body that now Thomas can touch it? Does the nature of Jesus' resurrected body change when it is in different locations? Had Jesus ascended to the Father and then descended again by the time he told Thomas he could touch his body? Many questions can be asked about all these things. Are there answers anywhere? The writer of the Gospel of Mary says that indeed there are answers. But in order to know the answers we must go back to conversations Jesus had with his disciples before he was crucified and buried.

Rewriting the Unbelief of the Disciples in Luke 24

But here another dimension comes into the Gospel of Mary. Much as we saw Lukan stories and topics blended with Johannine topics in InfThomas, so a number of Lukan topics blend into Johannine topics in the Gospel of Mary. When Mary runs to Simon Peter and the beloved disciple in John's Gospel, telling them, "They have taken the Lord out of the tomb, and we do not know where they have laid him," these two disciples believe Mary enough to run to the tomb themselves (20:2-4). And later when Mary goes to the disciples and announces, "I have seen the Lord," and tells them all the things he said to her, there is no indication the disciples do not believe her (v. 18).

But in the Gospel of Mary, after the disciples have heard Mary's report, Andrew says "I do not believe that the Savior said these things," and Peter "brings up similar concerns." Where does this disbelief of Mary come from? This is where the blending of Luke with John becomes important. In Luke 24 the disciples persistently "disbelieve" the women, among whom one is Mary Magdalene. When Mary Magdalene, Joanna, Mary the mother of James, and the other women go to the apostles and tell them about the empty tomb and the words the two men in dazzling clothes have spoken to them, "these words seemed to them an idle tale, and [the apostles] did not believe in them" (24:11). Indeed, even when Jesus suddenly stands among the eleven and says, "Why are you frightened, and why do doubts arise in your hearts? Look at my hands and my feet; see that it is I myself . . . ," still "in their joy they were disbelieving and still wondering" (v. 41). In Luke, then, the "disbelief" of Jesus' male disciples is a major topic.

In John's Gospel, in contrast, Thomas is singled out as "the unbelieving one" among the twelve (20:24-29). The rest of the disciples "rejoiced when they saw the Lord" (v. 20) and told Thomas, "We have seen the Lord" (v. 25), rather than remaining in disbelief. Even in John 21, which is considered an epilogue added to the Gospel, when the disciples see the risen Jesus along the shore, the narrator says they did not dare to ask him "'Who are you?' because they knew it was the Lord" (21:12). John also emphasizes that Jesus' disciples "believed" in him as early as the sign of the abundance of wine at the wedding at Cana (2:11). To be sure, they had to ask Jesus questions persistently because his message was extremely complex, indeed rather "philosophical" in its orientation. Judas betrayed Jesus because, according to the narrator, "Satan entered into him" (13:27), but John presents the rest of the twelve except Thomas asking questions for the purpose of more deeply understanding their belief in Jesus, rather than disbelieving Jesus, or disbelieving Mary Magdalene when she tells them about the empty tomb and the risen Jesus. Once we see that the topic of "disbelief" among the twelve is related to Luke, we will more readily see some other dimensions of Luke that blend into Johannine topics as the Gospel of Mary unfolds.

The Return of Matter to Its Root Nature at the End of Time

If the Gospel of Mary ends with events that blend Johannine topics with Lukan topics, how does it begin? Unfortunately we do not know what existed at the beginning of the Gospel, because the first six manuscript pages have been lost. When the text we have begins, someone asks Jesus, "Will matter then be destroyed or not?" Jesus answers: "Every nature, every modeled form, every creature, exists in and with each other. They will dissolve again into their own root nature. For the nature of matter is dissolved into what belongs to its nature" (2:1-4 in Miller; 7 in Ehrman-Pleše).

On the one hand, this discussion is related to 2 Peter 3:10-12:

[10]But the day of the Lord will come like a thief, and then the heavens will pass away with a loud noise, and the elements will be dissolved with fire, and the earth and everything that is done on it will be disclosed. [11]Since all these things are to be dissolved in this way, what sort of people ought you to be in leading lives of holiness and godli-

ness, [12]waiting for and hastening the coming of the day of God, because of which the heavens will be set ablaze and dissolved, and the elements will melt with fire?

From the perspective of 2 Peter, it appears that the elements of the heavens and earth will be destroyed into nothingness. During this period of time, however, there was a debate among philosophers and religious thinkers whether heaven and earth had been made "out of nothing" or had been made out of preexistent, formless matter. According to Karen L. King, only a few early philosophers like Eudorus of Alexandria (1st century B.C.E.) believed that matter had been created out of nothing, even though later this view became widely accepted. More people held the view of Plato that all things were created out of formless "matter" that was devoid of all "quality." In the "created sphere" this matter has quality and form. When it dissolves, however, it does not become nothing but dissolves "into its own parts" (King 45).

This is the view also presented in Gospel of Philip 53:14-23:

> Light and darkness, life and death, right and left, are brothers of one another. It is not possible to separate them from each other. For this reason, neither are the good good, nor the evil evil, nor is life life, nor death death. This is why each one will dissolve into its original source. But those who are exalted above the world will not be dissolved, for they are eternal. (Miller 337)

In addition, Origin of the World 127:3-5 has this description of the end of the world: "And the deficiency will be pulled by its root down into the darkness. And the light will go back up to its root" (Miller 337). This seems to present well an additional part of the understanding in the Gospel of Mary. Jesus responds that all things "intermingle" with one another when they exist in the created world, and when they dissolve they return to their "root nature," rather than simply disappearing into nothingness. This is important for the discussion that occurs next in the Gospel.

The Nature of Sin in the World

After Jesus' answer about things returning to their root nature when they are destroyed, Peter says he would like to know, "What is the sin of the world?" (3:2 Miller). Jesus answers, "There is no such thing as sin." Then he explains that people themselves "produce" sin when they act in accordance with the nature of adultery, "which is called 'sin'" (3:3-4). Then Jesus states that this is the reason "the Good" came among them, pursuing the good that belongs to every nature, to "set it within its root."

The thinking here seems to be related to the deep wisdom in the Gospels that people produce "fruit" according to "kind" through their actions (Luke 3:8-9; 6:43-45). People produce actions just as good trees produce good fruit and bad trees produce bad fruit. Therefore, "actions" produce fruit related to their "root nature," namely whether their root nature is good or bad. Both good and bad exist, of course, in relation to one another in God's created order. In the context of this thinking about good and bad, Jesus is understood as "the Good" who has come into the world to set every nature "within its root" (3:6 in Miller) to "energize," if you will, the good nature of things, especially in people. This idea of the divine as "the Good" comes especially from the philosopher Plato (King 51-52). Once Jesus has stated this, he explains that people get sick and die because they love what deceives them, rather then loving the Good.

At this point Jesus tells a little story about matter giving birth to "passion." This is a significant alternative to Paul's story in Romans 5:12 about sin giving birth to death in the world. Rather, it is related to the widespread view of the material world as characterized by sexual passion where male and female seek one another, in contrast to the divine realm, where male and female are thoroughly embedded in one another. In the Gospel of Mary, Jesus explains that passion has no "image," because it "derives from what is contrary to nature," which has no "desire" to become or possess anything other than it is. Since passion has no image, it produces a disturbing confusion throughout the whole body. The alternative, Jesus says, is to "become content at heart, while also remaining discontent." Indeed, Jesus says, "become contented only in the presence of every true Image of nature" (3:10-14 in Miller).

Preaching the Kingdom of the Son of Man

After this Jesus says to them: "Peace be with you! Acquire my peace within yourselves" (4:1 in Miller). This would seem to be exactly what Jesus was talking about in his discussion of the "root nature" of the Good. The root nature of the Good is peace rather than a disturbing confusion throughout the entire body. At this point, Jesus makes a statement that differs from some assertions he makes in the Gospel of Thomas: "Be on your guard so that no one deceives you by saying, 'Look over here' or 'Look over there.' For the Son of Man is within you. Follow after him. Those who search for him will find him" (Gospel of Mary 4:3). Thus Jesus does not say "the kingdom" is within you; rather "the Son of Man" is within you (cf. Luke 17:20-23; Gospel of Thomas 3). We will see how important this difference is as we continue.

Jesus' statements lead to a point where he tells them to go and "preach the good news about the kingdom," warning them not to lay down any rule beyond what he has determined for them, nor to "promulgate law like the lawgiver," or else they themselves will be dominated by law rather than the good news of the kingdom (4:8). This leaves the disciples in a state of confusion. After Jesus leaves, they are distressed, and they weep bitterly. This is, of course, exactly the problem about which Jesus has been speaking to them. Their bodies should be filled with peace rather than distress and weeping. We should also notice that the state of the disciples at this point is like Mary's state when she was standing by the empty tomb and wanted to know where someone had taken Jesus' corpse and laid it (John 20:11-15). Mary knows this state of being, because her body had experienced distress and despair that caused her to weep when she found the empty tomb and nobody knew where the body was. When the disciples reach complete despair they say, "How are we going to go out to the rest of the world to announce the good news about the kingdom of the Son of Man? If they didn't spare him, how will they spare us?" (5:1-3 in Miller). The problem is that they do not understand the nature of the Son of Man "within them," namely that he is "their root nature." At this point Mary speaks up. She knows two things: (1) the Son of Man within us "has united us and made us true human beings," and (2) her vision of the risen Jesus brought peace into her body at the moment of her deepest distress and confusion.

So, in the Gospel of Mary, instead of Peter standing up and taking leadership among the brothers as in Acts 1:15, Mary stands up and begins speaking. She greets them all, both brothers and sisters, saying, "Do not weep and be distressed nor let your hearts be troubled. For his grace will be with you all and will shelter you. Rather we should praise his greatness, for he has united us and made us true human beings" (5:4-8 in Miller; 9 in Ehrman-Pleše). Here Mary is saying things closely related to what Jesus says to his disciples in John 20:19-26, which in turn are related to what Jesus taught his disciples earlier. In that earlier setting, Jesus had taught them about his leaving of "peace" with them as he was going away. They are not to let their hearts be troubled or afraid. In the Gospel of John Jesus says they need to know that the ruler of this world has no power over them. At the end, he tells them, "Rise, let us be on our way" (John 14:27-31). The Gospel of Mary says that "When Mary said these things, she turned their mind toward the Good, and they began to discuss the words of the Savior" (5:9-10 in Miller; 9 in Ehrman-Pleše). This means that Mary turned their mind to the Son of Man within them, and they began to understand the relation of their inner "root nature" to the answers the Savior had given to their questions.

Mary Magdalene Tells the Disciples the Words of the Savior

Up to this point, Mary has shown herself to be a true leader among the disciples. As she has spoken, she has blended things Jesus emphasizes in John's Gospel with things he says in the Gospel of Thomas. But she has added a dimension about the Son of Man's being "their true nature within them." Peter, recognizing for at least a moment that Mary understands things they need to know, requests that Mary tell them "the words of the Savior that you remember." When Mary begins to speak, she speaks on an even higher level, a level one can only describe as philosophically theological. Anyone who has not been trained in philosophical theology will likely be left behind by the profound things Mary begins to teach the disciples.

When Peter speaks, he states openly that they all know that the Savior loved her "more than all other women." Moreover, he admits that she heard him say things that they have never heard. Therefore he asks her to tell them the words of the Savior she remembers. Mary responds positively, saying she will report things hidden from them; and she begins to speak (6:1-4 in Miller).

Mary begins by saying she saw "the Master in a vision" and spoke with him. Perhaps this vision is an expanded version of the conversation Mary had with Jesus in the garden after he had been resurrected. Possibly, however, it is a vision Mary had earlier, related to Peter, James, and John's vision of the transfigured Jesus in Mark 9:2 and its parallels in Matthew and Luke. According to Mary's account, the first thing Jesus did was congratulate her for not wavering at seeing him, because "where the mind is, there is the treasure." This is a reconfiguration of QLuke 12:34: "Where your heart is, there is your treasure also." In the Gospel of Mary, Jesus' saying focuses on the philosophical strength of the mind. We also should notice that Mary's strength of mind has allowed her to remain steady rather than being "startled and terrified" and thinking she was seeing a ghost, as the eleven disciples and their companions did when the risen Jesus suddenly stood among them and said "Peace be with you" in Luke 24:36-38. Mary remains calm, allowing her to engage in philosophical dialogue with Jesus. Therefore, she asks Jesus if a person who sees a vision sees it with the soul or with the spirit. Jesus answers, "He does not see it with the soul or the spirit, but the mind that exists between the two, and it is that which . . ." (7:1-6 in Miller) and here the text breaks off and four additional manuscript pages are missing.

We can make a number of observations, however, on the basis of the text we have. First, it is obvious in this account that Mary is known for having sayings from Jesus that the disciples do not have. Second, Mary's absence of fear when she sees Jesus in a vision immediately catches the reader's attention, since fear is such a common phenomenon in visions and is a noticeable phenomenon in the eleven disciples and their companions in Luke's Gospel. Mary's lack of fear indicates something very special about her. Third, Jesus' explanation that the mind, rather than the soul or spirit, sees the vision raises the status of Mary's intellectual abilities. Conventional tradition points to men, rather than women, as those capable of the highest intellectual pursuits. Mary is the one among the brothers and sisters who has truly philosophical capacities of understanding.

The Ascent of the Soul

When the text picks up again four pages later, Mary is describing the ascent of the soul out of the earthly, material realm. As the soul ascends, it must overcome, free itself from, and move beyond four Powers, whose names are Darkness (probably), Desire, Ignorance, and the seven Powers of Wrath.

As the fragmented text begins, Desire is telling the soul that it did not see the soul descend into the material realm, yet now it sees the soul "going up." Then Desire accuses the soul of lying to it, because the soul belongs to Desire. At this point the soul explains to Desire that it saw Desire when it descended, even though Desire did not see or know it. The soul tells Desire it mistook the garment the soul wore for the soul's true self, and therefore it did not recognize it as the soul. This discussion is reminiscent of the garment the person sheds in logion 37 of the Gospel of Thomas; that person is not afraid of the son of the Living one. After the soul says these things, it continues on its way, rejoicing greatly (9:2-7 in Miller).

After the soul overcomes Desire, it comes to Ignorance, the third Power. Ignorance examines the soul by asking where it is going and telling it that it is bound to earth by wickedness and must not judge Ignorance's statement as untrue. The soul responds, "Why do you judge me, since I have not passed judgment?" Then the soul tells Ignorance that the soul has been bound to earth but has not bound anything. Then it says that the Powers did not recognize it, though it recognizes that the universe will be dissolved, "both the things of earth and those of heaven" (9:8-15 in Miller).

When the soul has overcome Ignorance, the third Power, it goes upward and sees the fourth Power, the seven Powers of Wrath. The first form of Wrath is darkness, the second desire, the third ignorance, the fourth zeal for death, the fifth the kingdom of the flesh, the six the foolish wisdom of the flesh, and the seventh the wisdom of the wrathful person. These seven Powers of Wrath ask the soul: "Where are you coming from, human-killer, and where are you going, space-conqueror?" The soul replies saying, "What binds me has been slain, and what surrounds me has been destroyed, and my desire has been brought to an end, and ignorance has died." Then the soul explains that it was set free through another world and through a superior image that has released it from the chain of forgetfulness that exists in time. Then the soul says in another statement related to assertions we saw in the Gospel of Thomas: "From this hour on, for the time of the due season of the age, I will receive rest in silence" (9:16-29 in Miller; cf. Thomas 50).

After reporting these things, Mary becomes silent. This means, of course, that her own soul, spirit, and mind have entered at least momentarily into the peaceful silence associated with "eternal rest," which is one of the innermost attributes of God and the kingdom of light in the Gospel of Thomas. It appears that even her telling of the vision, therefore, is a journey of her mind that frees her soul and spirit from the earthly, material Powers of Darkness, Desire, Ignorance, and seven Powers of Wrath. Mary stops, because she has come to the end of what the Savior spoke to her.

The Disciples Dispute Mary's Words

At this point Andrew asks the brothers and sisters their opinion of what Mary has said and says he does not believe the Savior said these things, "for what she said appears to give views that are different from his thought" (10:1-2 in Miller; 17 in Ehrman-Pleše). Then Peter responds after thinking a bit, saying, "Has the Savior spoken secretly to a woman and not openly so that we would all hear?" Then he asserts that surely the Savior did not want to show that Mary is more worthy than his male disciples (10:3-4 in Miller; 17 in Ehrman-Pleše). At this point Mary weeps. This means, of course, that the unwillingness of Andrew and Peter to accept the truthful account she has given brings distress and grief to her soul and spirit something like her finding of the empty tomb and her inability to find where someone had taken the Savior's body. Through her tears Mary asks "her brother Peter" what he is imagining. Does he think she made all this up or that she is telling lies about the Savior? (10:5-6 in Miller).

At this point Levi speaks to Peter, telling him that he always gives in to his "perpetual inclination to anger." Perhaps Levi is thinking of Peter's response with the sword that cut off the right ear of the high priest's slave Malchus when they came to arrest Jesus (John 18:10-11). Peter certainly responded with hot-tempered anger there. This suggests, of course, that Peter continually struggles to overcome the seven earthly powers of wrath, which are darkness, desire, ignorance, death, realm of the flesh, foolish wisdom of the flesh, and wisdom of the wrathful person. Perhaps Levi would not say Peter is thoroughly ruled by these earthly material powers. But he is proposing that Peter has continual difficulty overcoming them. The result, Levi observes, is that Peter is now questioning Mary as if he were her adversary. Here it is important to remember how Mary has just characterized the four Powers of the earthly, material realm as adversaries of the soul. Peter is questioning Mary and asserting that she is lying, just as the Powers treated the soul in Mary's account when it was trying to ascend to the timeless realm of God's rest. Then Levi says, "For if the Savior made her worthy, just who do you think you are to reject her? For he knew her completely and loved her steadfastly" (10:7-10 in Miller; 18 in Ehrman-Pleše). The tradition of the Savior's love for Mary is developed even more in Gospel of Philip 63:34–64:10:

> And the companion of the [Savior is] . . . Mary Magdalene. [But the Savior] loved her more than all the disciples [and used to] kiss her [often] on her [mouth]. The rest of [the disciples were offended] by it. . . . They said to him, "Why do you love her more than all of us?" The Savior answered them, "Why do I not love you like her? When a blind man and one who sees are both together in darkness, they are

no different from one another. When the light comes, then he who sees will see the light, and he who is blind will remain in darkness."

Then Levi continues, telling the disciples that they all ought to be ashamed. Then he asserts, "Once we have clothed ourselves with the perfect Human, we should do what we were commanded and announce the good news, and not be laying down any rules or making laws." Then Levi (in the Greek) or all the disciples (in the Coptic) start going out to announce the good news (10:11-14 in Miller).

Conclusion

Who then do people say Jesus is in the Gospel of Mary? One major answer certainly is that he exhibits the characteristics of a wise philosopher, as Matthew answered in Gospel of Thomas 13:3 when Jesus asked his disciples to compare him to something. But beyond this, Jesus is "the perfect human," that "Son of Man" who is the perfect image from whom the original Adam was created. Indeed, he teaches "the kingdom of the Son of Man" rather than the kingdom of God. The Son of Man, or "the Human One" as some translate it, is "inside humans" in the form of the perfect human who overcomes fear; who knows the power, lure, and deceit of the earthly, material Powers; and who knows how to overcome them. Jesus is the Savior who preaches the good news of the kingdom of the perfect human, which is inside every human. So the question for the reader at the end of the Gospel of Mary is, "How will a person 'clothe oneself' with 'the perfect human'?" (10:11 in Miller; 18 in Ehrman-Pleše). Will a person accept the insight, understanding, and memory of Mary Magdalene so as to be able to overcome the powers of darkness, desire, ignorance, and the seven powers of wrath? If so, that person can learn the way the Savior taught people to enter into the kingdom of the perfect human.

We saw in an earlier chapter how the writer of the Infancy Gospel of Thomas found a way of "grounding" his story of the boy Jesus with the Lukan story of Jesus in the Jerusalem Temple at twelve years of age. There an "infancy gospel" of Jesus ends in a familiar way, bringing the story into a familiar relationship to Gospels inside the New Testament. In Gospels outside the New Testament , a strange beginning can be exciting if it leads to an end that is at least somewhat familiar. The Gospel of Mary ends with Mary Magdalene telling the details of her "vision" of Jesus to the eleven disciples after Jesus has left them, and their responsibility is to go out and preach the kingdom. Much of this sounds quite familiar. The particular way the ending is configured, however, takes us into quite new territory. Was the good news the disciples were supposed to preach really "the Gospel of the Son of Man who is within"? Actually, this may sound something like Paul's preaching of a gospel according to which "Christ is in me, and I am in Christ." But the particular way the Gospel of Mary presents the gospel sounds very different. From another angle, its ending sounds much like the Great Commission the risen Jesus gives the eleven disciples on a mountain at the end of Matthew's Gospel. Instead, however, of leaving with a commission to teach people "to obey everything that I have commanded you" (Matt 28:20), in the Gospel of Mary Levi tells Peter they must do what they are commanded, and announce the good news, "and not be laying down any rules or making laws" (10:13 in Miller). So, after a very strange beginning, the Gospel of Mary ends with a blend of quite familiar and quite unfamiliar things. This combination of familiar and unfamiliar is a good start in preparing us for the Gospel of Judas, which we will discuss in the next chapter. The question is if we will have the peace of mind and courage to discuss it. Perhaps the spirit of Mary Magdalene can help us if we falter or become confused or afraid! And if that alone does not work, perhaps Levi will pitch in and help us to accept Mary's memory that Jesus said, "Where the mind is, there is the treasure."

LEARNING ACTIVITIES

1. Read the story of Mary Magdalene and the other women's encounter with the risen Lord in Luke 24:1-11 and John 20:1-18.

2. Read about the destruction of earthly and heavenly elements in 2 Peter 3:10-12. Contrast this with the perspective found in Gospel of Philip 53:14-23 and Origin of the World 127:3-5.

3. Read how people produce "fruit" according to their "kind" in Matthew 7:17-20; 12:33//Luke 6:43-44.

4. Read Romans 5:12 and contrast its story of sin giving birth to death in the world with Gospel of Mary 3:10-14.

5. Read Jesus' statement about the kingdom being "within you" in Luke 17:20-23 alongside Gospel of Mary 4:3.

6. Read about Mary's response to the empty tomb in John 20:11-15.

7. Read Jesus' words of peace in John 20:19-26 and compare them with what Mary says in Gospel of Mary 5:4-8.

8. Read about the rest of God in Gospel of Thomas 50 and compare it with the soul's rest in Gospel of Mary 9:29.
9. Read Jesus' Great Commission in Matthew 28:18-20 alongside Levi's statement in Gospel of Mary 10:11-14.

BIBLIOGRAPHY

Ehrman, Bart D., and Zlatko Pleše. 2011. *The Apocryphal Gospels: Texts and Translations.* Oxford: Oxford University Press, pp. 587-605.

Foster, Paul. 2009. *The Apocryphal Gospels: A Very Short Introduction.* New York: Oxford University Press, pp. 124-30.

Foster, Paul (ed.). 2008. *The Non-Canonical Gospels.* New York: T & T Clark, pp. 43-53.

Gospel of Mary: http://www.earlychristianwritings.com/gospelmary.html.

King, Karen L. 2003. *The Gospel of Mary of Magdala: Jesus and the First Woman Apostle.* Santa Rosa: Polebridge.

Klauck, Hans-Josef. 2003. *Apocryphal Gospels: An Introduction.* New York: T & T Clark, pp. 160-69.

Miller, Robert J. 2010. *The Complete Gospels: Annotated Scholars Version.* 4th ed. revised and expanded. Santa Rosa: Polebridge, pp. 333-42.

Perkins, Pheme. 2007. *Introduction to the Synoptic Gospels.* Grand Rapids: Eerdmans, pp. 269-74.

Tuckett, Christopher, ed. 2007. *The Gospel of Mary.* Oxford: Oxford University Press.

11

You Came from the Immortal Aeon of Barbelo!

With the Gospel of Judas we move into a form of Christianity that emerged during the 2nd and 3rd centuries C.E. in which Christians thought there was a higher unknown, invisible God who is completely separated from creation and a second lower God who oversaw the creation of the world. One of the champions of this point of view was Marcion (ca. 85-160 C.E.), a Christian born and raised in Sinope in Pontus on the Black Sea with access to the area of ancient Babylonia and Assyria. When Marcion was a young adult he went to Rome, but after studying there he was driven out by the authorities for his errant views (142-144 C.E.). He went back to Pontus and started many churches in the East where people held what is now called a "Marcionite" view of Christianity. This view asserts that the unknown, invisible God of Jesus was a "new covenant" God of love who exists beyond creation in a realm of the fullness of God. In contrast, the Israelite God of the "old covenant" was a lower god, in philosophical terms a "demiurge," who created the world and rules over it with violence and wrath against anyone who does not "do his will." The influence of this "Marcionite" view became widespread and is even noticeable today among a significant number of Christians who distinguish between the Israelite God of wrath of the Old Testament and the God of love of the New Testament. For Gnostic Christians of the 2nd and 3rd centuries, the invisible God dwells in the realm of the Pleroma (Fullness). This Fullness is so "generative" that aspects of it, like light and life, "spill out" or "emerge out" of it. The common term for this spilling out or emerging is "emanation." Light, life, wisdom, and many other things "emanate" from the fullness, and these emanations are "creations" outside the realm of God's fullness.

In many Gnostic systems of belief, feminine Wisdom, whose name is Sophia (Greek for "wisdom"), emanated out of the Pleroma, and her passionate desires for the Unknown God caused sexual fluids to flow out of her body and create material things. Thus, the created world came into being out of "sexual" processes that create and re-create material things, including the physical, material bodies of humans. This means that all the created order operates on the basis of sexual procreation, and "procreated" things degenerate and die. Thus the created order is a "mortal flesh and blood" realm based on sexual procreation, a realm where things die or pass away, in contrast to the realm of the Pleroma, where things exist eternally in a "perfect form" of their nature. Many will recognize that the concept of perfect form in a "heavenly" realm shows influence from the philosopher Plato.

The Gospel of Judas and Sethian Gnosticism

The Gospel of Judas, which is the subject of this chapter, has a significant relation to a form of Gnosticism regularly called "Sethian Gnosticism" or simply "Sethianism." It also has relationships to other forms of Gnosticism, but the absence of large portions of the text as a result of careless activity with it by sellers and buyers makes it difficult for scholars to reach definite conclusions about some of the points of view in it (Robinson). We know for certain, however, that this Gospel has a special Gnostic focus on Seth, who was the third son of Adam and Eve. This son, according to Genesis 5:3, was a son in the "likeness" of Adam, a son "according to his image." For Sethians, this meant that Seth, in contrast to Cain and Abel, was the son of Adam and Eve who possessed the "image" out of which Adam was created in Genesis 1:27. Cain and Abel possessed the nature of "the man of dust" Adam whom God created in Genesis 2:7. The offspring of Seth down through time, in contrast, are a generation of elect people who bear the "image of Adam." This means that "the generation of Seth" is a divine incarnation of the original Adam, namely a generation of people who inherited the eternal image that comes from God through the "original Adam" of Genesis 1 rather than the "man of dust Adam" whom God created in Genesis 2. The unknown, invisible God can only be known, and the benefits of God's "eternal" redemption can only be transmitted, through the image of God in the original Adam.

The Gospel of Judas presents a particular form of Christian Sethian Gnosticism in which Jesus is a "Savior" who has come out of God's eternal "fullness" realm through "self-generation"; that is, he "emanated" out of God's realm through a process understood as "self-creation." This means that for Sethians, when John 1:3 says "All things came into being through the Logos Word," the "all things" that came into being included Jesus himself, who became life and light in the realm of creation. As a result of the Savior Jesus' eternal self-generated nature, Jesus' "home" is "the great and boundless Aeon" where "the great generation" dwells. In other words, "the place of light" to which Jesus refers in the Gospel of Thomas is visualized in the Gospel of Judas and spoken of not simply as "the kingdom" but as "the great and boundless Aeon" where the great generation (of Seth) dwells. The Savior Jesus can travel back and forth as he wishes between the realm of "the great generation" and the realm of creation, appearing and "leaving" his disciples again and again. Once we understand these things about this Gospel, we can go to its beginning, where Jesus makes his first "appearance" to the twelve disciples, and start to understand the very complicated things that happen in it.

The God of Jesus and the God of the Disciples

After a summary introduction, the Gospel begins with a scene that recalls the Caesarea Philippi scene in Mark, Matthew, and Luke and its reconfigurations in John 6 and Thomas 13. The disciples ask Jesus who he is, rather than Jesus asking them who they think he is. This occurs in a context where the disciples are gathered together practicing godliness by offering thanksgiving over bread (33.24–34.2). When Jesus laughs, they ask him, "Teacher, why are you laughing at our eucharist? We have done what is right." Jesus responds by saying he is not laughing at them but at their following of the will of "their" god. The distressing thing for the disciples is Jesus' reference to "their god," as though the god they are worshiping is different from the god to whom he is devoted. In no New Testament Gospel does Jesus suggest that any of his disciples worships a god other than the Father in heaven. Often the disciples do not understand properly, and this causes them not to be persistent in prayer or watchfulness or to flee when Jesus is arrested by authorities in Jerusalem. The worst problem seems to be Satan, who the Gospels say enters into Judas and at one point even influences Peter (Mark 8:33; Matt 16:23). But in the New Testament Gospels Jesus never suggests that the disciples worship some other god than his "Father in heaven."

Jesus' response causes the disciples to ask, "Teacher, are you not the son of our god?" Jesus responds to them, "How do you know me? Truly, I tell you, no generation will know me from the people who are among you" (34.13-18). This is noticeably different from John's Gospel, where Jesus says to his Father in heaven: "Now they know that everything you have given me is from you; for the words that you gave to me I have given to them, and they have received them and know in truth that I came from you; and they have believed that you sent me" (John 17:7-8; cf. 6:69; 7:28-29; 16:30). It is true that in one place in Matthew and Luke Jesus addresses his disciples as members of "a faithless and perverse generation" (Matt 17:17; Luke 9:41), because they are unable to cast an unclean spirit out of an epileptic boy (cf. Mark 9:19). Beyond this one instance, however, Jesus' assertions that people are members of a "wicked and perverse generation" apply to people who are not his disciples (Mark 8:38; Matt 12:39, 45; 16:4; Luke 9:41; 11:29). Neither in the Synoptic Gospels nor in John does Jesus ever imply that the disciples belong to a wicked and perverse generation that will never enter the kingdom, and he certainly never says they worship a god other than Jesus' Father in heaven. Indeed, how could Jesus ever suggest that the disciples' faithful Eucharistic performance of thanksgiving over bread could indicate that they worship a different god than his? One would think that people who gather to practice godliness by offering thanksgiving over bread would be those who know precisely who Jesus is and who worship God the Father to whom Jesus is devoted. To begin to understand this it will be helpful if we remind ourselves of two things: (1) there are a number of places in the Synoptic Gospels where Jesus is highly critical of Jewish ritual practices, and (2) there is a discussion of Jesus as the "bread from heaven" in John 6 that leads to very puzzling, complex issues about what kind of ritual activities, if any, Jesus' disciples should perform with bread.

Jesus and Jewish Ritual Practices in the Synoptic Gospels

In the Synoptic Gospels there are a number of Jewish ritual practices that Jesus does not follow or identifies as unnecessary when his disciples do not follow them. To clarify Jesus' criticism of the disciples' eating of the Eucharist, this chapter will focus only on rituals concerned with food. In Mark 7 and Matthew 15 Pharisees and scribes complain that Jesus' disciples do not wash their hands before they eat. Jesus' response is that the Pharisees and scribes make the word of God void by breaking a commandment of God to observe "the traditions of the elders." As the scene unfolds, Jesus asserts that whatever enters the mouth simply goes through the stomach into the sewer. In contrast, whatever comes out of the mouth proceeds from the heart, and this is what defiles (Mark 7:18-23; Matt 15:17-20). In Mark 7:19, the narrator adds that with this statement Jesus "made all foods clean."

The specific event in Mark 7 and Matthew 15 is not recounted in Luke, but in Luke 11 when Pharisees invite Jesus to dine with them they observe that Jesus "did not first wash before dinner" (11:38). In response Jesus criticizes the Pharisees for cleaning "the outside of the cup and of the dish" but "inside" they are "full of greed and wickedness" (v. 39). Then he instructs them to "give for alms those things that are within; and see, everything will be clean for you" (v. 41). In addition, in Jesus' mission instructions to the seventy in Luke 10:8 Jesus tells them to eat whatever is set before them.

Beyond the complaint that Jesus' disciples do not wash their hands and assertions that Jesus made every food clean, there are complaints that Jesus' disciples do not fast. Jesus explains that his disciples are not to fast "while the bridegroom is with them." Only when the bridegroom "is taken away from them" will they fast (Mark 2:18-20; Matt 9:14-15; Luke 5:33-35). But Jesus himself also comes under direct attack, being called "a glutton and a drunkard," namely one who does not follow ritual practices in either his eating or his drinking (QLuke 7:34//QMatt 11:19).

Eating Flesh, Drinking Blood, and the Last Supper in the Gospel of John

In addition to the issues about food in the Synoptic Gospels, John's Gospel sets the stage for helping us understand how certain Christians could come to a view that eating Jesus' flesh and drinking his blood are problematic. As we have seen in the chapter on the Gospel of John, Jesus' teaching about "eating" moves beyond issues of fasting and eating everything set before a person, and even beyond eating bread in remembrance of Jesus' crucified body and drinking "wine" as "the new covenant" in his blood. In John 6:53-57, as we recall, Jesus says:

> [53]Very truly, I tell you, unless you eat the flesh of the Son of Man and drink his blood, you have no life in you. [54]Those who eat my flesh and drink my blood will have eternal life, and I will raise them up on the last day; [55]for my flesh is true food and my blood is true drink.

⁵⁶Those who eat my flesh and drink my blood abide in me, and I in them. ⁵⁷Just as the living Father sent me, and I live because of the Father, so whoever eats me will live because of me.

As we saw in that earlier chapter, this language caused many of Jesus' disciples to turn back and no longer go about with him (v. 66). Indeed, in John Jesus does not call "twelve" to be special disciples who follow him. Rather, he ends up with twelve when "many other disciples" react against Jesus' teaching about eating his flesh and drinking his blood. After many fall away, "twelve" do not go away but faithfully follow Jesus. These are the twelve who become Jesus' special followers (including, of course, Judas, who would hand Jesus over). In this context Jesus asks them if they too will fall away, and Peter tells Jesus they will not go away like the others, because Jesus has "the words of eternal life" (v. 68).

From what I have presented above, one could think that it is absolutely clear in John 6 that Jesus asserts that it is necessary to "eat the flesh" and "drink the blood" of the Son of Man to have eternal life. But the sequence of statements by Jesus in this context is much more complex and difficult than this. After many of Jesus' disciples complain about what Jesus has said about eating his flesh and drinking his blood, Jesus changes his emphasis by focusing on "the spirit" rather than on flesh and blood. In response to the disciples' complaint Jesus says, "It is the spirit that gives life; the flesh is useless. The words I have spoken to you are spirit and life" (v. 63). So what should a believer do in terms of ritual practice? Is it necessary to have a ritual practice of eating the flesh and drinking the blood of the Son of Man to receive eternal life? Is there some kind of "spirit" practice with Jesus' words whereby a person can receive the spirit that gives life, or is there still some other ritual practice in which a believer should engage? If Jesus says flesh is "useless," shouldn't it be obvious there is no benefit to gathering in prayer over the Eucharist? Wouldn't it be natural for Jesus to laugh at people who gather together to be godly by eating the flesh and drinking the blood of Jesus? After all, it is the spirit that gives life. The flesh is useless!

Here it is important that we notice the additional statements by Jesus in John that no one can see the kingdom of God without being born from above (3:3), that the only way to enter the kingdom of God is to be "born of water and Spirit" (v. 5), and that what is born of flesh is flesh and what is born of the Spirit is spirit (v. 6). How can a person be born of Spirit? And of special importance here, is there a way to be born of Spirit through a ritual of eating the flesh and drinking the blood of the Son of Man?

At this point it is important to remind ourselves that the Last Supper in John is not a Passover meal in which Jesus says his disciples should eat bread as a remembrance of his crucified body or drink from the cup of wine in remembrance of the blood of the new covenant Jesus shed for the forgiveness of sins. Rather, there is a Last Supper which has a ritual of foot-washing followed by a new commandment: "Love one another. Just as I have loved you, you also should love one another. By this everyone will know that you are my disciples, if you have love for one another" (John 13:34-35). Reading the Gospel of John carefully, it can look as if Jesus has replaced the eating of his body and the drinking of the blood of the new covenant with a commandment to love one another. If the disciples want to do what Jesus told them at the Last Supper they should show their love for one another through a ritual of washing each other's feet, not by eating the flesh and drinking the blood of the Son of Man! Jesus says in John 13:17: "If you know these things, you are blessed if you do them" (cf. vv. 34-35). In addition Jesus says in John 14:12: "the one who believes in me will also do the works that I do and, in fact, will do greater works than these, because I am going to the Father." It looks as if it could be quite appropriate to understand Jesus in John as saying that, rather than focusing on a ritual Eucharist where people gather to eat the body and drink the blood of Jesus, "true disciples" will engage in rituals that "enact love for one another." Indeed, to believers who do this, "the Spirit of truth" will come, and believers will "know" this Spirit, because he will "abide" with them and be "in" them (14:17). So, according to John, what is "the will" of Jesus and what is "the will" of God concerning ritual practices believers should follow to receive eternal life? The answer, it would seem, is not absolutely clear. Therefore, perhaps we should not be surprised if all Christians did not believe the same thing about what ritual practices, if any, they should regularly follow both to remember Jesus properly and to fulfill God's will.

The Disciples' Eucharist and Judas's Identification of Jesus

In the Gospel of Judas, when Jesus explains to the disciples that they are simply following "the will of their god" when they gather and perform the Eucharist of thanksgiving, they get annoyed and angry. In fact, "they curse him in their hearts" (34.21-22). This is serious indeed. In the Synoptic Gospels, Pharisees and scribes "question in their hearts" and say Jesus "blasphemes," but Jesus' disciples never "curse" Jesus in their hearts. It is true that in the Caesarea Philippi story Peter "rebukes" Jesus for saying the Son of Man must be rejected, suffer, die, and after three days rise again (Mark 8:31 and parallels). But this is an angry moment a hearer can understand. Cursing Jesus in their hearts is something quite different. This indicates a kind of anger that completely turns the disciples against Jesus. Here Jesus' twelve disciples seem to be reacting against Jesus like those disciples in John 6 who turned away and refused to go with Jesus after he said it was necessary to eat the flesh and drink the blood of the Son of Man to receive eternal life (6:53-66)!

So the tables have been turned on the twelve, who think they are following Jesus' teaching properly when they practice "godliness" by regularly performing a priestly Eucharist of thanksgiving with bread. Somehow Jesus has become something altogether different from what they understood him to be. Isn't it clear from Matthew, Mark, Luke, and 1 Corinthians 11 that disciples are to gather to break bread and bless and drink from a cup of wine in memory of Jesus until he comes again? Has Jesus changed his mind about the coming of the kingdom and the time all of them will spend together in the future? Something is wrong, and the question is whether the disciples can get a clear answer to their confusion and anger.

When in the Gospel of Judas Jesus saw "their ignorance," he said, "Why this angry uproar? Has your god within you and [his . . .] vexed your souls? Whoever has the strength among you men, let him bring forward the perfect person, and let him stand in front of me!" (34.22–35.5). This is a challenge more severe than anything we have seen in the previous scenes of confrontation between Jesus and his disciples over his identity. In the Synoptic Gospels Jesus tells the disciples that they have hardened hearts, that their ears cannot hear, that their eyes cannot see, and that they cannot understand. But the direct way in which the narrator in the Gospel of Judas says Jesus saw "their ignorance" is truly problematic, especially because the disciples were seemingly doing exactly what they should be doing. In addition, in all the New Testament Gospels Jesus asks the disciples questions and they answer to the best of their ability. Even if they are wrong, some of them regularly respond on their own volition. To be sure, Peter is usually the first to respond, and he seems to respond automatically, so to speak. The challenge for someone to have the strength to "bring forward the perfect person" and "stand in front" of Jesus seems truly beyond anything anyone expects Jesus to say to his disciples.

First, all the disciples say, "We have strength" (35.7). This is, of course, what they say in the New Testament Gospels when Jesus tells them they will all fall away when he goes to the cross. Usually, as we know, Peter is the one who speaks, assuring Jesus that even if all the other disciples fall away he will not. But in the Gospel of Judas it is not Peter but Judas who speaks. After the disciples say they have the strength, "their spirits were not able to get up the courage to stand before him, except Judas Iscariot" (35.7-10). Judas has the courage to stand before Jesus, but he does not dare look Jesus in the eye. Rather, he turns away his face. But then he speaks, and what he says is remarkable! He says, "I know who you are and from what place you have come. You came from the immortal Aeon of Barbelo, and the one who sent you is he whose name I am not worthy to speak." So when Judas speaks it is not like when Thomas says in the Gospel of Thomas that his mouth is utterly unable to say who Jesus is. Judas claims he knows exactly who Jesus is. He also knows who it is who has "sent" Jesus, but he is not "worthy" to speak the name of the one who sent Jesus. Surely the one whose name Judas is not worthy to speak is YHWH, the God of Israel. But what is the immortal Aeon of Barbelo, which is the place from which Judas says Jesus has come?

The answer appears to lie, as we have stated above, in an awareness that the belief system that guides this Gospel is a form of Christian Sethian Gnosticism. Let us remind ourselves more fully now what this means. Overall, an important emphasis is on Seth, who is the third son of Adam, born in Adam's "likeness, according to his image," when Adam was one hundred thirty years old (Gen 5:3-8). Eve described the name of her son as the divine "establishing" of a replacement for the murdered Abel (4:25). Seth represents the line of righteous people before the flood from whom Noah came (Genesis 5) and is in the line of ancestors of Jesus according to Luke 3:38. In Gospel of Judas 49.5-17, "the Self-Generated One, the God of Light" reveals "the Incorruptible Generation of Seth" and the "seventy-two Luminaries in the Incorruptible Generation according to the will of the spirit" as the third and fourth realms of "luminaries" who "come into being."

The one who "brings into being" the Incorruptible Generation of Seth is the Son, who is the "Self-Generated One, the God of Light" who exists in the "great and boundless generation," which "no eye of angel has seen, no thought of heart has comprehended, nor was it called by my name" (47.5-13). Within this great and boundless Aeon, or "realm," is "the immortal Aeon of Barbelo," the Mother, Womb of Everything, Triple-Powered, First Power, First Thought, Forethought, Image of the Invisible Virginal Spirit, Glory, Mother-Father, First Man, Holy Spirit, Thrice-male, Triple-named"

(DeConick 36). Here one sees feminine aspects of God, the Trinity, and aspects of the Virgin Mary. Here is a speculative religious-philosophical system that moves far beyond the Gospel of Mary. For this reason, the information Jesus presents to his disciples and the dream-visions the disciples themselves see are much more complex than anything we saw in our last chapter.

After Judas says he "knows" who Jesus is, Jesus recognizes that Judas is thinking "about something exalted." Therefore, in an action similar to his action with Thomas in Gospel of Thomas 13:6, Jesus says to Judas, "Separate from them. I shall tell you the mysteries of the Kingdom, not so you will go there, but so that you will grieve greatly. For someone else will take your place so that the twelve [disciples] will still be complete before their god" (Gospel of Judas 35.24–36.4). Here, of course, Jesus appears to be referring to Matthias, who was chosen by lot to replace Judas in Acts 1:26. The sad news for Judas is that his knowing "the mysteries of the Kingdom" will not provide a way for him to go there. Also, it is alarming that Jesus once more refers to the god of the twelve disciples as "their god" rather than his own heavenly Father. At this point Judas asks Jesus when he will tell him the mysteries of the kingdom and when "the great day of light" will dawn for the generation. But without saying more, Jesus leaves Judas (36.5-10).

Jesus and the Great and Holy Generation

When Jesus appears to his disciples the next morning, they ask him, "Teacher where did you go? What did you do when you left us?" (36.11-15). This is something like John 13:36–14:8, where the disciples ask Jesus a series of questions such as "Where are you going?" and "Can we go where you are going?" In the Gospel of Judas, the disciples want to know where Jesus went and did while he was away from them. Jesus' answer is remarkable: "I went to another great holy generation" (36.15-17). As a result of the Sethian cosmic system introduced above, it is clear that Jesus left the earthly realm and went up to the "great and holy generation" in the "great and boundless Aeon." Jesus is in no way limited to the earthly realm for his activity. Anytime he wishes, he can be present in the great and boundless Aeon or can appear to his disciples on earth. This is not like the pre-resurrection Jesus in John's Gospel, who "at a particular time" goes back to the Father. Rather, in the Gospel of Judas Jesus' body is like the resurrection body of Jesus that could "be present" among the disciples and then disappear as in Luke 24 and John 20–21. It is a very special "body." It is the body of the Son who Self-Generated out of a luminous cloud as the God of Light (47.14-21). But we will see below that there is even a bit more to the story of Jesus' body than this.

When Jesus tells his disciples he went to "another great and holy generation," his disciples say, "Lord, who is the great generation more exalted and holier than us, (a generation) not in these realms?" (36.18-21). Jesus laughs and asks them why they are wondering in their heart about the strong and holy generation, since "whoever is born of this realm will not see that generation" (37.2-3). Here it is important for us to remember that in John 3:6 Jesus distinguishes between "those born of flesh," who are flesh, and "those born of Spirit," who are Spirit, and that Jesus asserts in John 3:3 that "no one can see the kingdom of God without being born from above." In the Gospel of Judas it seems clear that Jesus is telling the twelve disciples that, in Johannine terms, they are "born of the generation of flesh" rather than "born of the generation of Spirit."

Jesus goes on to say that no army of angels of the stars rule over that "great generation," "nor will people of mortal birth be able to associate with it," and that "[the] generation of people among [you] is from the human generation" (37.4-8, 11-12). Again, this seems very close to Jesus' statements to Nicodemus in John that "No one can enter the kingdom of God without being born of water and Spirit. What is born of the flesh is flesh, and what is born of the Spirit is spirit" (3:5-6). But there has obviously been a major expansion of thinking about this by the time of the writing of the Gospel of Judas. Sethian Gnostics have taken Johannine topics and meanings and expanded them into an elaborate system of understanding and belief that moves far beyond anything envisioned in John. Moreover, the Gospel of Judas has moved in a direction that makes fun of the Eucharist, which seems totally startling to a person who regularly blends Jesus' statements in John with the account of the Last Supper in the Synoptic Gospels. When Jesus' disciples hear his explanation of where he went and his assertion that they will never be able to go there, they are so troubled in their spirits that they are unable to say a thing (37.17-20).

The Disciples' Vision

When Jesus comes to the disciples another day, they tell him they have seen a vision. Then they tell Jesus about "a great temple with a large altar in it and twelve men" who they say are priests. They describe a crowd of people serving at the altar who wait until the priests finish making their offerings (37.20–38.11). When Jesus asks them what the priests were like, they say some were sacrificing their own children, others were sacrificing their wives as a gift, and all were humiliating each other. Some were sleeping with men, some were committing murder, and still others were committing various other sins and lawless acts. "And the men standing beside the altar were calling upon your Name." And while they were doing all their murderous deeds, the sacrifices burned on the altar. When the disciples complete their description, they are quiet because they are troubled (38.12–39.5).

When Jesus interprets the disciples' dream-vision for them, he explains that they themselves are those whom they saw presenting offerings on the altar. Indeed, Jesus says, "That one is the god you worship, and the twelve men you saw are you. And the animals that were brought for sacrifice are those you saw, who are the crowd of people that you lead astray" (39.18-27). This is, of course, a brutal attack on all the priestly rituals the disciples perform in the name of Jesus. To understand it in relation to what is normally considered "standard" Christian belief, it is important that we return to the Synoptic Gospels again for a moment to see Jesus' complaint about those who closely follow priestly ritualistic practices. When Jesus explains to his disciples in Mark 7 the problem with focusing on priestly rituals rather than on "what comes out of a person," he lists the ways people act when they are defiled by the things that come out of their hearts. It is remarkable how similar the "evils" Jesus lists in Mark 7:21-22 (cf. Matt 15:19) are to the evils the disciples describe about those participating in the priestly rituals in Gospel of Judas 38.16-23. In Mark 7:21-22 Jesus describes the actions that come out from within the heart and defile as "fornication, theft, murder, adultery, avarice, wickedness, deceit, licentiousness, envy, slander, pride, and folly." The twelve priests in the Gospel of Judas commit fornication, murder, avarice, wickedness, licentiousness, slander (against the name of Jesus), and folly (38.16-23). They do all these things while "calling upon Jesus' [Name]" (38.24-26). Their actions are described as "murderous deeds" (39.2), which is third in Jesus' list in Mark 7:21. So Jesus' twelve disciples are portrayed as unwittingly and unknowingly victimized by priestly rituals that cause them to defile themselves by participating in "outside" rituals, rather than cleansing all the evils that "come out of the heart and defile a person." It appears, then, that the twelve disciples are performing the terrible acts Jesus describes in Mark 7 as coming from the hearts of those who focus on "outside" rituals. Instead of focusing on the "outside," they should instead be focusing on rituals that "clean the inside," that is, that purify what comes out of the heart.

The version of Sethian Gnosticism represented by the Gospel of Judas is a stream of early Christianity that despised all the institutional rituals of baptism, Eucharist, and thanksgiving offerings formulated, practiced, and regularized within the church (DeConick 3-21). So who is Jesus in this Gospel? Not only one who does not wash his hands before eating, fast at proper times, or keep proper eating and drinking laws, as we see in the Synoptic Gospels. Jesus' interpretation of the disciples' dream-vision implies that the disciples' Eucharistic meal perpetuates bloody sacrifices that violate God's commandments not to commit adultery or murder and not to offer human sacrifices. Jesus is proposing that any commemoration of him through sacrificial priestly acts represents devotion to a "lower God" who encourages barbarous, murderous acts as a way of honoring him. This is an assault on virtually all the rituals the leaders of the "proto-orthodox" church were establishing during the 2nd and 3rd centuries C.E. The Gospel of Judas was written by a person in a widespread movement within early Christianity that was objecting to this "priestly ritualistic" approach to belief in Jesus. The alternative they recommended and perpetuated appears to have been mystical-philosophical activities that could release them from the "earth-bound" generation and give them access to the "great and holy generation" that dwells in the great and boundless Aeon (DeConick 22-42).

Judas's Dream-Vision

Another time Jesus appears to Judas, Judas tells Jesus he has seen a dream-vision. When Jesus hears this he laughs, asks Judas why he competes with the other disciples, and addresses him as "O Thirteenth Daimon" [or "Demon"]. Then Jesus tells him to "speak up" for himself, telling him he will "bear with" him (44.15-23). At this point Judas begins to tell Jesus his vision, explaining to Jesus that the twelve disciples threw stones at him and chased him while he was seeing it. He tells Jesus he saw a house so large his eyes could not measure it. Important people surrounded the house, which had a grass roof. In the middle of the house was a crowd of people. Then Judas asks Jesus to take him inside the house with the people (44.23–45.12). Jesus tells Judas his star has led him astray. Then Jesus adds, "No one born of any mortal is worthy to enter the house which you saw, because that place is reserved for the saints." Again this reminds us of Jesus' statement in John 3:3 that "no one can see the kingdom of God without being born from above." Jesus' statement also is close to Paul's statement in 1 Corinthians 15:50 that "flesh and blood cannot inherit the kingdom of God." Jesus' statements in the Gospel of Judas often seem quite strange, but many statements in the New Testament have a significant relationship to what he says in this Gospel.

As Jesus continues to speak to Judas, he explains that neither the sun, the moon, nor the day will rule in the realm where Judas has seen the house where the saints will stand forever with the holy angels. Then Jesus says, "I have told you the mysteries of the Kingdom and I have taught you about the error of the stars" (45.12–46.2). Jesus does not describe the kingdom as the place of light, as in the Gospel of Thomas, but in relation to heaven and earth, which have been created. Thus Genesis 1 lies in the background here. In the kingdom, Jesus says, sun, moon, day, and stars do not rule as they rule over heaven and earth. The kingdom, then, is a realm "beyond the created world." Then in a fragmented verse Jesus refers to people or something "sent" "over the twelve realms" (46.3-4).

At this point Judas tells Jesus, "Enough," and insists, "At no time may my seed control the Archons" (45.5-7). It appears that in text now lost to us Jesus told Judas that Judas himself is the one sent to rule over the twelve realms or Archons in the created realm of heaven and earth. Then Jesus repeats that Judas "will grieve much more, seeing the Kingdom and all its generation" (46.11-13). So Judas asks Jesus what advantage it is for him that Jesus separated him "from that generation." Jesus explains to him, "You will become the Thirteenth, and you will be cursed by the other generations and will rule over them" (46.18-24). Then he repeats that Judas himself will not ascend to the holy generation (46.25–47.1).

Jesus and Judas at End of Gospel of Judas

After Jesus interprets Judas' dream-vision for him, he teaches him "the secrets that no human has seen." He tells him about "a great and boundless Aeon" "whose extent no generation of angels has seen, [in] which is the great Invisible [Spirit], that no eye of an [angel] has seen, no thought of the heart has comprehended, nor was it called by any name." Then he gives Judas a long account of the emanation and creation of all things in the universe (47.1–53.7), and Judas raises questions that Jesus answers in 53.8–56.10. This finally leads to Jesus' discussion of Judas' fate in 56.11–57.15, where Jesus tells Judas, "Behold you have been told everything." Then Jesus tells Judas to lift up his eyes and see the cloud with the light in it and the stars around it (57.16-18). Jesus explains that the star that is leading is Judas' star (57.19-20). Judas lifts his eyes and sees the cloud, and at this point the text says, "he entered it" (57.23).

There is a dispute among interpreters whether this "he" refers to Judas or Jesus. April DeConick argues on the basis of Sethian Gnostic views in the *Apocryphon of John, On the Origin of the World,* and the *Holy Book of the Great Invisible Spirit* that it is Judas who entered the cloud (118-20). From her perspective, "In Sethian tradition, this particular stellar cloud is the cloud where Ialdabaoth lives, enthroned in the thirteenth heaven." Ialdabaoth's mother Sophia created the cloud, which contains thirteen heavens: twelve heavens below ruled by twelve angels, and a thirteenth heaven above, where Ialdabaoth dwells. In DeConick's view, the Gospel of Judas presents Judas entering the cloud and ascending to the thirteenth heaven where his star rules alongside Ialdabaoth over the twelve stars of the disciples (who include Matthias as Judas' replacement: 36.1-4).

Marvin Meyer has recently argued that "recovered fragments confirm that at the end of the *Gospel of Judas* it is Jesus who enters the luminous cloud," not Judas (21). People standing on the ground hear a voice coming out of the cloud, saying, ". . . great generation . . . image . . . and . . . in(?) . . ." Then Judas sees Jesus no more and at once there is a commotion among the Jews (57.21–58.8). This interpretation of the text proposes that the "great generation" Jesus ascends in the luminous cloud to the great and boundless Aeon, where the great generation lives. Judas is the only witness to Jesus' ascension. This leaves Judas on earth, and he hands "the man that clothes Jesus" (56.19-20; 58.25-26) over to the priests to be sacrificed.

Meyer's interpretation of Jesus entering the luminous cloud brings to mind both the Transfiguration accounts in the Synoptic Gospels (Mark 9:7-8; Matt 17:5-6; Luke 9:34-35) and Jesus' ascension into heaven in Acts 1. In the Gospel of Judas, when Jesus enters the cloud, the stars of the disciples gather as witnesses, as the disciples gathered in the account of Jesus' ascension in Acts 1:8-9. Judas's star leads the stars of the other disciples. As Meyer says, "Near the beginning of the text Judas takes the lead in his profession of Jesus, and near the end he takes the lead as witness to the ascension of Jesus" (21).

The surprising thing at the end of the Gospel of Judas is the presence of two manifestations of Jesus: (1) Jesus the member of the great generation who intermittently appears on earth and leaves and (2) Jesus the man who clothes Jesus on earth, whom Judas hands over to the scribes to be sacrificed.

Conclusion

So who do people say Jesus is in the Gospel of Judas? The ending of the Gospel is as important for explaining Jesus' identity as the earlier parts. There the Passover is near and priests are seeking how to kill Jesus. This leads to the arrest of Jesus through Judas's betrayal of him. The text that exists begins with the high priests murmuring because Jesus has gone into the guest room for his prayer (58.9-12). Some scribes watch carefully in order to arrest Jesus during the prayer (58.12-16). The scribes are afraid of the people, since Jesus is held "by all as a prophet" (58.16-18). The scribes approach Judas, asking him what he is doing here, and propose that he is "the disciple of Jesus" (58.20-22). Judas answers them "as they wished" and received some money (58.23-25). Then Judas handed Jesus over to them. And here the Gospel ends.

The ending appears to provide the key to many of the issues throughout this Gospel. The problem is that even the ending has lost portions of text. One thing seems absolutely clear: Judas worships a lower god, the god who oversees the created world and "wills" that people in the created realm perform priestly rituals. Jesus, in contrast, has an intimate relation to a higher god, the god who is manifest in "the great and boundless Aeon," which only people who are not born of flesh can enter. If it is Judas who enters the luminous cloud at the end, he surely ascends in the cloud to the Thirteenth Aeon to rule over the created order alongside Ialdabaoth, who wills that people on earth perform priestly rituals. But if Jesus enters the cloud, as Marvin Meyer and his associates claim on the basis of recently edited fragments, then the ending of the Gospel presents an "ascension" of Jesus that revises the ascension in Acts 1 in relation to Jesus' presence in the cloud in the Synoptic accounts of the Transfiguration. From this perspective, Jesus enters the luminous cloud and ascends to the great and boundless Aeon, where people born of the spirit will dwell.

A short comment at the end of the Gospel creates a further surprise: Jesus tells Judas he will hand over "the man who bears" Jesus, not Jesus himself, to be sacrificed. Perhaps some of the lost portions of the earlier part of the text gave some clue or even made some direct statement about Jesus having two "beings," an earthly being "borne by a man" and a heavenly being who can travel back and forth between the earthly realm and the great and boundless Aeon and finally ascends to that special realm to dwell with the great and holy generation. But the portions of the text that now exist have no earlier reference to an earthly Jesus and a divine Jesus.

The earthly and divine forms of Jesus in this Gospel lead us naturally to our next chapter on the Acts of John, where there also are a "human" Jesus who dies on the cross and a "heavenly" Jesus who does not die when the human Jesus dies. Especially as a result of the fragmentary nature of the Gospel of Judas, we probably will never be able to answer with certainty some of the questions we have about the nature of Jesus in it. In the Acts of John, however, we see a divine Jesus who participates in earthly forms of Jesus. So, let us stop this chapter here and proceed to the next chapter, which presents a divine Jesus with highly interesting relationships to Jesus in the Gospel of Judas.

LEARNING ACTIVITIES

1. Read Genesis 5:3 to see where Seth is introduced as a son "according to the image" of Adam. Compare this description with Genesis 1:27 and note the contrast with the description of the "man of dust" in Genesis 2:7.

2. Read John 1:3 to see the central role the Gospel ascribes to the Logos in bringing "all things into being."

3. Compare Gospel of Judas 33.24–34.2 with the reconfigurations of the Caesarea Philippi scene of Mark, Matthew, and Luke in John 6 and Gospel of Thomas 13. Note the implication of the Gospel of Judas passage that the disciples worship a different god from Jesus' god.

4. Read Mark 7:18-23//Matthew 15:17-20 and Luke 11:37-41, where Jesus criticizes ritual practices of the Pharisees, to see a likely background for Jesus' critique of the Eucharistic performances of his disciples in the Gospel of Judas.

5. Read the statements about birth from above and the contrast between Spirit and flesh in John 3:3-8 to begin to understand how the Gospel of Judas's Jesus can disapprove of the focus on the body of flesh implied by the Eucharistic practices of his disciples.

6. Read John 13:17, 34-35; 14:12 to recall that John replaces the Synoptic Gospels' emphasis on eating the body of Jesus and drinking his blood

with the "love commandment," which becomes the means for enacting true discipleship.

7. Read Gospel of Judas 34.21-22 alongside John 6:53-56. Note how the disciples' cursing of Jesus in the Gospel of Judas approximates the reaction of the initial followers who turn away from Jesus in John.

8. Compare Gospel of Judas 35.24–36.4 with Gospel of Thomas 13:6. Observe how the responses to Judas and Thomas, respectively, represent Jesus' approval of their answers.

9. Read Luke 24 and John 20–21 to see the special ability of Jesus' resurrection body to be present at one moment with his disciples only to disappear again. Note the similarity of this body with the one we find in Gospel of Judas, particularly as represented by Jesus' response in 36.15-17.

10. To see how the Gospel of Judas condemns a focus on "outside" rituals, compare the "evils" described by the disciples from their dream-vision in Gospel of Judas 38.16–38.23 with those listed by Jesus in Mark 7:21-22.

11. Compare Jesus' (?) entry into the cloud in Gospel of Judas 57.23 with the Transfiguration accounts in the Synoptic Gospels (Mark 9:7-8; Matt 17:5-6; Luke 9:34-35) and Jesus' ascension into heaven in Acts 1.

BIBLIOGRAPHY

DeConick, April D. 2007. *The Thirteenth Apostle: What the Gospel of Judas Really Says.* New York: Continuum.

Ehrman, Bart D. 2006. *The Lost Gospel of Judas Iscariot: A New Look at Betrayer and Betrayed.* New York: Oxford University Press.

Foster, Paul. 2009. *The Apocryphal Gospels: A Very Short Introduction.* New York: Oxford University Press, pp. 118-123.

Foster, Paul (ed.). 2008. *The Non-Canonical Gospels.* New York: T & T Clark, pp. 84-109.

The Gospel of Judas together with the Letter of Peter to Philip, James, and a Book of Allogenes from Codex Tchacos. 2007. Coptic text ed. Rodolphe Kasser and Gregor Wurst. Introductions, Translations, and Notes by Rodolphe Kasser, Marvin Meyer, Gregor Wurst, and François Gaudard. Washington: National Geographic.

Gospel of Judas: http://www.nationalgeographic.com/lostgospel/pdf/GospelofJudas.pdf.

Meyer, Marvin. 2011. *The Gospel of Judas: On a Night with Judas Iscariot.* Eugene: Cascade.

Robinson, James M. 2007. *The Secrets of Judas: The Story of the Misunderstood Disciple and His Lost Gospel.* San Francisco: HarperSanFrancisco.

Strousma, G. H. 2004. "Christ's Laughter: Docetic Origins Reconsidered." *Journal of Early Christian Literature* 12:267-88.

12

I Saw You above the Cross of Light!

In the previous chapter we saw Judas identify Jesus as one who has "come from the immortal Aeon of Barbelo," and the one who sent Jesus as "he whose name I am not worthy to speak" (Gospel of Judas 35.15-20). The surprising thing toward the end of that Gospel was to discover that Jesus had two forms: (1) a "great generation" Jesus who traveled freely back and forth between the earth and the "great and boundless Aeon" and (2) a "man" who bore Jesus on earth, whom Judas handed over to be sacrificed.

A Human and Divine Jesus in Acts of John

The Acts of John, which is the subject of this chapter, also presents a double Jesus: a human Jesus and a divine Jesus who has no flesh. But here the situation is more complex. When Jesus is on earth with his disciples, his material and non-material substance flow back and forth, making Jesus sometimes a solid, physical body and at other times a soft, non-physical substance. In addition, sometimes Jesus looks like a child, at other times he looks like an old man, and at still other times he looks like a normal adult. When the human Jesus is suffering and dying on the cross, the divine Jesus appears to the disciple John in a cave and speaks to him. In the midst of this, there is no Last Supper. Rather, Jesus sings and dances a hymn-dance that initiates the disciples into the redemptive mystery of his suffering and death.

One of the most interesting things from the perspective of our previous chapters is the way certain scenes in the Acts of John blend contexts and

topics related to Luke's Gospel with topics and perspectives related to
John's Gospel. We recall how topics and scenes related to Luke and John
are explicitly blended together in InfThomas, beginning with a Johannine
topic as Jesus "plays creation" and ending with a version of the Lukan story
about Jesus in the Temple at twelve years of age. We also recall how
InfJames starts with circumstances around the birth of Mary closely related to Luke's presentation of the birth of John the Baptist. As the story
continues, however, the Logos/Word through whom all things come into
being in John is the agency for the pre-born Jesus to be present in Mary's
womb. Then Mary gives birth to Jesus as "the light who comes into the
world and becomes flesh." We will also see in the Acts of John scenes related to Luke blended with topics related to John as this chapter unfolds.
We will also see statements and concepts especially related to some of the
mysterious things in the Gospels of Thomas and Judas.

Drusiana's Experience of Jesus
in the Form of John and a Young Man

The beginning portion of the Acts of John tells of a series of events focused
on John the son of Zebedee after Jesus' death, resurrection, and exaltation
to heaven. The important portion for our consideration begins where
John, who is in Ephesus as the result of a vision that told him to go there,
tells the Ephesians about his time with Jesus before Jesus was crucified
(87). He tells his story to the Ephesians to help them deal with a perplexing
statement by a woman named Drusiana, to whom Jesus appeared when
she was in a tomb where her husband had put her after she refused to have
sexual relations with him any longer. After Drusiana was out of the tomb,
she told the Ephesians: "The Lord appeared to me in the tomb in the form
of John and in that of a young man" (87). John's speech to the Ephesians is
designed to clarify this double form of Jesus. In other words, John's speech
to the Ephesians is something like Mary Magdalene's speech to the disciples in the Gospel of Mary when the disciples are confused about things
they have seen and heard. John begins his speech by telling the Ephesians
they "have experienced nothing strange or incredible" in their perception
of the Lord, since even he and the apostles experienced strange things
when they were with Jesus.

The Disciples See Jesus in Different Forms

As John speaks in Acts of John 87, he tells the Ephesians a revised version of Jesus' calling of himself and his brother James, both sons of Zebedee, while they were fishing (cf. Mark 1:19-20//Matt 4:21-22). When Jesus calls John and James to the shore, James sees him as a child, but John sees him as a man who is handsome, fair, and cheerful-looking. James tells John he does not see what John sees, but he agrees to go to the shore to "see what this means" (88). When John and James bring the boat to shore, Jesus helps them beach the boat. Then as they follow Jesus, John suddenly sees Jesus as a bald-headed man "with a thick flowing beard." To James, however, Jesus looks like "a young man whose beard was just beginning" (89). Both of them wonder about the meaning of "the vision" they see, and as they follow Jesus they become even more perplexed about it. But then an even more amazing sight appears to John. When John looks closely at Jesus, he sees that Jesus' eyes are always open, never blinking. In addition, at times Jesus looks like a small, unattractive man, and at other times Jesus looks as if he extends up into heaven (89).

In an attempt to help the Ephesians understand the strange things that happened to James and himself, John tells them a revised version of John 13:23, "One of his disciples — the one whom Jesus loved — was reclining (at table) next to him." John identifies himself as "the one whom Jesus loved" and tells the Ephesians that whenever Jesus reclined at table, he would take him to his breast, and when John would touch Jesus' breast sometimes it was smooth and soft, and sometimes it was "hard like rock." John tells the Ephesians that this left him perplexed in his mind and he would say to himself, "Why do I find it so?" (89).

Then John tells the Ephesians a revised version of the Transfiguration story in Luke 9:28-36. We saw in a previous chapter that in Luke Jesus routinely goes to some special place to pray. Once Jesus took John, James, and Peter with him to "the mountain" to pray, and while Jesus was praying, the disciples saw "the appearance of his face change" and "his clothes become dazzling white" (9:29). In Acts of John 90, John says Jesus used to go regularly to this mountain to pray. Then he tells about a particular time Jesus took him, James, and Peter with him and they saw a light on Jesus "such that a man who uses mortal speech cannot describe what it was like." Here John's statement sounds like Thomas's statement in Gospel of Thomas 13, "My mouth is utterly unable to say what you are like." It also is related to

Judas's statement in the Gospel of Judas when Judas says he is "not worthy to speak" the name of the one who sent Jesus.

Another time in Acts of John when Jesus took John, James, and Peter with him and Jesus was at a distance praying, since John knew that Jesus loved him, he went quietly up to Jesus and stood behind him, looking at his hind parts. This is like Moses, when he saw the hind parts of God when God moved past him on the mountain (Exod 33:18-23). When John came up behind Jesus, he saw Jesus "not dressed in clothes at all," but stripped of the clothes his disciples usually saw him wear, and not looking "like a man at all." From our chapter on the Gospel of Thomas, we know that John is seeing Jesus without his "earthly garments," which a person takes off to go naked (without one's "earthly" body) into the realm of the kingdom (cf. Thomas 22, 37). In addition, John saw Jesus' feet as "white as snow," causing the ground to be lit up by his feet. Here John is seeing Jesus in relation to the "Ancient of Days" (God) in Daniel 7:9, whose clothing was "white as snow" and whose throne (underneath) was "fiery flames." When John saw that Jesus' head stretched up to heaven, he cried out. This caused Jesus to turn around, and when he turned around Jesus looked to John like a small man. Jesus grabbed John's beard, pulled it, and said, "John, do not be faithless, but believing, and not inquisitive." The words "do not be faithless, but believing" are exactly the words Jesus speaks to Thomas in John 20:27, translated in the NRSV as "Do not doubt but believe." In response, John asked Jesus what he did that he was not supposed to do, but Jesus did not respond. Then, John tells the Ephesians, the place where Jesus grabbed his beard ached for thirty days, so that John said to Jesus, "Lord, if your playful tug has caused such pain, what (would it be like) if you had dealt me a blow?" Jesus said to him, "Let it be your concern from now on not to tempt him that cannot be tempted" (90). This confusing statement by Jesus about "temptation" seems to mean that Jesus will not yield to the temptation simply to take the form of God, but he accepts the task of regularly taking an earthly form.

As John continues to describe their time on the mountain with Jesus, he says that Peter and James became angry that John was talking to Jesus, so they motioned to him to come to them and leave Jesus alone. Then Peter and James asked John who it was who had spoken with Jesus when he was on the mountain top, "For we heard them both speaking." In response to the question by Peter and James, John thought about Jesus' "abundant grace and his unity within many faces and his unceasing wisdom that looks after us." Here the story seems to be blending Jesus' speaking with

Moses and Elijah in the Transfiguration account in Luke 9:30 and a special feature that will now appear in John's speech where at times Jesus' earthly form "talks with" Jesus' non-material divine form! John tells Peter that if they ask Jesus he will explain to them to whom he was talking on the mountain (90).

Then John tells a story that seems to be related to the disciples' sleeping when Jesus was praying in the Garden of Gethsemane. John relocates this topic of "sleeping" to a time when all the disciples were sleeping in one house at Gennesaret and Jesus was with them. John says he wrapped himself up in his cloak in such a way that he could watch what Jesus was doing. Here the Acts of John story reverses Jesus' statements to the disciples that they should "keep awake" (Mark 14:34-41//Matt 26:38-45). Jesus tells John to go to sleep! John watches Jesus while pretending to sleep, and he sees "another like Jesus coming down" and hears this other Jesus saying, "Jesus, the men you have chosen still disbelieve you." Then the earthly Jesus says, "you are right, for they are men" (92).

Then John tells the Ephesians what he calls "another glory" which is simply a summary of things he has said before. He says:

> Sometimes when I meant to touch him I encountered a material, solid body; but at other times again when I felt him, his substance was immaterial and incorporeal, and as if it did not exist at all. (93)

Then John tells another story that revises Lukan stories, in this instance merging the three stories in Luke 7:36-50; 11:37-52; and 14:1-24 in which Pharisees invite Jesus home for dinner. John says: "And if ever he were invited by one of the Pharisees and went (where) he was invited, we went with him." Then he says that each of the disciples and Jesus were given a loaf of bread by the host. Jesus would bless his loaf and divide it among his disciples, and "every man was satisfied by that little (piece), and our loaves were kept intact, so that those who had invited him were amazed" (93).

Astonishing Experiences with Jesus

Then John tells that he wanted to see Jesus' footprint in the earth when he walked with him. He never saw a footprint, however, and in fact at times he saw Jesus "raising himself from the earth" (93). John explains that he is telling the Ephesians these things to encourage their faith in Jesus, "for his miracles and wonderful works must not be told for the moment, for they are unspeakable and, perhaps, can neither be uttered nor heard" (93). This is a very important moment in the Acts of John. In my understanding it reverses the process of proclamation in the New Testament Gospels. In the canonical Gospels, there is a perception that Jesus' miracles are an avenue or gateway "toward" understanding and "being able to describe" who Jesus is. Through the miracles, the New Testament Gospels show Jesus to be in particular "the Son of God." This is explic.tly clear in John 20:30-31: "Now Jesus did many other signs in the presence of his disciples, which are not written in this book. But these things are written so that you may come to believe that Jesus is the Messiah, the Son of God, and that through believing you may have life in his name." In the Acts of John, in contrast, John tells miraculous things about Jesus in a manner intended to lead the hearer to say the kind of thing Thomas says in Gospel of Thomas 13: "My mouth is utterly unable to say what you are like." The goal, then, is to say that Jesus is so totally unlike any other being — human, angel, spirit, or whatever — that it is impossible to say who he is. In other words, in the world of both Thomas and the Acts of John, Jesus is really "beyond all words." Thus, instead of clarifying Jesus' identity by comparing him to other people, like Moses, Elijah, Elisha, Isaiah, or John the Baptist, or even to angels like Gabriel or Michael, the approach is to say that Jesus is "unlike any other being." In the end it is "utterly impossible" to find words to describe who he is.

Experiences Surrounding Jesus' Death

Once John has reached the point in his story where he asserts that the miraculous nature of Jesus is so profound that the nature of his miracles and wonderful works are "unspeakable" and "can neither be uttered nor heard," John tells about activities and circumstances surrounding Jesus' death that produce long lists of words that present the nature of Jesus' "fullness." Here we see the Acts of John extending the tradition in John 1:16, in which the narrator says, "From his fullness we have all received, grace upon grace" (cf. Col 1:19). This tradition of presenting Jesus as possessing "the fullness of God" while he is "on earth" is distinctly different from the Synoptic Gospels, where the narrators describe Jesus in relation to various kinds of beings people know in the earthly realm — sages, prophets, apocalyptic seers, miracle workers, priests, and angels who carry out specific tasks on earth for God. We are accustomed to think about Jesus in these Gospels in positive terms, namely as a "special human being" whose perceptions and powers transcend "ordinary humans."

When we enter the world of the Acts of John, the issue is whether we should think of the Jesus of the Synoptic Gospels as "full of exceptional humanness" or "empty of full divinity." All the storylines in the New Testament that describe Jesus in relation to humans and even to angels presuppose certain kinds of "emptiness" of divinity within Jesus' humanity while he is on earth. The early Christian hymn in Philippians 2:5-11 states this clearly when it asserts that Jesus "emptied himself, taking the form of a slave, being born in human likeness" (2:7). Jesus' time on earth is understood to be a time of "emptiness," a time in which Jesus was indeed in the lowest form of humanity, a slave. The Synoptic Gospels and the Epistle to the Hebrews do not speak of Jesus as having the complete emptiness of a slave but as a human being obedient to God's will. As it says in Hebrews 5:7: "In the days of his flesh, Jesus offered up prayers and supplications, with loud cries and tears, to the one who was able to save him from death, and he was heard because of his reverent submission." In the Synoptic Gospels, in turn, Jesus tells God: "Abba, Father, for you all things are possible; remove this cup from me; yet, not what I will, but what you will" (Mark 14:36; cf. Matt 26:39; Luke 22:42).[1] In these storylines, Jesus has an "emptiness" of full divinity that requires him to be obedient to the "full" will of God, and in turn God raises him from death and exalts him to heaven.

In contrast, the Acts of John presents Jesus on earth "in divine fullness." This causes continual changing of form within Jesus while he is on earth, and just before Jesus' arrest, trial, and crucifixion Jesus sings and dances a hymn that ritually initiates his disciples into this divine fullness while he is on earth.

Immediately after describing Jesus' miracles as unspeakable, John begins to tell the final events of Jesus' time on earth. The traditional "Last Supper" ritual is replaced by a hymn-dance ritual in which Jesus initiates his disciples both spiritually and bodily into the mysteries of his suffering and death. But we must remember that John's Gospel, which the Acts of John is expanding and reconfiguring, has no ritual of eating bread and drinking wine in memory of Christ's suffering and death at the Last Supper. Rather, in the Gospel Jesus performs a ritual of foot-washing in which Jesus models the new commandment he gives them, that they love one an-

---

1. See John 12:27, where Jesus is limited to doing God's will on earth, even in all his "fullness."

other as he has loved them. In the Acts of John, the hymn-dance Jesus performs with his disciples moves beyond Jesus as a model of love and enacts
a process by which the disciples come to "know" who Jesus is and at the
same time to "know" who they themselves are. We see, therefore, a "Gnostic" (coming to "know") ritual replacing both the Last Supper ritual of the
Synoptic Gospels (and 1 Cor 11:23-26) and the foot-washing ceremony in
John 13:2-17.

On the basis of various things John tells us in the Acts of John plus
other things we know from the Gospel of John, I suggest that we can re-
construct fairly well what would have happened at a Last Supper if John
had recounted one in the Acts.[2] During the Supper, Jesus would have taken
a loaf of bread, blessed it, and given it to the disciples, and, as the disciples
ate, "every man" would have been "satisfied by that little piece" (93). While
they were reclining at the table, the beloved disciple would have been lean-
ing on Jesus' breast (John 13:23), and sometimes Jesus' breast would have
felt "smooth and soft, but sometimes hard like rock" (89, 93). If there had
been a cup at the Supper (there is no cup in John 13!), Jesus probably would
have asked the disciples to pour water into it, then when Jesus blessed it
and passed it to his disciples, the water would have been wine (John 2:6-
10). The disciples' drinking of the wine would have been a sign to them
that "revealed Jesus' glory" and would have caused them to "believe in
him" (2:11). If Jesus would have washed their feet, he would have said
something like, "As God is washing (glorifying) me, so I am washing you
(making you clean) so you will be able to come to the Father" (cf. John
13:8-11; Acts of John 95:11, 26-27). Among the episodes, Jesus would have
told Judas that he worships a "traitor God" rather than Jesus' Father in
heaven (96:44). None of this would have been a decisive ritual for the disciples' future "remembering" or "going to the Father" after Jesus' death,
resurrection, and ascension, however. Rather, the hymn-dance is the ritual
that "initiates" Jesus' disciples into the mystery of salvation and redemp-

---

2. Just before John's death in the Acts of John, he celebrates a Eucharistic meal of bread
with the believers gathered with him (109-10). There is no cup, and there is no other ritual.
John asks for bread and prays a long thanksgiving prayer in which he glorifies "the way" of
the Lord Jesus. The prayer contains relationships both to the hymn-dance and John's vision
of the Cross of Light analyzed below as it refers to Father, Son, entrance door, grace, resurrection, and being called these names "for your sakes." After the prayer, John breaks the
bread, gives it to all, prays for each person "that he might be worthy of the grace of the Lord
and his most holy eucharist," partakes of it himself, and ends saying, "To me also let there be
a portion with you, and peace be with you, my beloved."

tion through Jesus. Let us explore this hymn-dance in some detail to see how it functions as the disciples' ritual for remembering and redemptively participating in Jesus' suffering and death.

Jesus' Hymn-Dance with His Disciples

Moving directly from his assertion that Jesus' miracles and wonderful works are "unspeakable" and can neither be "uttered nor heard," John tells the Ephesians about a "hymn to the Father" that Jesus sang and danced with his disciples "before he was arrested by the lawless Jews" (94). This event revises Mark 14:26//Matthew 26:30: "When they had sung the hymn, they went out to the Mount of Olives." Interpreters consider "the hymn" at the end of the Passover in the Synoptic Gospels to be Psalms 113–118. In the Acts of John, John says that Jesus "assembled us all and said, 'Before I am delivered to them, let us sing a hymn to the Father, and so go to meet what lies before (us).'" The hymn is thus a unifying ritual that initiates Jesus and his disciples into his suffering and death in its "full" cosmic form. In other words, as the disciples join in the hymn and dance with Jesus they ritually participate with their bodies, minds, spirits, and souls in "the fullness of Jesus' suffering and death," which initiates them into their own transition from earth to the eternal realm of God.

The hymn starts with five repetitions of "Glory be to thee, . . ." ending in "Glory be to thy Glory" as they circle around Jesus and answer him with "Amen." The five repetitions present a progressive texture of "Glory be to thee," adding Father, Logos, Grace, Spirit, and Holy One, until they add "thy Glory" in the sixth repetition. The sixth repetition seems to have a relation to the sixth day of creation, the day on which God created humans in God's "image." Those who sing the hymn are praising God the Father for Jesus' glory as it first became visible in humans on the sixth day of creation, when God created humans "in the image of God" on earth (cf. Gen 1:27). Jesus, as the Logos "image of God," is the "glory" of God come to earth at a later time so that humans can participate in the image of God anew (or "from above") through Jesus' suffering and death on earth (cf. John 3:3).

Then the hymn contains a sequential praise statement: "We praise thee, Father; We thank thee, Light; In whom darkness dwelleth not. Amen" (93). Here the praise focuses on the relation of Jesus as Light to God the Father. The hymn interweaves Grace, Holy One, and Glory as it moves to a final focus on the Light in whom no darkness dwells.

Then the hymn moves to the rationale for singing the hymn: "And why we give thanks, I tell you: I will to be saved, and I will to save. Amen" (95). The form of this statement in terms of "I will to" immediately raises a question concerning the form of the additional statements that elaborate Jesus' statement "I will to be saved, and I will to save." It appears to me that Jesus' repetitive statements "I will to . . ." blend Jesus' statement in Luke 22:15, "With desire I desire to eat this Passover with you before I suffer," with John 14:10: "The words that I say to you I do not speak on my own; but the Father who dwells in me does his works." In Acts of John, the "will" of Jesus who exists in "God's fullness" is "the will of God," rather than the will of the human Jesus who prays in the Synoptic Gospels: "Not my will but your will be done" (Mark 14:36 and parallels). In the Acts, Jesus' will is God's will. As Jesus leads his disciples in the "rationale" of the hymn-dance, he elaborates major dimensions of "his will" to be saved (by doing the will of the Father) followed by statements of his will "to save" those who believe in him. If the statement "I will to be saved, and I will to save. Amen" is an overall thesis of the rationale for singing the hymn, the next section of the hymn presents topics that play on active and passive events that Jesus wills to happen for the purpose of producing redemption for humans:

> "I will to be loosed, and I will to loose. Amen."
> "I will to be wounded, and I will to wound. Amen."
> "I will to be born, and I will to bear. Amen."
> "I will to eat, and I will to be eaten. Amen."
> "I will to hear, and I will to be heard. Amen."
> "I will to be thought, being wholly thought. Amen."
> "I will to be washed, and I will to wash. Amen."

A division of the strophes of the hymn in the manner I have displayed them above makes the statement about washing the seventh in the sequence. If it is the seventh, it could, of course, be related to the Sabbath, the day on which one "rests in God." Usually, however, the final statement is presented as the eighth statement. This final statement, whether it is the seventh or the eighth, functions as Jesus' creation of a new world for the believer, ending in a step of "being washed" through Jesus for redemption in God.

First there is a set of three actions "on" Jesus while he is on earth, related to three actions Jesus himself "wills" to perform on earth: loosing, wounding, and bearing. The meaning of the "bearing" seems very clear: Jesus is pleased to do the will of his Father that he be born on earth and bear the burdens of humanity. The loosing perhaps refers to being loosed from earth so he can go to the Father, which Jesus desires for both himself and his followers. The meaning of the wounding is less clear. Jesus wills to be wounded, so that he will fulfill the Father's desire that he suffer. But whom does Jesus "will to wound"? One might think it is Satan he wills to wound, but Satan plays only a minor role in the Acts of John. Does Jesus will to wound the hearts of believers, so they can enter into the redemption of his suffering and death? It might be that the dancers who participate in the "wounding of the Logos" (101) will experience a "wounding of their own hearts and souls," which initiates them into God's process of redemption. In other words, it is possible that when the hymn-dance initiates Jesus' disciples into the wounding of the Logos, this participation wounds their own hearts and souls. This may help us see how the Acts presents an alternative to Paul's ritual of baptism "into Christ's death and resurrection." Instead of Paul's imagery of participating in Jesus' death and resurrection by going down into water and coming back up, the imagery is of Jesus' disciples participating in Jesus' suffering and death by dancing around Jesus in a circle, as the stars in the heavens participate in and actually create the unity of the universe by going round and round in their orbits. As the disciples circle Jesus, they say, "Amen," to Jesus' progressive statements, which lead them through his suffering and death into "being washed" into God through their unifying action. In other words, as they sing and dance, the disciples' actions unify them with Jesus, with God, and with the universe.

After the first set of three passive-active actions, there are two "active" actions Jesus wills to perform, eating and hearing, which lead to actions Jesus wills those who believe in him to perform: eating him and hearing him. Then there is the manifestation of Jesus as Logos/Thought: "I will to be thought, being wholly thought." Last is the topic that summarizes Jesus' washing of his disciples' feet in the Last Supper in John 13: "I will to be washed, and I will to wash. Amen." This statement transforms language about God's glorification of Jesus in John's Gospel to language about God's "washing" of Jesus: Jesus wishes to be glorified (washed) by God. In relation to his own washing by God (his being glorified), he washes his disciples "into God's redemption."

In the Gospel of John, Jesus' action of washing the disciples' feet inducts them into the new commandment "that you love one another. Just as I have loved you, you also should love one another. By this everyone will know that you are my disciples, if you have love for one another" (John 13:34-35). The foot-washing also gives the disciples "a share with" Jesus

(v. 8). In the Acts of John, the final statement in the hymn transforms the foot-washing into a hymn-dance ritual whereby the disciples experience "knowing who Jesus is" and "knowing who they themselves are," which leads to their "coming to the Father" through Jesus (cf. John 14:6-7). Jesus washes his disciples through words he says while his disciples dance around him in a circle. He thus initiates his disciples into his coming suffering and death through the hymn-dance rather than through a ritual of eating bread, of drinking from a cup, or of washing their feet.

At this point there is a shift beyond the rationale for the singing and dancing to "Grace dancing." The wording is remarkable as it asserts that in this next section "Grace dances." In other words, as Jesus and the disciples sing and dance, Grace dances with, in, and through them. First there is a three-step sequence that builds on the QLuke 7:32//QMatt 11:17 tradition where children play weddings and funerals, as Jesus played a wedding and John the Baptist played a funeral. In the Acts of John, Jesus plays both: (1) "I will to pipe: Dance, all of you. Amen." (2) "I will to mourn: Beat your breasts, all. Amen." This is, of course, a blending of Jesus' joyful mission to the poor and outcast (which is like a wedding feast) with his painful experience of rejection, suffering, and death (which is like a funeral).

Then comes a third step: (3) "(The) one Ogdoad sings praises with us. Amen." The Ogdoad are the yoked male/female "syzygies" in the Pleroma, the realm of divine fullness, in Gnostic systems of belief. So here all the "beings" in the "Fullness" of God in the realm above are the first to sing praises with Jesus and his disciples in this step in the hymn.

Then the hymn moves from the Ogdoad (eight) to "the twelfth number": "The twelfth number dances on high. Amen":

1. "To the Universe belongs the dancer. Amen."
2. "He who does not dance does not know what happens. Amen."
3. "I will to flee, and I will to remain. Amen."
4. "I will to order, and I will to be ordered. Amen."
5. "I will to be made one, and I will to unite. Amen."
6. "I have no house, and I have houses. Amen."
7. "I have no place, and I have places. Amen."
8. "I have no temple and I have temples. Amen."
9. "I am a lamp to you (singular) who looks at me. Amen."
10. "I am a mirror to you who knows me. Amen."
11. "I am a door to you (who) knocks on me. Amen."
12. "I am a way to you (the) traveler. Amen." (95)

While the Ogdoad (the eight number) dwells in the Fullness (Pleroma), the twelve number (like the twelve disciples related to the twelve tribes) dwells in relation to the Universe outside the realm of the Fullness (DeConick 113-16). In the sequence of twelve, one sees various "universe" or "earthly" manifestations through whom Jesus offers access to the Fullness "if" they sing and dance with him. The most important steps in this sequence are 9 through 12, where Jesus is the lamp, mirror, door, and way. As the lamp, Jesus shines as the Light in the world. As the mirror, Jesus functions as the one whom the disciples look at, and when they see Jesus, they "see" both Jesus and themselves and come to "know" both who Jesus is and who they themselves are. As the door, Jesus is the opening through which the disciples can go from earth to the eternal realm. As the way, Jesus is the path for the "traveler" to follow Jesus from earth to the eternal realm.

After Grace dances in, with, and through Jesus and the disciples, the hymn moves into a long sequence (96) that is too complex to interpret in detail here. In brief, the sequence moves from "if you follow my dance" at the beginning to "if you know how to suffer" toward the end. Those who follow Jesus' dance will see who is speaking, but they will keep silent about Jesus' mysteries. They will consider the passion of man that Jesus suffers as what the Logos did when he was sent by the Father. Those who see the suffering will be moved toward wisdom whereby they know who Jesus is, when he goes forth, and what he now is and is not. Then the sequence moves to "if they know how to suffer." Those who know how to suffer will be able not to suffer. What they do not know, Jesus will teach them (cf. John 13:12-15). Jesus is their God, and Jesus is "not" the God of their traitor.

At this point we reach an amazing parallel to the two Gods (the God of Jesus and the God of Judas the traitor), which we have discussed in the previous chapter on the Gospel of Judas. At the end, Jesus asks his disciples to say with him in a shorter form than in the opening of the hymn (94): "Glory be to thee, Father; Glory be to thee, Word; Glory be to thee, [Holy] Spirit. Amen." With this sequence, the participants in the hymn-dance are being initiated into "the mysteries" of Jesus' story. In the Acts of John, then, Christianity is functioning as a Mediterranean mystery religion (Dewey 74-80).

There are two important steps to the mystery. First, in Acts of John 96 Jesus says, "Obeying my dance, see yourself in me who am speaking, and seeing what I do, be silent about my mysteries." In relation to people who are initiated into the Mediterranean mystery religions, the people being initiated into the mysteries of Jesus are to remain silent about what they have seen, heard, and done. Second, in 96:11-13 Jesus says, "Who I am, you will know when I go away. What I now appear to be, that I am not. (What I am) you will see when you come" (Kaestli, response to Dewey, 84). Even though the disciples have been initiated into the mysteries of redemption through Jesus, the images they will carry in their mind will not allow them to see Jesus "fully as he is." Here we are seeing the two stages of Mediterranean mysteries: the "lesser" mysteries and the "greater" mysteries. The hymn-dance introduces Jesus' disciples into the lesser mysteries. After these mysteries, still "what he appears to be" to them "he is not." They will only be able to see him "as he really is" when they are initiated into the "greater mysteries" which actually lead them to the Father.

Excursus on Initiation into the
Lesser and Greater Mysteries in Acts of John

Pieter J. Lalleman (1998: 52-66) has formulated a highly learned argument, supported by his detailed analysis of expansions of the Acts of John, that the Acts presents the disciple John initiating the Ephesians into the mysteries of the Savior through two stages. The first stage is John's telling the Ephesians about the day-to-day experiences the disciples had with Jesus while he was on earth. The second stage, then, is John's telling the Ephesians of the hymn-dance and the vision of the Cross of Light in the cave.

If an interpreter focuses on Jesus' initiation of John into the mysteries rather than John's initiation of the Ephesians into the mysteries, the hymn-dance functions as John's initiation into the "lesser mysteries" along with the rest of the disciples. These lesser mysteries initiate John and the rest of the disciples into "primary" experiences of understanding who Jesus is and who they themselves are through singing and dancing about Jesus' suffering. After these lesser mysteries, Jesus introduces John into the "greater mysteries," where Jesus shows John the vision of the Cross of Light and explains the "deeper mysteries" about Jesus' suffering to John.

Perhaps one of the strongest pieces of evidence to support the concept of the hymn-dance as the first, "lesser," initiation and the vision of the Cross of Light as the second, "greater," initiation are the two statements by Jesus about "my mysteries" and "a mystery" in the two contexts. First is Jesus' statement in the hymn-dance: "Now if you follow my dance, see yourself in Me who am speaking, and when you have seen what I do, keep silence about my mysteries" (96). Second is Jesus' statement to John when he sees the vision of the Cross of Light: "So then I suffered none of those things which they will say of me; even that suffering which I showed to you and to the rest in my dance, I will that it be called a mystery" (101).

The "lesser" initiation presents an activity whereby the initiates enter into redemption through Jesus' suffering. The "greater" initiation occurs through a vision to John, which leads John into the mysterious truth that the Logos "suffered not, yet he did suffer" (101).

John's Vision of the Cross of Light

After the lesser mystery of the hymn-dance, John tells the Ephesians that when the dance was over Jesus "went out." The disciples "were like men amazed or fast asleep," and they "fled this way and that." Then, when John saw Jesus suffer, he did not wait by Jesus but "fled to the Mount of Olives and wept at what had come to pass." When Jesus was hung on the cross on Friday, at the sixth hour "there came a darkness over the whole earth." Then, he says, "My Lord stood in the middle of the cave and gave light to it." If we would put this in the terms of InfJames, after Jesus came into the world as light in a cave where Mary gave birth, during his crucifixion he went as light into the cave where John fled, so that he could be "a light" to John's understanding. Here Jesus is leading John to the "greater mysteries." When Jesus appears as the Light in the cave, the Light speaks, saying: "John, for the people below I am being crucified and pierced with lances and reeds, and given vinegar and gall to drink. But to you I am speaking, and listen to what I speak. I put into your mind to come up to this mountain so that you may hear what a disciple would learn from his teacher and a man from God."

As the Light speaks, we are seeing Jesus initiate John into the "greater mysteries." This occurs in the form of a vision of "the Cross of Light." After Jesus tells John he put the idea into Jesus' mind to come up to the cave on the mountain, Jesus shows John a Cross of Light "firmly fixed, and around the Cross a great crown, which has no single form; and in it (the Cross) is one form and the same likeness." Then John sees "the Lord himself above the Cross, having no shape but only a kind of voice." The voice, John says, was "not that voice which we knew, but one that was sweet and gentle and truly (the voice) of God." This voice said: "John, there must (be) one man (to) hear these things from me: for I need one who is ready to hear." Then Jesus explains the Cross of Light to John through a list of names and earthly things the reader knows from the Gospel of John. Indeed, most of the names and earthly things are present in Jesus' "I am" sayings in John's Gospel. Jesus tells John that the Cross of Light is sometimes called: Logos, mind, Jesus, Christ, door, way, bread, seed, resurrection, Son, Father,

Spirit, life, truth, faith, grace. Then Jesus ends with: "So (the Cross of Light is called) for men's sake" (98).

After Jesus introduces these names and earthly things to John so that John can begin to understand the nature of the Cross of Light, Jesus describes the nature of the Cross of Light with terms such as Jesus uses in the Gospel of Mary to describe "the nature of things." Jesus tells John that "in truth" the Cross of Light "as known in itself and spoken to us" is: "the distinction of all things; the strong uplifting of what is firmly fixed out of what is unstable; and the harmony of wisdom, being wisdom in harmony." Then Jesus explains that there are "places on the right and on the left; powers; authorities; principalities and the demons; activities; threatenings; passions; devils; Satan; and the inferior root from which the nature of transient things proceeded" (98). Here we see both the complexity and philosophical nature of the "greater mysteries" about Jesus into which John is being initiated. Reflecting back on the Gospel of Mary, and indeed the Gospel of Judas, it can be interesting to think about the visions of both Mary Magdalene and Judas as initiations into "greater mysteries." The irony in the Gospel of Judas, of course, is that Judas himself is not to go into the "great and boundless Aeon" which he sees.

As Jesus continues to initiate John into the greater mysteries, he explains that the Cross of Light has "united all things by the word" and "has separated off what is transitory and inferior." This means that the Cross of Light is the boundary between the mortal realm, where everything decays, dies, or is destroyed, and the eternal realm, where the Fullness of God dwells. It is important that we recall at this point the moment in the "lesser mysteries" when the participants sing and dance through a sequence in which Jesus is Logos/Word, mind, door, and way. There the initiates sing and dance their way into Jesus as the bridge between the earthly world and the divine realm as "speech" (Logos/Word) and "mind" (reasoning) that function as the "door" and the "way." Those "lesser mysteries" are closely related to Jesus' function in John's Gospel. The "greater mystery" moves beyond Jesus as speech/Logos, mind, door, and way, which provide initial access to God's eternal realm through singing and dancing Jesus' suffering and death, to a vision of the Cross of Light, which unites the earthly realm with the divine realm by being "the harmony of wisdom" and "wisdom in harmony." From the perspective of the Acts of John, the Cross of Light is the "tunnel" or "passageway" that unites the "inner mind of God" with the "inner nature" of God's ordered world of creation through the perfect unity of Jesus' will with God's will.

As Jesus continues to speak to John, he distinguishes the Cross of Light from the wooden cross John will see when he goes down to where Jesus was crucified. Then Jesus asserts: "nor am I the (man) who is on the cross, (I) whom now you do not see but only hear (my) voice." Then Jesus describes himself: "I was taken to be what I am not, I who am not what for many others I was; but what they will say of me is mean and unworthy of me." Then Jesus says: "Since [the crucifixion] the place of (my?) rest is neither (to be) seen nor told, much more shall I, the Lord of this (place), be neither seen (nor told)." Here we are very close to the description in the Gospel of Judas of the "great and boundless Aeon" which no eye has seen, nor ear heard, nor . . ." In the Acts of John Jesus exists in the eternal realm of God's fullness after the crucifixion, which has a nature highly similar to the "great and boundless Aeon" in the Gospel of Judas. Instead of all the disciples' seeing Jesus go there, however, only John sees Jesus there.

Then Jesus explains the nature of things around the wooden cross, the form of the cross in its "inferior nature." He says, "Ignore the many and despise those who are outside the mystery; for you must know that I am wholly with the Father, and the Father with me" (100; cf. John 14:11). Also he says: "So then I suffered none of those things which they will say of me, even that suffering which I showed to you, and to the rest in my dance, I will that it be called a mystery" (101). Finally he says, "What I am is known to me alone, and no one else" (101).

In the Acts of John, the cosmic feature in InfJames where "the world stopped, yet it did not stop" moves into the inner nature of Jesus' suffering and death. He suffered, yet he did not suffer; he did not suffer, yet he did suffer; he was pierced, yet he was not wounded; he was hanged, yet he was not hanged; blood flowed from him, yet it did not flow. These statements attempt to describe actions in human time with what are perhaps best called "processes in eternal non-time," when, as John says in Acts of John 93, the miracles and wonderful works of Jesus are unspeakable, and indeed "neither uttered nor heard." What they say of Jesus (in the human realm) he did not endure (in the eternal realm), but what they do not say (in the human realm), those things he did suffer (in the eternal realm). He will secretly show John what these are, for he knows John will understand. Jesus says: "You must know me as the torment of the Logos, the piercing of the Logos, the blood of the Logos, the wounding of the Logos, the fastening of the Logos, the death of the Logos" (101). These are all eternal processes within the Logos. "So I speak, discarding the man(hood). The first then (that) you must know (is) the Logos; then you shall know the Lord, and thirdly the man, and what he has suffered" (101). One who has come to know the eternal Logos knows the Lord. Then that person will really understand what the man Jesus suffered. The human suffering he suffered really was the suffering of the eternal processes of God.

John Talks to Those at the Crucifixion

Then Jesus was taken up, "without any of the multitude seeing him." And when John went down, he laughed at them all, since Jesus had told him what they had said about him. John held this one thing fast in his mind, "that the Lord had performed everything as a symbol and a dispensation for the conversion and salvation of man" (102). This "laughing" by John has a relation to Jesus' laughing at his disciples in the Gospel of Judas. Jesus laughs at those who think he has suffered and died, because only the earthly form of Jesus has suffered and died. The divine Jesus has not really died. In the Acts of John, John also knows this, so he laughs at those "below" who think Jesus has died. Yet John also knows that the divine Logos has enacted "divine suffering and death" as a way of bringing humans into the eternal realm of God's fullness. Thus, what humans know "is and is not" literally true; it is "metaphor" or "symbol" at the same time. Here we see how John's understanding of Jesus has "moved beyond" other people's understanding as a result of his initiation into the higher mysteries of redemption through the Cross of Light.

Then John asks his "brothers" to worship Jesus, because they "have seen the grace of the Lord and his affection towards us" (103). They have obtained mercy from him "with the disposition of our soul" (103). John asks them to worship "him who was made man (apart from) this body" (103). In addition John says: "Let us watch, since he is at hand even now in prisons for our sakes, and in tombs, in bonds and dungeons, in reproaches and insults, by sea and on dry land, in torments, sentences, conspiracies, plots and punishments; in a word he is with all of us, and with the sufferers he suffers himself" (103). Here we see that Jesus is "everywhere." He is not limited in any way, but he himself is everywhere, as in Gospel of Thomas 77: "I am the light that is over all things. I am all. . . . Split a piece of wood; I am there. Lift up a stone, and you will find me there." Then John says: "If he is called upon by any of us he does not hold out against hearing us, but being everywhere he hears us all, and now also myself and Drusiana, being the God of those who are imprisoned, bringing us help through his own compassion" (103).

Then John assures the disciples that he is not exhorting them to worship a man, but "God unchangeable, God invincible, God higher than all authority, and all power, and older and mightier than all the angels and creatures that are spoken of, and all ages" (104). Then he assures them that if they "abide in him and are built up in him," they "shall possess" their "soul indestructible" (104). Here John finishes and goes out with Andronicus, husband of Drusiana, for a walk. Drusiana follows at a distance, to see the things performed by John "and to hear his word at all times in the Lord" (105).

Conclusion

So who is Jesus in the Acts of John? Jesus is "the fullness of God." This fullness is so expansive that no title like "Son of God," "Savior," "Lord," or even "God" can properly describe and explain who Jesus is. The only choice is to introduce a long string of words to describe the nature of Jesus. But more than this, it is necessary to introduce actions along with words to describe the nature of Jesus. Also, it is necessary to describe the nature of Jesus on earth and the nature of Jesus in the eternal realm of God's fullness.

It may be helpful if we return, for a moment, to the cave in InfJames where Jesus came as light into the world and gradually receded into the flesh of a suckling baby. In the Acts of John, Jesus is the light in the world that "looks different" to people in different circumstances. In other words, Jesus as "the light" is not "actually" or "simply" flesh. This light is the fullness of God. People have difficulty "seeing" this light. Therefore, depending on their angle of vision, their distance from Jesus or closeness to him, and their readiness or lack of readiness to see him, they see "the light" differently. It appears that, as in the Gospel of Mary, there is an awareness that "mind," which exists between soul and spirit, sees the light of the fullness of God. John is given the special privilege of seeing Jesus as "the Cross of Light" who forms "the way" from earth to the divine realm. So his "vision" moves beyond Mary Magdalene's vision of talking with the risen Savior. Instead of simply talking with Jesus, John sees a "formless" Jesus "above" "the Cross of Light" and hears "the sweet, gentle voice" of Jesus, which is a voice different from the one the disciples heard while Jesus was on earth. For John, the Cross of Light is an avenue for seeing beyond the earthly realm into the eternal realm beyond. John's vision, then, is different from the dream-visions of Judas and the twelve disciples in the

Gospel of Judas. Instead of visions that include houses or temples, John's vision sees the heavenly form of Jesus' suffering and death as "the Cross of Light."

One of the amazing things about the Acts of John is that John tells the Ephesians both the "lesser mysteries" and the "higher mysteries" about Jesus. One of the noticeable things about the Greek mysteries is that people who are initiated into them "actually do not tell" what they did and saw during the initiation ceremony. They "keep silent," as they have been instructed to do. In contrast, John "tells" the mysteries Jesus tells him to "keep silent" about. Here we may see a special feature of Christianity in its Mediterranean context. Underlying Christian belief is the conviction that a person must "tell" what God has revealed through Jesus Christ. As many emerging Christians became Gnostic, they emphasized the "deep mysteries" surrounding Jesus, God, the universe, and themselves! They considered these mysteries to be "beyond explanation." No words could explain the miraculous nature of these mysteries. Still, however, Christians "preached" these mysteries as "gospel" — good news about Jesus, God, and the world. When told to "be silent," they went out and "told what happened to them." And this, we have seen, spans a list of early Christian writings from the Gospel of Mark at the beginning of Gospel writing to the Acts of John, which embeds a Gospel in an account of the Acts of the apostle John. This "telling what is impossible to tell" has been present in Christianity throughout all the centuries, and we can anticipate that it will continue throughout the centuries that are yet to come.

LEARNING ACTIVITIES

1. Read Mark 1:19-20//Matthew 4:21-22. Observe how Acts of John 87–89 revises the calling of James and John.

2. Read Acts of John 89 alongside John 13:23. Note how Acts of John stresses the incomprehensible nature of Jesus' presence.

3. Read the Transfiguration account in Luke 9:28-36, which Acts of John reconfigures in 90–91. Observe how John's characterization of what he, James, and Peter witness resembles Thomas' confession in Gospel of Thomas 13, namely, that his "mouth is utterly unable to say" what Jesus is truly like.

4. As an example of how Acts of John revises stories found in the third canonical gospel, read Acts of John 90 alongside stories about Jesus' dealings with the Pharisees in Luke 7:36-50; 11:37-52; and 14:1-24.

5. Read Philippians 2:5-11; Hebrews 5:7; Mark 14:36; and John 12:27 to get a sense for how the New Testament generally presupposes a certain limiting of Jesus' divinity during his earthly ministry. Contrast this with the Acts of John's presentation of Jesus maintaining the fullness of deity during his time on earth.

6. Read Mark 14:26//Matthew 26:30. Note how Acts of John 94 recasts the Synoptic account so that the singing of the hymn becomes a unifying ritual.

7. Read Luke 22:15 and John 13:10 and observe how Acts of John 95 blends these verses from Luke and John so as to underscore how Jesus' will is really God's will.

8. Read Gospel of Thomas 77 and compare its statement about the omnipresence of Jesus with the similar sentiment one finds in Acts of John 103.

BIBLIOGRAPHY

Acts of John: http://www.earlychristianwritings.com/actsjohn.html.

Bowe, Barbara E. 1999. "Dancing into the Divine: The Hymn of the Dance in the Acts of John." *Journal of Early Christian Studies* 7:83-104.

Bremmer, J. N. (ed.). 1995. *The Apocryphal Acts of John.* Studies on the Apocryphal Acts of the Apostles 1. Kampen: Kok Pharos.

Cameron, Ron (ed.). 1982. *The Other Gospels: Non-Canonical Gospel Texts.* Philadelphia: Westminster, pp. 87-96.

Culpepper, R. A. 2000. *John, the Son of Zebedee: The Life of a Legend.* Studies on Personalities of the New Testament. Edinburgh: T & T Clark.

DeConick, April D. 2007. *The Thirteenth Apostle: What the Gospel of Judas Really Says.* New York: Continuum.

Dewey, Arthur J. 1986. "The Hymn in the *Acts of John:* Dance as Hermeneutic." *Semeia* 38:67-80, with response by Jean-Daniel Kaestli, 81-88.

Elliott, J. Keith. 1993. *The Apocryphal New Testament.* Oxford: Clarendon, pp. 303-49.

Junod, Eric, and Jean-Daniel Kaestli. 1983. *Acta Johannis.* 2 volumes. Corpus Christianorum, Series Apocryphorum 1. Turnhout: Brepols.

Klauck, Hans-Josef. *The Apocryphal Acts of the Apostles: An Introduction.* Waco: Baylor University Press, 2008, pp. 15-45.

Lalleman, Pieter J. 1998. *The Acts of John: A Two Stage Initiation into Johannine Gnosticism.* Studies on the Apocryphal Acts of the Apostles 4. Leuven: Leuven University Press.

Pervo, Richard I. 1992. "Johannine Trajectories in the Acts of John." *Apocrypha* 3:47-68.

Pulver, Max. 1955. "Jesus' Round Dance and Crucifixion According to the Acts of John." In O. Froebe-Kapteyn (ed.), *The Mysteries*. Bollingen Series 30, vol. 2. Princeton: Princeton University Press.

Schneider, Paul G. 1990. *The Mystery of the Acts of John: An Interpretation of the Hymn and the Dance in the Light of Acts' Theology*. Ph.D. dissertation. New York: Columbia University.

Strousma, G. H. 2004. "Christ's Laughter: Docetic Origins Reconsidered." *Journal of Early Christian Literature* 12:267-288.

Conclusion

The chapter on the Acts of John seemed an appropriate way to end this book, because people truly do "see" Jesus very differently from one another. Where one person sees a rabbi, another person sees a prophet. Where one person sees an observant Jew, another person sees a Cynic-like boundary breaker. Where one person sees a miracle worker, another sees an apocalyptic seer. Where one person sees a person who loves food and wine, another person sees a priest. Perhaps there also are issues concerning the stage of life at which people see Jesus. Where one person may see Jesus as a rebellious "young adult," another person may see Jesus as "wise beyond his years." Where one person may see Jesus as "childlike" in his playfulness, humor, and free spirit, another person may see Jesus as totally "serious" in his concern about over-ritualized religious practice and lack of concern about the poor and outcast.

In chapter 1 we saw how the Q Gospel presents Jesus as greater than his messenger, John the Baptist. Early followers of Jesus began with prophetic expectations they had from traditions about Moses, Elijah, Elisha, Solomon, and Jonah and from sayings they knew in the prophetic writings of Isaiah and Malachi. We also saw how Jesus' use of the phrase "the Son of Man" in the Q Gospel presented Jesus' joyous lifestyle as a dramatic contrast to John the Baptist's severe, ascetic lifestyle. As we pursued how Jesus is greater than John the Baptist in the Q Gospel, we became aware of Jesus' actual enactment of the kingdom of God, rather than simply his announcing it and preparing people for it by calling them to repent and be baptized. Jesus especially enacts the kingdom in the Q Gospel through his restoration of malfunctioning human bodies through healing. Also, Jesus' demeanor and activity are joyous, characterized by the joy at weddings, in contrast to the activity of John the Baptist, who is compared to weeping and mourning at funerals. In Q, Jesus is known for his table fellowship with tax collectors and sinners, which appears to be a context in which he celebrates their inclusion in God's kingdom.

As we continued our exploration of the Q Gospel in chapter 2, we saw how the phrase "the Son of Man" could refer to a heavenly being who would come in the future to verify the truth of Jesus' proclamation of the coming of the kingdom of God. Moreover, we saw that as soon as followers of Jesus believed that Jesus had been raised from death into heaven they were convinced that the heavenly Son of Man who would come in the future would be Jesus himself. This Jesus, they also believed, would establish the twelve disciples on thrones judging the twelve tribes of Israel. Just as Ben Sira says in 4:15 that "Those who obey her [Wisdom] will judge the nations," so in the Q Gospel Jesus promises the twelve disciples they will sit on thrones judging the twelve tribes of Israel.

Chapter 3 showed us how in Mark's Gospel Jesus disappoints the disciples by arguing that "the Son of Man" must suffer, be rejected, be killed, and after three days rise up. An amazing thing about Mark is that the disciples never do accept Jesus' view of a suffering-dying-rising Son of Man/ Messiah. They flee when Jesus is arrested (14:50), and Peter even denies that he ever was with Jesus (vv. 66-72). The result is that none of Jesus' disciples sees Jesus die on the cross or sees the empty tomb. None of them participates in the burial of Jesus, in contrast to disciples of John the Baptist, who took John's body and buried it in a tomb (6:29). Rather, Mary Magdalene, Mary the mother of James the younger, and Salome see Jesus die on the cross (15:40), and they see the empty tomb when they bring spices on the first day of the week to anoint Jesus' body (16:1-2). But the narrator of Mark says that the women did not tell the disciples or anyone else about the tomb, because they were afraid (v. 8). This is a remarkable ending, since all hearers/readers will actually know, on the basis of 13:9-11, that the disciples accepted a life of derision and punishment to "proclaim the gospel to all nations" after Jesus' death. The ending appears to be designed to build within the hearer/reader a feeling of necessity to tell the story, since the women did not tell it. And the hearer/reader knows the story was told, because the story now exists as a public story in the Gospel.

Mark also uses the term "Son of God" to describe Jesus as the suffering, rejected, dying, rising Son of Man Messiah. By the time we receive the written form of Mark's Gospel, the opening verse announces "The beginning of the gospel of Jesus Messiah, the Son of God" (1:1). When Jesus is baptized, the heavens split apart when Jesus is coming out of the water, the Spirit descends like a dove on him, and a voice from heaven says, "You are my Son, the Beloved; with you I am well pleased" (v. 11). At various points in the story, unclean spirits shout out to Jesus, "You are the Son of God" (cf. 3:11; 5:7). When Jesus is transfigured on a high mountain so that his clothes become dazzling white, a voice comes out of the cloud saying, "This is my Son, the Beloved, listen to him" (9:7). After Jesus is arrested and the high priest asks Jesus if he is "the Son of the Blessed One," Jesus says, "I am; and you will see the Son of Man seated at the right hand of the Power, and coming with the clouds of heaven" (14:62). Then when Jesus gives a loud cry and breathes his last on the cross, the Roman centurion, seeing that he died in this way, said, "Truly this man was God's Son!" (15:39). In the end, then, in Mark a person outside Jesus' inner circle of disciples sees and understands the true nature of Jesus' messiahship. The Messiah of the Judeans, which is the title above the cross where Jesus is hanging (15:26), is a suffering, rejected, dying Messiah.

When the Roman centurion sees Jesus' death, he calls Jesus God's Son, but when Jesus talks about suffering, rejection, and death he uses the title "the Son of Man." For some early messianic Jewish followers of Jesus, the term Son of Man had become a special way to think through belief in Jesus as a suffering, rejected, dying Messiah of Israel. But it would not be a phrase a Roman centurion would understand. Also, there is no evidence that the centurion considers any possibility that as God's Son Jesus will rise from the dead. In contrast, some women are told about Jesus' resurrection when they find an empty tomb instead of a tomb with Jesus' corpse in it. But they do not tell anyone! The hearers/readers of Mark's Gospel also hear about the resurrection of Jesus. And everyone should know about it, right? Jesus repeated over and over again in Mark 8–10 that the Son of Man would be rejected, killed, and buried and after three days rise up.

In chapter 4 we became aware of how the Gospel of Matthew expands Mark into a twenty-eight-chapter Gospel containing five major sermons of Jesus, with the first and last sermon being three chapters long. In these five sermons, Jesus presents "gospel Torah" that blends topics from prophetic literature, wisdom sayings, and Psalms of David from the Old Testament/ Hebrew Bible. In the midst of this, Peter identifies Jesus as "the Messiah, the Son of the Living God" (16:16). This Messiah is "the son of David, the son of Abraham" (1:1). But he is also the Messiah who was taken to Egypt while he was an infant and was "called" out of Egypt to be God's son in the form of a new Moses who taught a new version of the Torah (2:15; 5:21-48). The end result is the presentation of Jesus as a Messiah who both teaches and enacts a new Torah that correlates individual people's inner spirituality with their outward practices on a daily basis (25:31-46).

Matthew 16:13-20 contains an expanded version of the Markan Caesarea Philippi story in which Jesus establishes Peter as the rock on which he will build his Messiah "assembly," commonly called "church." Where two or three gather in Jesus' name, this church functions as a community on earth whose actions are embedded in the will and action of Jesus' "Father in heaven." Guided by gospel Torah, this community is instructed by Jesus to practice forgiveness that exceeds "perfect forgiveness" and to nurture actions by its members that fulfill God's righteousness on a daily basis without realizing they are doing so. Perhaps we should have little surprise that Christian writers during the second and third centuries C.E. repeated in their writings more words from Matthew, which is the longest Gospel in the New Testament, than any other New Testament Gospel. In addition, we should observe that this amazingly rich and complex Gospel moved into a position of preeminence during the first four centuries as the first Gospel in the New Testament. If a person opens the New Testament to read it from beginning to end, the first book is Matthew.

In chapter 5 we saw how Luke's Gospel presents Jesus as a praying prophet-Messiah anointed with the Spirit. He brings good news to the poor and heals people. He confronts scribes and Pharisees prophetically, challenging them to accept not only sinners but also the crippled, the blind, and the lame (14:21). In addition, he seeks and saves the lost. It is informative that this anointed prophetic Messiah does not remain silent during the process of his crucifixion, as he does in Mark and Matthew. Rather, while hanging on the cross he prays to God to forgive those who are crucifying him, saying, "Father, forgive them; for they do not know what they are doing" (23:34). Then to the criminal who has spoken out against the other criminal who was mocking Jesus' status as Messiah Jesus says, "Truly I tell you, you will be with me in Paradise" (v. 43). Then, this spirit- and oil-anointed prophetic Messiah does not cry out, "My God, my God, why have you forsaken me?" as in Mark 15:34//Matthew 27:46. Instead, he gives the spirit with which he was anointed back to God, crying out with a loud voice, "Father, into your hand I commit my spirit" (23:46).

When Jesus has given his spirit back to God in Luke, the stage is ready for God to give his Holy Spirit to Jesus' followers in Acts 2. But before this happens, there is another event of great importance. When the centurion at the foot of the cross sees Jesus die, instead of saying, "Truly this man was God's Son" (Mark 15:39//Matt 27:54), he says, "Certainly this man was *dikaios*" (Luke 23:47). The Greek word *dikaios* regularly means "righteous," and in this context it means "innocent." In Luke, there is no question about Jesus being God's Son. The reader has known this identity for Jesus ever since the angel Gabriel came to Mary and told her she would have a child (1:32). Rather, the question was what God's Son would do with his anointment with both spirit and oil. The answer Luke presents is an anointed life focused on food, healing, and justice for the poor supported by a life of prayer. Justice and well-being, Jesus the specially anointed Messiah says, can occur only through love and generosity nurtured through prayer and enacted by those who possess an abundance of God's blessings. As Jesus dies in Luke, the centurion at the foot of the cross says that Jesus himself is righteous, innocent of any wrongdoing, in contrast to what those who have killed him think.

In chapter 6 we learned that John's Gospel also contains a scene in which Simon Peter speaks up for the twelve disciples, identifying Jesus in a context of disagreement and dispute. When Peter speaks, he asserts that Jesus is "the Holy One of God" who has "the words of eternal life" (6:68-69). In John the dispute is not over the Son of Man's suffering, death, and resurrection. Rather, the dispute is over "eating the flesh and drinking the blood of the Son of Man" (6:51-58).

As we explored Jesus' identity in John, we observed the absence in Jesus' Last Supper with his disciples (John 13) of any "institution of a ritual" concerning eating bread and drinking wine in relation to Jesus' body and blood. Rather, Jesus' Last Supper features a foot-washing ritual and a "new commandment" that Jesus' disciples "love one another." This means that in John's Gospel Jesus' identity is "embedded" in a "foot-washing" action of love and service and in a commandment to "love one another" rather than in a "ritual of remembrance" that focuses on eating bread and drinking wine.

As we explored the relation between John 6 and Jesus' Last Supper in John 13, we observed that Jesus' "final statement" in John 6 about eating and drinking is that "It is the spirit that gives life; the flesh is useless. The words that I have spoken to you are spirit and life" (6:62-63). These "final statements" in John 6 raise a serious question concerning proper ritual activity in emerging Christianity in relation to Jesus as "the bread from heaven" who "has the words of eternal life." What kinds of "regular ritual activities" will enact "proper remembrance" of Jesus and lead believers in

Jesus into proper actions and beliefs? We have seen in subsequent chapters that the Gospel of John introduced topics and issues concerning Jesus as light and life that later writers would explore in elaborate ways and, in some instances, portray in remarkable ways. In the centuries to come, John's presentation of Jesus' identity was so full of meaning, significance, and divinity that a selection of Johannine topics and issues were present in one way or another in virtually every new presentation of Jesus thereafter.

Chapter 7 showed us how the Gospel of Thomas presents Jesus as a manifestation of God who transcends angelic forms, all forms of wisdom tradition, and even a Word-flesh personage. He is a self-generated manifestation of the one whose name is unutterable. His presence is known through a human-like image with a voice that speaks words that can help the chosen ones in the world return to the place of light.

In Thomas, then, Jesus is not "the Word who was with God," as in John. Also, Jesus is not "life" through whom all things were created. Rather, Jesus is the Living One who is "the light over all things" who emanated from God the Living Father, in whom are motion and rest. When Jesus emanated from the Father as the light over all things, this light established itself as the place of light, which is the kingdom. This place of light contains both the beginning and end of time; that is, it is both the beginning and the end. It also contains the motion and rest of God the Father.

In the Gospel of Thomas, all the elect have come from the place of light and will return to it when they seek and find the kingdom through the Living One, namely Jesus, who is in their presence. Jesus' sayings are the means by which they can come to this knowledge, become "kings of wisdom" who rule over all others in the created world, take off their earthly clothing, and return to the place of light, which is the kingdom, where they will dwell in the motion and rest of God the Father.

When Jesus asks the disciples to compare him to something, the challenge before them is amazingly difficult. Simon Peter gives quite a good answer when he suggests that Jesus is a righteous heavenly messenger. But his answer is not good enough, because angels assist God within "time" to bring in God's kingdom on earth. Jesus, in contrast to angels, functions outside time as "the light over all." While Matthew's answer that Jesus is a wise philosopher could seem to be more appropriate, since Jesus' mode of thinking is so complex, in many ways it is a less perceptive answer than Peter's. In the Gospel of Thomas, Jesus is a personage far beyond any human being like a philosopher.

Thomas's answer, in contrast to both Peter's and Matthew's, is right on target: the mouth of no human is able to properly express who Jesus is! Humans must speak, of course. But none of their words are able to explain what an incredible personage Jesus is. The only remedy is to have sayings from Jesus, the Living One. When people seek until they find within Jesus' sayings, they will be disturbed when they find. When they are disturbed, however, they will begin to marvel. When they marvel, then they will begin to know the Living One who is in their presence. And when they know the Living One, they will know that they themselves have come from the place of light, and they will take off their earthly clothes and return to the place of light. Then in the place of light they will dwell in the motion and rest of the Living Father.

In chapter 8 we saw how in the Infancy Gospel of Thomas some Christians during the 2nd and 3rd centuries blended aspects of Luke with John to present Jesus as "the Word" even as a boy. This blending of the two Gospels gave writers an opportunity to explore the nature of God's powerful "creating" word, which immediately brings what it says into being. When the "human" Jesus is born as a little child and only gradually grows up into adulthood, it is not easy for him to control his powerful "word" so that he does not do more damage than good.

One of the remarkable things about InfThomas is its presentation of Jesus in the context of the Greek educational system of *paideia*, in which learning the Greek alphabet was the beginning process for becoming a "civilized" person. How would Jesus as "boy Word" respond to a Greek teacher who was accustomed to striking his students with a stick as part of his "taming" of unruly children? Also, would the "boy Word" ever submit to the process of changing from destructive action to benevolent action by means of learning "Greek letters"? What, then, was to be the relation of the Greek educational *paideia* system to teaching about the Bible and about Jesus? These issues remained very important throughout the 3rd, 4th, and 5th centuries c.e. Indeed, Augustine addressed the issue of the relation of Christian thinking, belief, and practice to classical education and oratory in many of his writings until his death in the 5th century (d. 430 c.e.). Even in the 21st century the question of the relation of Christian belief and understanding to public school education is with us. In InfThomas, Jesus learns by age eight through his own internal wisdom to control the power of his speech. Thereafter he uses his power only "to save people" rather than to destroy them.

In chapter 9 we learned how the Infancy Gospel of James is a "four-gospel-in-one" story about the birth of Jesus. The story begins with an extension of the Lukan story of the births of John the Baptist and Jesus back-wards to the birth of Mary, reworking aspects of the birth of Samuel in 1 Samuel 1–2 in the process. As the story proceeds, the writer subtly inter-weaves topics and meanings from John and at one point even Mark. So who do people say Jesus is in InfJames? He seems to be a Lukan, Matthean, Markan, and Johannine Jesus who makes the world stand still, and yet it does not. This caused us to recall how around 180 C.E. a Christian named Tatian created a "four-gospel-in-one." Scholars call this Gospel the Diatessaron, which means "through four" in Greek. Tatian created his "one gospel" by interweaving virtually all the verses in Matthew, Mark, Luke, and John. His began, naturally, with "In the beginning was the Word," and after the prologue from John presented the Lukan story of the birth of John the Baptist. After this, he wove together the Lukan and Matthean stories of Jesus' birth and continued to pull Luke, Matthew, Mark, and John together story by story until the end. In InfJames, the narrator weaves aspects of all four gospels together, creating a "Synoptic Gospels" environment into which Jesus comes into the world as light who becomes flesh, as stated in John's Gospel.

Chapter 10 showed us how the Gospel of Mary presents Jesus with characteristics of a wise philosopher as it opens with Jesus explaining how earthly matter returns to its root nature when it is destroyed. Then toward the end of the story Mary Magdalene remembers that the Savior said, "Where the mind is, there is the treasure." As the Gospel unfolds, Jesus emerges as "the perfect Human," the "Son of Man" who is the perfect im-age from whom the original Adam was created. Indeed, Jesus teaches "the kingdom of the Son of Man," rather than the kingdom of God. The Son of Man, or "the Human One" as some translate it, is "inside humans" in the form of the perfect human who overcomes fear, who knows the power, lure, and deceit of the earthly, material Powers, and who knows how to overcome them. Jesus is the Savior who preaches the good news of the kingdom of the perfect human, which is inside every human. So the ques-tion for the reader at the end of the Gospel of Mary is, "How will a person 'clothe oneself' with 'the perfect human'?" Will a person accept the insight, understanding, and memory of Mary Magdalene so as to be able to over-come the powers of darkness, desire, ignorance, and the seven powers of wrath? If so, that person can learn the way the Savior taught people to en-ter the kingdom of the perfect human.

We saw how the Gospel of Mary ends with Mary telling the details of her "vision" of Jesus to the eleven disciples after Jesus has left them and charging them to go out and preach the kingdom. Much of this sounds quite familiar. The particular way the ending is configured, however, takes us into quite new territory. Was the good news the disciples were supposed to preach really "the Gospel of the Son of Man who is within"? Actually, this may sound something like Paul's preaching of a gospel whereby he says "Christ is in me, and I am in Christ." But the particular way the Gospel of Mary presents the gospel sounds very different. From another angle, the ending of the Gospel sounds much like the Great Commission the risen Jesus gives the eleven disciples on a mountain at the end of Matthew.

So, after a very strange beginning, the Gospel of Mary ends with a blend of quite familiar and quite unfamiliar things. The truly unusual thing, however, is the role of Mary Magdalene as the one who helps the disciples move beyond their faltering, confusion, and fear. Using her mind, which the Savior taught her was her special treasure, she grasps the very difficult concepts Jesus teaches when the rest of the disciples cannot. Thus, when the male disciples are afraid and confused, Mary courageously speaks to them, giving them the courage to go out and preach the kingdom. What a change in emerging Christianity for Mary Magdalene, rather than Peter, to play this role among the disciples!

In chapter 11 we entered the strange world of the Gospel of Judas. At the end of this Gospel, the Passover is near and priests are seeking how to kill Jesus. This leads to his arrest through Judas's betrayal of him. The text that exists begins with the high priests murmuring because Jesus has gone into the guest room for his prayer, with scribes watching carefully so as to arrest Jesus during the prayer. But they are afraid of the people, since Jesus is held "by all as a prophet." The scribes identify Judas as "the disciple of Jesus" and give him money. Then Judas hands Jesus over to them. And there the Gospel ends.

The ending appears to provide the key to many of the issues throughout the Gospel of Judas, but it is obscured by the loss of portions of the text. It seems clear that Judas worships a lower god, the god who oversees the created world and "wills" that people perform priestly rituals. Jesus, in contrast, has an intimate relation to a higher god, the god who is manifest in "the great and boundless Aeon" that only people who are not born of flesh can enter. It is disputed whether Judas or Jesus enters the luminous cloud at the end. If Judas enters it, he surely ascends in the cloud to the Thirteenth Aeon to rule over the created order alongside Ialdabaoth, who wills that people on earth perform priestly rituals. If Jesus enters the cloud, as Marvin Meyer and his associates claim on the basis of recently edited fragments, then the ending of the Gospel presents an "ascension" of Jesus that revises the ascension in Acts 1 in relation to Jesus' presence in the cloud in the Synoptic accounts of the Transfiguration. From this perspective, Jesus enters the cloud and ascends to the great and boundless Aeon where people born of the Spirit will dwell.

A short comment at the end of the Gospel of Judas creates a further surprise: Jesus tells Judas he will hand over "the man who bears" Jesus, not Jesus himself, to be sacrificed. Perhaps some of the lost portions of the earlier part of the text said something about Jesus having two "beings," an earthly being "borne by a man" and a heavenly being who could travel back and forth between the earthly realm and the great and boundless Aeon.

The earthly and divine forms of Jesus in the Gospel of Judas led us naturally to the twelfth chapter, on the Acts of John. There also a "human" Jesus dies on the cross and a "heavenly" Jesus does not die. Especially as a result of the fragmentary nature of the Gospel of Judas, we probably will never be able to answer with certainty some questions we have about the nature of Jesus there. In the Acts of John, however, we clearly see a divine Jesus who participates in earthly forms of Jesus.

In chapter 12 we saw how in the Acts of John Jesus is "the fullness of God." This fullness is so expansive that no title like Son of God, Savior, Lord, or even God can properly describe and explain who Jesus is. The only choice is to introduce a long string of words to describe the nature of Jesus. But more than this, it is necessary to introduce actions along with words to describe the nature of Jesus. Also, it is necessary to describe both the nature of Jesus on earth and the nature of Jesus in the eternal realm of God's fullness.

In the Acts of John, Jesus is the light in the world that "looks different" to people in different circumstances. This light is the fullness of God. People have difficulty "seeing" this light. Therefore, depending on their perspective and their degree of readiness to see him, they see "the light" differently. It appears that, as in the Gospel of Mary, there is an awareness that "mind," which exists between soul and spirit, sees the light of the fullness of God. In the Acts, John is given the special privilege of seeing Jesus as "the Cross of Light" who forms "the way" from earth to the divine realm. So his "vision" moves beyond Mary Magdalene's vision of talking with the risen Savior. Instead of simply talking with Jesus, John sees a "formless" Jesus "above the Cross of Light" and hears "the sweet, gentle voice" of Jesus, which is different from the voice the disciples heard from Jesus while he was on earth. For John, the Cross of Light is an avenue for seeing beyond the earthly realm into the eternal realm beyond. John's vision, then, is different from the dream-visions of Judas and the twelve disciples in the Gospel of Judas. Instead of visions that include houses or temples, John's vision sees the heavenly form of Jesus' suffering and death as "the Cross of Light."

Though initiates into the Greek mysteries kept silent about the mysteries, in the Acts John tells the Ephesians about both the "lesser mysteries" and the "higher mysteries" about Jesus, even though Jesus has told him to "keep silent" about the mysteries. Here we may see a special feature of Christianity in its Mediterranean context. Underlying Christian belief is the conviction that a person must "tell" what God has revealed through Jesus Christ. As many emerging Christians became Gnostic, they emphasized the "deep mysteries" surrounding Jesus, God, the universe, and themselves and considered these mysteries "beyond explanation." But still they preached these mysteries as "gospel" — good news about Jesus, God, and the world. When told to "be silent," they then went out and "told what happened to them." This, we have seen, is true of a list of early Christian writings from the Gospel of Mark to the Acts of John, and it has continued in Christianity throughout all the centuries.

Index of Names and Subjects

Abel, 189

Abraham: in the Gospel of Matthew's genealogy, 57; in Jewish tradition, 17, 93

Acts, book of, 8

Acts of John, 8, 204, 225-26, 238-39; astonishing experiences with Jesus in, 211-12; Drusiana's experience of Jesus in the form of John and a young man in, 208; experiences surrounding Jesus' death in, 212-15; how the disciples see Jesus (in different forms), 209-11; a human and divine Jesus in, 207-8; initiation into the lesser and greater mysteries in, 220-22, 226, 239; Jesus' hymn-dance with his disciples in, 207, 213, 214, 215-20; John's celebration of a Eucharistic meal in, 214n2; John's talk with those at the crucifixion, 224-25; John's vision of the Cross of Light in, 221-24, 225-26, 238-39; who Jesus is in the Acts of John ("the fullness of God"), 225, 238. *See also* Acts of John, hymn in

Acts of John, hymn in, 215-20; active actions of Jesus (eating and hearing) in, 217; active actions Jesus wills those who believe in him to perform (eating him and hearing him) in, 217; Christianity as a Mediterranean mystery religion in, 219-21; "Grace dancing" in, 218-19; Jesus' "I will" statements in, 216; manifestation of Jesus as Logos/Thought in, 217; passive-active actions involving Jesus (loosing, wounding, and bearing) in, 216-17; the rationale for singing the hymn, 216; repetitions of "Glory be to thee . . ." in, 215; the sequence of twelve numbers in, 218-19; sequential praise statement in, 215; three-step sequence in, 218; as a unifying ritual, 215; "washing" of Jesus in, 217-18

Adam, 35, 189; "image" of, 189; the "man of dust Adam" (Genesis 2), 35, 189; the "original Adam" or "Original Man" (Genesis 1), 35, 36, 189

Amos, 17

"Ancient of Days" (or "Ancient One"), in the book of Daniel, 33-34, 210

Andrew, in the Gospel of Mary, 176, 183-84

angels, 1, 33, 37, 51, 54, 72, 79, 118, 145, 161, 171, 175, 212, 213, 234; angel/messengers and John the Baptist, 21-22; Gabriel, 24, 75, 77, 78, 94, 159, 166, 167, 212; in the Infancy Gospel of

Index of Scripture and Other Ancient Texts